THE WILD GARDEN

THE WILD GARDEN

EXPANDED EDITION

by

WILLIAM ROBINSON

with new chapters and photography by

RICK DARKE

TIMBER PRESS
Portland • London

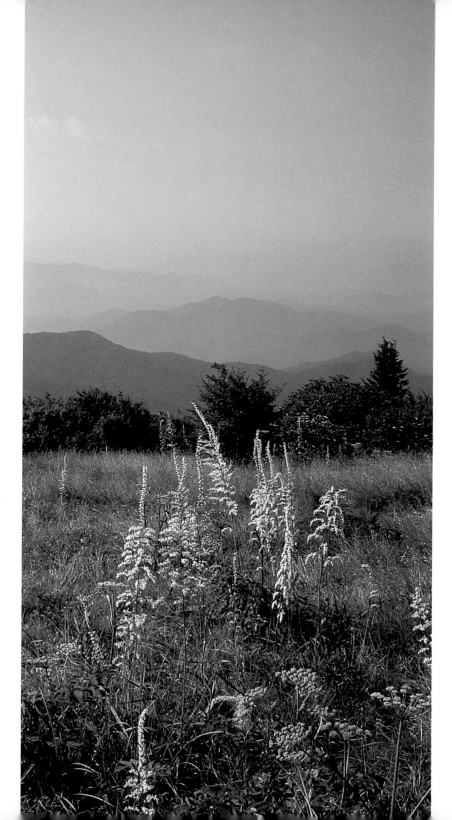

Frontispiece: Mt. Cuba Center, Greenville, Delaware. This page: Eastern featherbells (*Stenanthium gramineum*) growing wild in a high meadow in the Smoky Mountains of North Carolina.

Published in 2009 by Timber Press, Inc.

The Haseltine Building
133 S.W. Second Avenue, Suite 450
Portland, Oregon 97204-3527
www.timberpress.com

2 The Quadrant
135 Salusbury Road
London NW6 6RJ
www.timberpress.co.uk

Printed in China
Designed by Susan Applegate

Library of Congress Cataloging-in-Publication Data

Robinson, W. (William), 1838–1935.
    The wild garden / William Robinson; with new chapters and photography by Rick Darke.—Expanded ed.
        p. cm.
    Expansion of: 5th ed. 1895.
    Includes bibliographical references and index.
    ISBN-13: 978-0-88192-955-3
    1. Wild flower gardening. 2. Wild flower gardening—Great Britain. 3. Wild flowers—Great Britain. 4. Exotic plants—Great Britain. I. Darke, Rick. II. Title.
    SB439.R615 2009
    635.9′676—dc22   2009019448

A catalog record for this book is also available from the British Library.

CONTENTS

INTRODUCTION

to
William Robinson
and the
Expanded Edition of *The Wild Garden*

First published in 1870 and evolving through seven editions in William Robinson's lifetime (1838–1935), *The Wild Garden* promoted an authentically naturalistic and genuinely low-maintenance approach based upon Robinson's considerable experience as a gardener, a botanist, and a direct observer of diverse habitats. The book was ground-breaking and hugely influential in its day, and is stunningly relevant to twenty-first century gardeners and landscape stewards seeking to combine esthetic design with dynamic biological diversity and sustainable management practices.

Rich with humor and strong opinion, *The Wild Garden*'s text is full of spirit and speaks of Robinson's enormous personal energy. A prolific writer and editor, the Irish-born Robinson made a successful career of telling the English how they might be more practical and imaginative gardeners—no mean trick in any day. When *The Wild Garden* first appeared, the prevailing taste in British and European Continental garden design was for meticulously contrived displays of tropical annuals newly introduced from South America. Robinson's condemnation of this style as rote and wasteful was highly controversial and yet his vision of gardens based upon flowing arrangements of locally adapted winter-hardy plants eventually triumphed and has proved the most enduring.

Robinson's lifelong friend Gertrude Jekyll was strongly influenced by *The Wild Garden*, and her own garden at Munstead Wood and many of her designs for others heartily embraced approaches outlined in *The Wild Garden*. Robinson's philosophies benefited from being very much in sync with the increasingly

FAR LEFT The West Garden at Gravetye Manor in July 2005.

popular British Arts and Crafts movement's ethics linking beauty with utility and promoting an appreciation of local materials and patterns. England's increasing industrialization was re-making much of the countryside and eliminating or modifying beyond recognition many of the semi-wild places previously taken for granted. Robinson's idea of conserving some of this wildness within gardens was well-reasoned and well-timed.

Though Robinson was just thirty-two when the first edition of *The Wild Garden* appeared, he brought to it a wealth of experience and knowledge. Robinson's professional career began in Ireland, as a gardener for the private estates Curraghmore House and, later, Ballykilcavan. He left Ireland for England in 1861 armed with a letter of introduction from David Moore, the director of Ireland's National Botanic Garden in Glasnevin, Dublin, and secured a position with the Royal Botanic Society's garden in Regent's Park, London. Robinson was responsible for the herbaceous plantings, which then included a small section of British wildflowers. Here he began developing his extensive field knowledge of the English flora, exploring the countryside to study plants in their habitats and to collect material for the garden. In 1863 he received support for a month-long tour of botanical gardens and nurseries in England, Scotland, and Ireland which considerably broadened his knowledge of the world's flora in cultivation.

Robinson's career as a writer began in earnest that year with a long series of articles describing the tour, running until 1865 in *The Gardener's Chronicle*. His further touring, writing, and work for the Royal Botanic

Society obviously made a fine impression among his peers: in 1866 he was elected as a Fellow of the Linnean Society, his nomination sponsored by Charles Darwin and many other preeminent British scientists and horticulturists. Later that year Robinson resigned his position at Regent's Park to devote himself to further studies and to his ambitions as a writer and publisher.

Long visits to France beginning in 1867 resulted in Robinson's first two books; *Gleanings from French Gardens* (1868) and *The Parks, Promenades and Gardens of Paris* (1869). His 1868 travels were devoted to high mountain and alpine habitats in France, Switzerland, and Italy, and from these Robinson produced *Alpine Flowers for English Gardens*, published in 1870, the same year as *Mushroom Culture* and *The Wild Garden*.

Robinson also sailed to North America in August 1870, traveling by train across the continent and back just a year after the First Transcontinental Railroad was completed. He returned to England in December, and although this was too late to provide material for the first edition of *The Wild Garden*, his observations of diverse North American natural habitats and the connections he made with leading botanists deeply informed his subsequent writing and books, including the fifth edition of *The Wild Garden*. In New England Robinson met Harvard's Asa Gray, who was then the leading expert on the North American flora. In New York he visited Central Park, just then nearing completion, with its superintendent and principal designer Frederick Law Olmsted. Robinson got his first glimpse of the desert on his way to California, where he explored the high Sierras with the assistance of California's great botanists Albert Kellogg and Henry Bolander.

In 1871 Robinson launched his weekly journal, *The Garden*, and served as its editor for twenty-nine years. Devoted to a wide array of garden and landscape subjects, *The Garden* drew from Robinson's extraordinary connections and included contributions from many of the period's most knowledgeable, progressive thinkers and doers. He began using engravings done from original works of accomplished artists to illustrate *The Garden*, a practice he eventually introduced to his books. The second edition (1881) of The *Wild Garden* benefited greatly from this, with its pages enlivened by nearly a hundred illustrations by British artist Alfred Parsons. The exquisite line drawings and engravings from Parsons' paintings portrayed individual plants

Detail from an engraving of one of Alfred Parsons's paintings that first appeared in the 1881 edition of *The Wild Garden*.

and broad landscapes and were retained in all later editions.

Robinson was clearly proud of *The Wild Garden* and recognized the enduring relevance of the concept. Many of his later books included a chapter on the wild garden, including his immensely successful title *The English Flower-Garden* (1883) and *The Garden Beautiful: Home Woods, Home Landscape* (1906).

William Robinson's purchase of Gravetye Manor in 1885 at last afforded the opportunity to explore wild gardening on intimate terms and on a grand scale. Located in West Sussex near East Grinstead, Gravetye (pronounced *grave-tie*) was built of stone in 1598 for local iron master Richard Infield and his wife Katherine. Though the manor house was in disrepair,

it was solidly constructed, handsomely proportioned, and beautifully positioned halfway up a south-facing slope with sweeping views of the Sussex Weald and Ashdown Forest.

Robinson spent the remaining fifty years of his life at Gravetye, first living in the Moat Cottage, a smaller farmhouse nearby on the estate, while Gravetye Manor was repaired and improved to his requirements. In 1882 the Southern Railway had introduced service connecting the neighboring village of West Hoathly to London's Victoria Station. This service allowed Robinson to commute by train from Gravetye to his offices in London's Covent Garden.

Robinson built terraces and gardens near the house and edited the woods and views on the estate, while planting thousands of trees and shrubs and naturalizing hundreds of thousands of bulbs and other herbaceous species wherever they would thrive. He added to Gravetye's lands, eventually assembling an estate of over a thousand contiguous acres. Robinson wrote about the evolution of Gravetye Manor and its gardens in *Gravetye Manor: Or, Twenty Years' Work Round an Old Manor House* (1911) and in *My Wood Fires and Their Story* (1917).

The influence of *The Wild Garden* grew steadily during Robinson's lifetime, extending far beyond England to Continental Europe and North America. German garden architect Willy Lange read the book, and his concept of the *Naturgarten* (nature garden), emphasizing the use of native plants in ecological

association, was heavily influenced by it. Frederick Law Olmsted owned a copy of *The Wild Garden* and shared his enthusiasm for Robinson's ideas with Calvert Vaux, with whom he worked on the design of The Rambles in New York's Central Park. Robinson actively corresponded with Charles S. Sargent, the United States' most distinguished dendrologist and director of the Arnold Arboretum, who repeatedly featured Robinson's work in his publication *Garden and Forest: A Journal of Horticulture, Landscape Art, and Forestry* (1888–1897). Wilhelm Miller, editor of *Country Life in America*, visited William Robinson at Gravetye in 1908 and wrote about Robinson's wild gardening concepts in his book *What England Can Teach Us About Gardening* (1911). American landscape architect

FAR LEFT Gravetye Manor soon after Robinson's purchase, with clearing of the grounds and alterations to the house underway (reproduced from Robinson's photo album, courtesy Gravetye Manor).

LEFT Another early image from Robinson's photo album showing the passage from the stables to the manor house with naturalized plantings nearly covering the dry-laid stone walls.

The south view in late
December from an upper
window at Gravetye Manor.

Warren Manning was familiar with Robinson's book and in his 1906 entry for *Bailey's Cyclopedia of American Horticulture* he attributed to Robinson both the idea and the name of wild gardening.

The aim of this expanded edition is to introduce *The Wild Garden* to a new generation of readers, and to expand upon William Robinson's wild garden concept in a modern ecological context. The first new chapter, "Reading *The Wild Garden*," selects passages from Robinson's original text and discusses their relevance to today's gardeners. The next chapter, "The Wild Garden in the Twenty-first Century," illustrates Robinsonian wild gardening in a broad array of current gardens, beginning with Gravetye and continuing through woodland, meadow, waterside, and post-industrial wildscapes.

Following this, the fifth edition of *The Wild Garden* (1895), which best represents the book in its mature and fully illustrated form, is reproduced in its entirety along with all original illustrations and the index. The page size has been enlarged from the original five and one-half inches by eight and one-half inches, and the text has been reset in modern typeface, increasing readability and allowing all illustrations to be oriented so they may be viewed without turning the book on its side, as was necessary with many landscape images in the original book. Recent

photographs of Gravetye are interspersed on pages
separate from the historic text. Robinson's prefer-
ences for plant names, spellings, capitalization, and
punctuation are generally retained, although typos
and certain formatting inconsistencies have been cor-
rected where Robinson's intent is clear. A few of his
longest paragraphs have been divided into smaller
paragraphs to improve readability, and all lists have
been alphabetized for ease of use.

New to this expanded addition are a list of up-
to-date nomenclature of the plants described in the
book, a bibliography of sources referred to in the historic text as well as in the new chapters, and an index
to the new material.

This edition owes much to the generosity of many
people and gardening institutions who recognize the
continuing inspiration to be found in William Robinson's remarkable book. I'm especially grateful to the
gardens photographed for this book; to Andrew Russell and Mark Raffan at Gravetye; to historian and
Robinson scholar Judith Tankard; to Melinda Zoeh-
rer, my inspired companion at Gravetye in all seasons;
to all the good folks at Timber Press; and to Peter
Herbert for a half century's dedication to preserving
the literary legacy and the very substance of Robinson's wild garden.

Robinson's interior refinements at
Gravetye Manor included molded
plaster ceilings depicting plants
from the wild garden. This section
features English oak (*Quercus robur*).

READING *THE WILD GARDEN*

THOUGH NEITHER LARGE NOR LENGTHY, *The Wild Garden* is so densely packed with ideas and details it merits reading and re-reading. For all of us seeking creative, practical approaches to today's challenges and opportunities—balancing culture and environment, native and exotic, consumption and sustainability— William Robinson's inspired responses to the same issues more than a century ago offer historical perspective and suggest current strategies.

The Wild Garden opens with the following quote from Sydney Smith (1771–1845), an Oxford-educated Anglican clergyman and moral philosopher celebrated for his wit and wisdom:

> I went to stay at a very grand and beautiful place in the country where the grounds are said to be laid out with consummate taste. For the first three or four days I was enchanted. It seemed so much better than Nature, that I began to wish the earth had been laid out according to the latest principles of improvement. In three days'

time I was tired to death; a Thistle, a heap of dead bushes, anything that wore the appearance of accident and want of intention was quite a relief. I used to escape from the made grounds and walk upon the adjacent goose common, where the cart ruts, gravel pits, bumps, coarse ungentlemanlike Grass, and all the varieties produced by neglect were a thousand times more gratifying.

It is easy to see why Smith's words resonated with Robinson: they celebrate variety and autonomy, the core

FAR LEFT A grass path defined by foot travel passes under a large English oak bordering the pond below Gravetye's south-facing slope in late July. In William Robinson's time and now, the wild garden at Gravetye has offered many such casual opportunities for observation and discovery.

values of the wild gardening concept. Both Smith and Robinson were railing against the monotony of order, and both recognized the diversity and serendipity that often result from a lessening of control.

Robinson included two forewords in the fifth edition, one originally written in 1881 for the second edition and another in 1894 to introduce the fifth. In both forewords Robinson felt the need to clarify his meaning of the "wild garden," saying it had been widely misunderstood. He emphatically states that the wild garden "has nothing to do with the old idea of the 'Wilderness'," nor does it equate to the "picturesque garden," which although it may be picturesque, is the "result of ceaseless care." The essence of his idea is placing plants "where they will thrive without further care." Robinson goes on to explain that the wild garden can co-exist with more structured plantings nearer to the house, and that it is not merely "a garden run wild" but a more practical and enduring approach especially suited to "the outer fringes of the lawn" and for "grove, park, copse or by woodland walks or drives."

Robinson's vision of the wild garden was clearly cosmopolitan, promoting a global mix of locally adapted plants, such as "the Winter Aconite flowering under a grove of naked trees in February" or "the blue Apennine Anemone staining an English wood blue before the coming of our Bluebells." The "Explanatory" (Chapter I) describes "naturalizing many beautiful plants of many regions of the earth in our fields, woods and copses, outer parts of pleasure grounds, and in neglected places in almost every kind of garden." Robinson's perspective is that of an Englishman who understands the relatively limited diversity in the British native flora and who appreciates the vast richness of hardy species occurring in other lands.

Among the many reasons given in support of wild gardening, Robinson suggests that many desirable plants may be too strong in their growth for anywhere but the wild garden. He cites "the Golden Rods, and other plants of the great order Compositæ, which merely overrun the choicer and more beautiful border-flowers when planted amongst them." As an extreme example, he cautions that "the Great Japanese Knot-worts (*Polygonum*) are certainly better planted outside of the flower-garden."

To a present-day North American gardener, the mention of *Polygonum cuspidatum* is most likely to raise the topic of exotic species and their impact on long-established regional ecologies. It is important to remember that Robinson's England of 1870–1935 had already been heavily impacted by human activity for many centuries, and virtually all of the forests, ponds, and meadows in his sphere were, in fact, managed landscapes. Robinson's concerns were purely practical, based upon the perceived amount of human effort required to maintain the desired vegetation. In nearly the same period, the Olmsted office introduced *Polygonum cuspidatum* to countless parks and other public landscapes in North America, valuing the plant for its nearly year-round interest and adaptability. More than a century of experience has revealed this plant to be manageable in England but a liability under many North American conditions.

Chapters following the "Explanatory" read like a collection of essays, and in fact many were written and revised at different times before appearing as they do in the fifth edition. Some directly promote and expand upon the philosophy of wild gardening, while others discuss plants, planting, or management practices in great detail. Robinson occasionally explains his motivation for publishing the book in 1870 and reflects on what he's learned in years since, sometimes including questions or observations sent to him by letter from readers in England and North America. His model of reflection and refinement is a good one for gardeners in any age.

Chapter II, "Example from Hardy Bulbs in Grass of Lawns or Meadows," makes a case against closely mowed turf that could have been written today. Robinson suggests a portion of lawn "as smooth as a carpet" should be sufficient, and that there is no need to regularly mow "the long and pleasant grass" in other parts of the grounds. Never shy about voicing his opinion, he calls extensive mowing "ridiculous work" and a "costly mistake."

Robinson is aiming for dual utilities: preserving the beauty of tall grasses intermingled with wildflowers, and managing grassy areas productively for hay. His subsequent experience proved the practicality of this idea, and in his foreword of 1894 he wrote,

> The best thing I have learnt from my own wild gardening is that we may grow without care many lovely early bulbs in the turf of meadows (i.e., fields mown for hay) without in the least interfering with the use of the fields.

Recognizing a human tendency to arrange objects in formal order, Robinson states that flowering bulbs

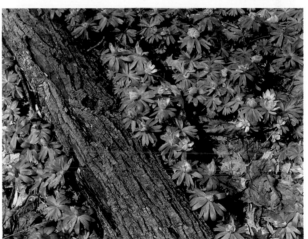

TOP Swallowtail butterfly and thistle in a former pasture in Delaware.

ABOVE Naturalized along a stream bank in a Pennsylvania woodland, this population of winter aconite (*Eranthis hyemalis*) has endured without care for decades by self-sowing.

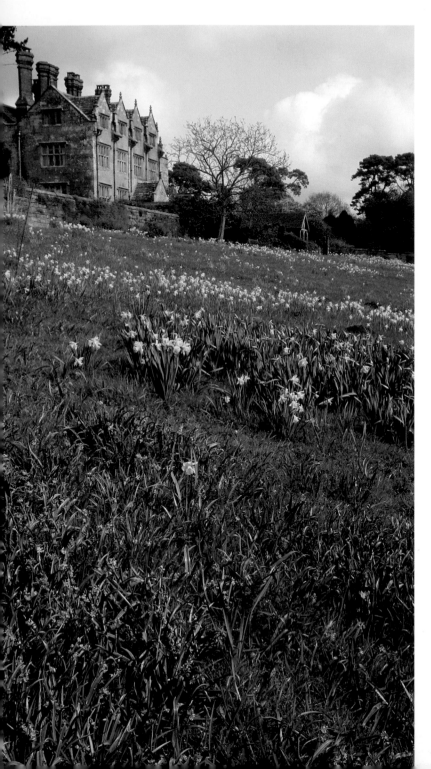

planted in grass should be "in natural groups or prettily fringed colonies, growing to and fro as they like after planting." He repeats his favored theme of looking to wild-growing populations for design inspiration, suggesting that "[l]essons in this grouping are to be had in woods, copses, heaths, and meadows, by those who look about them as they go."

As if to emphasize the botanical training he relied upon throughout his own horticultural career, Robinson's next two chapters each profile a plant family suited to the wild garden. He begins Chapter III, "Example from the Forget-me-not Family," with the artistic observation that although "Nature, say some, is sparing of her deep true blues," this family (the *Boraginaceae*) includes many deep and delicate blue-flowered species which will thrive in the wild garden, such as *Lithospermum*, *Mertensia*, *Myosotis*, *Pulmonaria*, and *Symphytum*. Robinson comments that although *Mertensia sibirica* is more commonly cultivated, the rare *Mertensia virginica* is "one of the loveliest of spring flowers" and that planting it in a moist location near a stream will ensure its survival.

The buttercup family, *Ranunculaceae*, is profiled in Chapter IV, "Example from the Globe Flower Order." Although Robinson includes peonies, which botanists now place in their own family, *Paeoniaceae*, he describes a number of genera many modern gardeners might be surprised to know are close relatives in the buttercup family: *Anemone*, *Clematis*, *Delphinium*, *Eranthis*, *Helleborus*, *Hepatica*, *Ranunculus*, and *Trollius*. Gardeners who follow modern trends may also be amused by Robinson's note that "recently many kinds of *Helleborus* have been added to our gardens." Robinson values the showy flowers of the often-cultivated Christmas

FAR LEFT *Scilla* and *Narcissus* bloom in late March in Gravetye's grassy south-facing meadow. These are among the many early bulbs Robinson successfully naturalized in his hay meadows. Others which have endured include *Crocus*, *Erythronium*, *Fritillaria*, *Leucojum*, *Muscari*, and *Ornithogalum*.

LEFT European native dog's-tooth violet (*Erythronium dens-canis*) blooms in late March in rough grass at Gravetye.

BELOW Virginia bluebells (*Mertensia virginica*) carpet the Susquehanna River floodplain in Maryland, growing under big deciduous trees and among small pawpaws (*Asimina triloba*). Natural genetic diversity is evident in this wild population, which includes a range of flower colors from clear blue to pink and pure white.

Rose (*Helleborus niger*); however, he recommends the superior foliage and growth habit of many new introductions and suggests these sturdy species could be naturalized on banks and slopes.

Alfred Parsons' illustration of a North American Joe-pye-weed introduces Chapter V, "Plants chiefly fitted for the Wild Garden." Identified only as a type of erect composite, it is certainly a *Eupatorium* species and is most likely *Eupatorium fistulosum. Eupatorium purpureum*, a name long misapplied to *Eupatorium fistulosum*, is listed later in the book. Robinson's point in this short chapter is that many vigorous species that are too large or coarse to fit in refined borders are ideally suited to the wild garden. He suggests that although the individual flowers may be subtle, such plants are often quite beautiful when grown in large colonies. He laments that when he first wrote *The Wild Garden*, many of the genera he recommends, including *Aster, Eupatorium, Phytolacca, Solidago, Veratrum*, and *Vernonia*, were not in cultivation outside of botanic gardens.

Robinson turns from sunny sites to explore the potential of a variety of more shaded and non-traditional niches in Chapter VI, "Ditches, Shady Lanes, Copses, and Hedgerows." Beginning with ditches, he suggests the plentiful moisture in such sites provides growing conditions for a great variety of unusual and beautiful plants including the white wood Lily (*Trillium grandiflorum*) and twin-flower (*Linnaea borealis*). He draws from his own observations in North America, telling of low wet areas in the woods and at their edges that were filled with handsome ferns. In 1871, following his return from America, Robinson published an article titled "The Bog Garden" in his journal *The*

Garden, in which he described "beauty in the ditches and pools of black water beside the road, fringed with sweet-scented Button Bush (*Cephalanthus occidentalis*), with a profusion of royal (*Osmunda regalis*) and other stately ferns, and often filled with masses of pretty Sagittarias." Robinson's penchant for first-hand observation and his habit of noting plant associations in wild habitats provided a wealth of information for his books and ideas for his garden.

In Robinson's time few gardeners paid much attention to the living hedgerows defining the rural countryside or the neglected spaces bordering cities, but Robinson certainly did. In keeping with his vision of the garden continuing far beyond dooryard formality, he celebrates hedgerows as the essence of beautifully vibrant wildness and as direct inspiration for the wild garden:

> Our wild flowers take possession of the hedges that seam the land, often draping them with such inimitable grace that half the conservatories in the country, with their small red pots, are poor compared with a few yards' length of the blossomy hedgerow verdure.

Complaining that vines are too often "tortured into forms in gardens," he suggests much greater beauty and utility results from allowing them to adapt to conditions on the site, citing a wide array of amenable climbers including clematis, honeysuckle, wild roses, Canadian moonseed, hardy jasmines, *Smilax, Aristolochia*, and Virginia creeper. In the ground layer below climbers and shrubs, Robinson envisions a mix of durable, often colonizing species including

LEFT A continuous carpet of naturalized *Anemone*, *Helleborus*, and *Scilla* species blooms in late March at Sissinghurst.

BELOW Buttercups naturalized in a Delaware meadow garden define a simple grass path. The path was mowed more recently than the rest of the meadow, yet early enough for the buttercups to regrow and bloom. Flowering is especially heavy in the path since plants here have less competition from the meadow grasses.

LEFT While traveling in North America, Robinson observed that royal fern (*Osmunda regalis*) preferred constantly moist habitats. He promoted the wild garden as a place to experiment with plants that are rarely cultivated in traditional full-sun gardens, including species "that do not care for sunny hillsides or meadows, but take shelter in woods, are happy deep between rocks, or in caves beneath the great boulders on many a mountain gorge, and garland the flanks of rock that guard the rivers on their way through the hills."

BELOW All perfect examples of the vigorous plants William Robinson promotes as ideally suited to wild gardens, *Eupatorium*, *Solidago*, and *Vernonia* species bloom in August in a moist sunny meadow in western Pennsylvania. The meadow was cleared long ago for use as a pasture, and these local natives have naturalized in the sunny habitat it now affords.

ostrich ferns (*Matteuccia struthiopteris*), lily of the valley, Canadian bloodroot, Solomon's-seal, mayapples, and asters.

As England's increasing industrialization made iron fences available, traditional living fences were beginning to fall out of favor. Robinson was dismayed by this, in part because of the loss of shelter provided by living fences for livestock and other animals. He defends the living fence as "the most satisfactory and the least expensive in the long run, and the most beautiful in its effect upon the landscape and for its varied life." Describing the constant or even annual clipping of living fences unnecessary, Robinson encourages periodic pruning only as needed to renew hedging shrubs and trees.

Chapter VII, "Climbers for Trees and Bushes," portrays additional vining species with flowering or foliage appeal that are suited as draperies over living woody plants, both deciduous and evergreen. Robinson's consistent message is that there is a great deal of beauty and ease of maintenance to be achieved if we entrust our plantings with a bit more freedom.

The traditional approach to the ground layer among shrub and tree plantings in Victorian-era English gardens was to fill it with tropical annuals during the growing season, to dig the beds in autumn, and leave them bare until the following spring. This practice was labor intensive and resulted in large portions of gardens being utterly devoid of living diversity during the winter season, and was in these ways similar to the twenty-first century practice of annually applying bare mulch as a principal groundcover. In Victorian gardens, autumn leaves were routinely raked and

disposed of much as they often are in modern residential gardens.

Robinson saw the folly in all this, and in Chapter VIII, "Shrubbery, Plantation, and Wood," proposed the following rule: "never show the naked earth: clothe it." He details the successful strategy he developed for covering the ground and retaining the leaves beneath his tree plantations at Gravetye. Robinson naturalized

Wisteria frutescens, a southeastern North American species that is more restrained in its growth than eastern Asian types, climbs freely on a flowering dogwood (*Cornus florida*). Robinson preferred living fences of trees and shrubs for defining spaces in the landscape, and recommended they could be further enlivened by climbers.

durable, colonizing herbaceous plants under his trees, allowing their dormant winter growth to stand and keep fallen leaves in place. This accumulation of leaves served as natural mulch and eventually decayed, adding to the soil. Among the herbaceous plants he recommends for this purpose are asters (which Robinson often called Starwort), spreading geraniums, lyme grass (*Elymus*), and alum root (*Heuchera*). Obviously pleased with this labor-saving device, Robinson writes,

> Before we planted in this way weeds were a constant trouble, but the vigorous colonies of plants wanted all the good of the ground for themselves, and took care of the weed for us! Certainly there was very much less trouble than an ordinary mixed border; there was no staking of any kind, and the stems were not cut down till late in spring: they looked very pretty in winter.

Robinson found wild woodlands infinitely intriguing, and in the *The Wild Garden* he seems almost in awe of them. "A thousand things may be suggested to us woods" he writes, and goes on almost apologetically, saying his little book can't possibly cover all the lessons to be learned from the world's diverse woodland habitats. After briefly describing plant associations in a variety of English woods, he reproduces a letter sent to him by W. Falconer, described as "an observer," detailing "what goes on in the woods of New England." Falconer's account is a fine example of first-hand observation, describing plants and plant associations, preferred habitat niches, and the seasonality of the forest. This example serves Robinson well as an encouragement to observant gardeners.

To prove the practicality of naturalizing woodland plants, and to draw from experience beyond his own at Gravetye, Robinson reports on the success of Mr. Wilson, an English gardener whose property of a few acres includes oak woods bordered by a stream, a boggy area, and a sunny slope. Taking advantage of these diverse growing conditions, Wilson has naturalized an impressive array of woodland denizens from around the world. Modern American gardeners may be surprised to learn that so many North American species still uncommon in cultivation, including *Galax aphylla*, *Gaultheria procumbens*, *Lilium superbum*, *Shortia galacifolia*, and *Xerophyllum asphodeloides*, were thriving in Wilson's wild woodland garden more than a century ago.

Taking a break from discussing specific plants, Robinson looks broadly at the design of pathways for wild gardens in Chapter IX, "Woodland Drives and Grass Walks." He argues against the "primitive and wholly inartistic idea" that the proper way to make a drive is to line it with closely spaced trees, and instead suggests a more open pattern of trees with hardy shrubs and ferns in the foreground.

Garden walks paved with stone, cast paving blocks, or asphalt are now the most common; however, in Robinson's era most were grass or gravel. For most of his life Robinson was an avid walker, and he clearly appreciated the pleasure of walking on grass "through pretty woodland scenery, over park, hill, or by stream or river." Though admitting "good firm walks" nearest the house were sometimes practical necessities, he promotes grass as the most economical and satisfying surface for walks in the more casual

TOP LEFT *Erythronium americanum*, known as trout lily or dog's-tooth-violet, blooms in mid-April in a Maryland woodland. Robinson occasionally relied upon the observations of correspondents to place such plants in ecological context for readers, as with this excerpt from Mr. Falconer of New England: "In low copses, in rich deposits of vegetable mould, it grows around here in the utmost profusion. In one place by the side of a wood is a sort of ditch, which is filled with water in winter, but is dry in summer, wherein is collected a mass of leaf-soil. Here the Yellow Dog's-tooth Violet runs riot, and forms the densest kind of matted sod, all bespeckled with yellow blossoms before a tree has spread a leaf."

TOP RIGHT Marsh-marigold (*Caltha palustris*) blooms in mid-April, growing wild in a wet deciduous Michigan woodland. Wide-ranging in temperate regions of the Northern Hemisphere, this species is native to both North America and Europe. In Chapter VIII Robinson reports Mr. Wilson's success with marsh-marigolds in his English woods, placed in "a deep bog where one might sink knee-deep in soft mud."

RIGHT Perfectly illustrating Robinson's suggestions, the foreground in this woodland drive in West Virginia is occupied by durable masses of hay-scented fern (*Dennstaedtia punctulobula*) and mountain laurel (*Kalmia latifolia*).

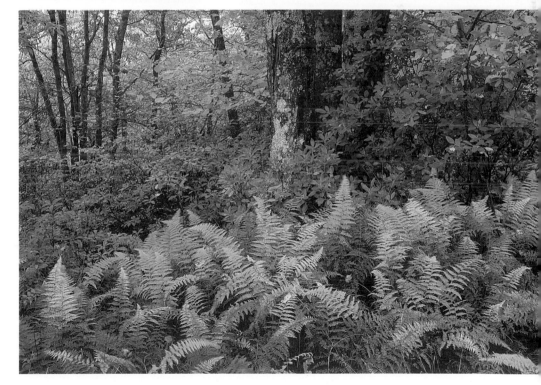

parts of the garden. When laying out and constructing grass walks Robinson states, "The line of ground should be studied for both ease in walking and mowing, and for the sake of the best views." He also understood the importance of paying close attention to drainage, so that his grass paths were walkable during winter and other wet times of year.

Robinson understood that few gardeners, including those well acquainted with the terrestrial wildflowers of their region, knew much about the great diversity of wetland and aquatic species. In Chapter X, "The Brook-side, Water and Bog Gardens," he describes possibilities for naturalizing such plants in the wild garden, frequently relying on his own first-hand observations of moist habitats in Europe and North America. He sees opportunity not just in ponds and similar open water, but in bogs and along the margins of brooks as they ripple through rocks or meander through glades or meadows.

Deploring the eroded banks so common to garden ponds, Robinson makes a case for naturalizing a diversity of moisture-loving species to occupy and stabilize the margins. Promoting a commonly overlooked but very graceful British native sedge, he suggests, "*Carex pendula* is excellent for the margins of water, its elegant drooping spikes being quite distinct in their way." He continues this grassy theme, recommending other sedges including *Cyperus longus*, *Scirpus lacustris* (now known as *Schoenoplectus tabernaemontani*), plus the narrow-leaved and common cat-tails,

Typha angustifolia and *Typha latifolia*. For flowering interest and contrasting texture, he suggests a variety of *Iris* species along with arrow-head (*Sagittaria*), *Pontederia cordata*, and other broad-leaved plants. Robinson reminds readers that creating such plant associations, as opposed to static monocultures, results in a "succession of effects" showing the "succession of life on the same spot of ground."

Robinson writes at length about the joys of naturalizing hardy waterlilies and their relatives in ponds and lakes, but cautions that the mix of vegetation should be managed so that portions of the water surface remain open. On the topic of bogs, he sounds very much like a modern-day conservationist, lamenting that "we have been so long encroaching upon bogs that some of us come to regard these as exceptional tracts." Though recognizing that few gardens have natural bogs or marshes in their midst, he makes a case for the adaptability of many bog and marsh species, and suggests that moist areas in the wild garden might provide homes for them. He promotes this idea with a brief survey of bog and marsh habitats, ranging from gentian-filled bogs in Bavarian alpine regions to low bogs in eastern North America rich with pitcher-plants (*Sarracenia*), golden club (*Orontium*), and swamp magnolia (which Robinson knew as *Magnolia glauca* but which was long since changed to *Magnolia virginiana*). Indeed, many of the bog species Robinson speaks of have proved adaptable to naturalizing in moist garden niches.

FAR LEFT AND CENTER Two paths at Mt. Cuba Center in Delaware beautifully illustrate Robinson's choice of grass surfaces for walks in wild gardens.

LEFT The pond margins in this German garden are beautifully clothed with two of Robinson's favorite sedges for naturalizing, *Cyperus longus* (center) and *Carex pendula* (right).

FAR LEFT TOP Robinson was acquainted with the white waterlily, *Nymphaea odorata*, from his 1870 trip to North America. He admired the fragrant white flowers and the ease with which this species can be naturalized in wild garden ponds and lakes.

FAR LEFT CENTER Naturalized cat-tails and Joe-pye-weed hold the margins of a Pennsylvania pond garden, providing a mix of form, texture, and flowering interest through the seasons.

ABOVE Cardinal flower (*Lobelia cardinalis*) blooms in August in a wet Pennsylvania habitat. Recalling his travels in 1870, Robinson writes, "In North America day after day, even from the railroads, one sees the vivid spikes of the Cardinal-flower springing from the wet peaty hollows."

LEFT Waterlilies and common cat-tails are naturalized in this German pond garden, which is gently managed to keep some of the water surface open and reflective, as Robinson recommends.

The hugely popular rock gardens of the Victorian era often featured prominent and sometimes pre-posterously arranged rocks with plants grown on or in-between them. Robinson strongly disliked the style but appreciated the special range of growing conditions often present in rocky and other sharply drained habitats. In Chapter XI, "Wild Gardening on Walls, Rocks, or Ruins," he looks at possibilities for naturalizing plants that would not likely survive in the flat ground of traditional planting beds. Many of Robinson's ideas for the wild garden resulted from observing common patterns and events, and in this chapter he asks readers to look closely at rocky mountain sites, and at growing niches in walls, stone banks, broken-down stone fences, and similar ruins to understand why so many plants thrive in such places.

Hybrid roses have been dominant for so long that it is easy to forget there is a wealth of garden-worthy species roses especially suited for the wild garden, and this is Robinson's point in Chapter XII, "Wild and other Roses in the Wild Garden." He acknowledges the appeal of well-tended hybrid tea roses but suggests that "[w]ithout the good gardener's spade and knife they would soon become a tangle with less meaning and beauty than the Wild Brier." Robinson values the elegant, often fragrant flowers, the carefree adaptability, and the good form common to many species roses. He recalls a trip he once made to Lyon, France, in search of tea roses, during which a friend pointed out that the wild yellow rose, *Rosa foetida*, grew locally. This prompted Robinson to buy a copy of *Étude des Fleurs*, a botanical flora of the region, to become better informed about wild roses. His chapter in *The Wild*

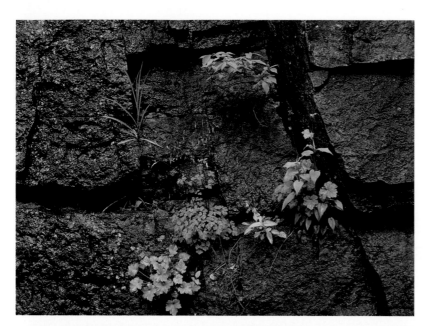

LEFT A nearly vertical rock face in the Virginia mountains supports a wild mix of *Aquilegia*, *Aster*, *Heuchera*, *Penstemon*, and other herbaceous plants. Water seeping over the stone surface and into the crevices provides adequate moisture without creating waterlogged conditions which would be especially injurious in winter.

BELOW Mossy rock walls at Birch Farm nursery have for decades provided well-drained habitat for a variety of naturalized ferns, sedums, geraniums, columbines, and other hardy plants. Walter Ingwersen, a specialist in alpine plants and a friend of William Robinson's, started the nursery in 1927 on Gravetye land leased from Robinson. Ingwersen's sons Will and Paul maintained the business, within walking distance of Gravetye Manor, until 2008.

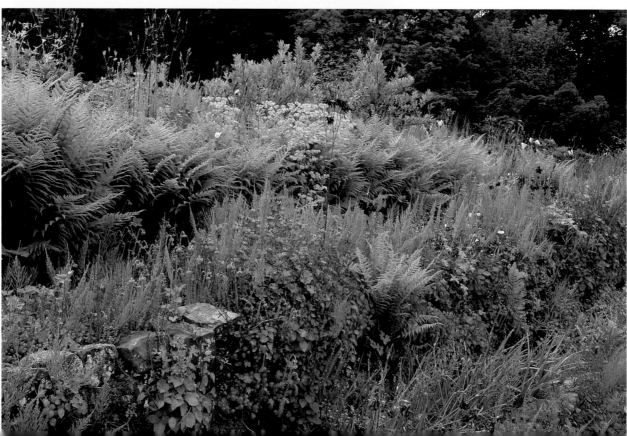

Garden remains a persuasive introduction to the diversity and merit of wild species roses, and is likely to spur modern gardens to learn about roses native to their own region, as well as suitable exotics.

Though steadily gaining in popularity, the idea of wild gardening remained at the periphery of conventional style throughout Robinson's lifetime and he continually felt the need to justify its merits. By the time the fifth edition was published (1894), *The Wild Garden* had been in print nearly a quarter century and had inspired a number of gardeners who wrote to Robinson of their experiments and successes. He first published many of these accounts in his journal *The Garden*, and then included especially relevant extracts in the fifth edition.

Chapter XIII, "Some Results," is devoted to the practical application of the wild gardening concept, drawing from Robinson's own experience and that of correspondents. Results illustrating wild gardening in a range of conditions and garden habitats are described. Stonecrops (*Sedum*) and saxifrage (*Saxifraga*) thrive on steeply sloped gravel while lavenders (*Lavandula*) and rock-roses (*Cistus*) cover the banks of a high sunny walk. Robinson tells of dead trees trimmed but allowed to stand as support for vines including clematis, roses, and Virginia creeper (*Parthenocissus quinquefolia*). He points out the opportunity presented when "an old tree falls and tosses up a mass of soil and roots." Promoting the fertile shade of woodland wild gardens, he predicts, "The wild garden of the future will be also the true home of all the larger hardy Ferns."

One example from a correspondent is startlingly progressive from a modern ecological perspective. It details uncovering (today we'd call it "daylighting") a stream that had been diverted underground in a tile culvert, and of establishing a wild garden along its course, teeming with marsh-marigolds, irises, ferns, sedges, rushes, and more. Echoing Stanley Smith's sentiments, Robinson suggests that much of "the beautiful in Nature, as it can be illustrated in gardens," is "rather the result of accident than design." He again criticizes gardens comprised of mere collections, those organized dryly by plant classification, and those with excessive geometrical order. For Robinson, the ideal gardening spirit seeks a living dynamic. As he states, "It is the *life* we want."

Robinson begins Chapter XIV, "Hardy Exotic Flowering Plants for the Wild Garden," with a short discussion on acquiring plants and follows with plant profiles in approximate alphabetical order by genus. The chapter is almost entirely devoted to herbaceous perennials. It's interesting to contrast Robinson's ease with raising plants from seed with the modern practice of purchasing vegetatively propagated perennials in pots. His profiles most typically include brief descriptions and comments on esthetics, but are most often focused on siting plants with regard to available growing conditions.

Robinson's intention is to provide examples, not a complete list, and to his credit many of the plants he mentions have proved durable choices for north temperate gardens. Quite a few, such as *Epimedium*, *Helleborus*, and *Sedum*, are among the most adaptable, water-conserving, deer-defying choices for contemporary low-input landscapes. North American gardeners may be surprised to see how many of their indigenous species Robinson includes. His list of exotics for British gardens features many genera that are only recently

Evening Light Through Warrens Wood, Gravetye 1903, by Henry G. Moon. Though a number of highly accomplished artists painted Gravetye at Robinson's invitation, Henry Moon (1857–1905) was best attuned to the wilder parts of the garden and the working landscapes surrounding it. Moon began working with Robinson as principal botanical illustrator for *The Garden*, and his drawings and paintings were prominent in many of Robinson's other journals and books. Moon visited Gravetye repeatedly, once staying most of the summer to paint outdoors. His oil of Warrens Wood portrays a vibrant mosaic formed by the light, layering, and patterns along a path in Robinson's woodland wild garden.

LEFT Naturalized common snowdrops (*Galanthus nivalis*) bloom in late winter in Pennsylvania. Drought and heat tolerant, water-conserving and deer-proof, snowdrops exemplify the durable choices Robinson recommends as hardy exotic flowering plants for the wild garden.

BELOW Naturalized daffodils bloom in grass between apples and crabapples at Ashland Hollow in Delaware. Regarding *Narcissus*, Robinson wrote, "Of all the planting I have ever made, the planting of these in the grass has given the greatest pleasure and the most lasting."

LEFT Willow gentian (*Gentiana asclepiadea*) flowering in August in a moist but not wet location in a German garden. Robinson observed this handsome species blooming in mountain woods in Switzerland.

BELOW Hellebores, hostas, and *Epimedium*, which Robinson called barren-wort, are naturalized in John Cram's mossy woodland garden in North Carolina. All are among Robinson's recommended exotic genera for the wild garden.

TOP LEFT Bird's-foot violet (*Viola pedata*) blooms on a steep rocky slope in the Virginia mountains. Robinson suggests growing this violet on "sandy level places or on rocky banks," which perfectly match the preferred North American habitats of this species.

TOP RIGHT Robinson promotes *Dodecatheon meadia*, called American cowslip or shooting-star, which he knew to occur "in rich woods in Pennsylvania, Ohio, to Wisconsin and southwestward, in America."

ABOVE Bloodroot (*Sanguinaria canadensis*) blooms in April in Delaware woods. No matter what their origin, plants that would thrive under similar conditions were of interest to Robinson. He suggests combining North American bloodroot with the Eurasian native winter aconite (*Eranthis hyemalis*) "under the branches of deciduous trees."

ABOVE LEFT AND RIGHT Seeds of common milkweed (*Asclepias syriaca*) lay against a frosted leaf of cinnamon fern in the Pennsylvania autumn. The silky strands attached to the seeds explain Robinson's prefered name for this genus, "silkweed." He was aware of the great diversity of hardy North American species, ranging from drought-tolerant butterfly milkweed (*Aslepias tuberosa*) to "water-side" species such as swamp milkweed (*Asclepias incarnata*). He recognizes that, although few have been introduced to England, many are ideal subjects for the wild garden.

LEFT Goldenrods and late thoroughwort (*Eupatorium serotinum*) bloom in great sweeps in late summer in a moist Delaware meadow. For the most dramatic effect in the wild garden, Robinson recommends planting such species in bold quantities.

coming into wider cultivation in America including *Arisaema, Aruncus, Asclepias, Dodecatheon, Eupatorium, Monarda, Parthenocissus, Phytolacca, Sanguinaria, Silphium, Solidago, Trillium, Vernonia, Viola,* and many ferns.

Robinson was aware of the sturdy beauty of North American asters, their relatives, and their companions, the warm-season grasses, long before meadow and prairie gardens entered popular imagination. He writes with great enthusiasm about the suitability of asters (which he calls starworts), goldenrods, and *Vernonia* species for the wild garden and of their contribution to the autumn landscape.

Chapter XV, "Selections of Hardy Exotic Plants for the Wild Garden," opens with a bit of timeless advice for gardeners interested in a truly resource-conserving approach to sustainable planting:

> As to soil, the best way is to avoid the trouble of preparing it; the point is to adapt the plant to the soil—in peaty places to place plants that thrive in peat, in clay soils those that thrive in clays, and so on.

The remainder of the chapter consists of plant lists organized by adaptability to various growing conditions or by plant growth habit. Though some of the categories seem fairly standard, Robinson's suggested applications are often inventive. His selection of "Trailers and Climbers" is promoted as useful for "rocks, precipitous banks, sides of bridges, river-banks, ruins." Although Robinson wrote these words in the West Sussex countryside, they could easily be applied to modern urban settings. His lists organized by soil type and available moisture are also quite modern in

their utility. As if anticipating the dwindling water resources of our current age, Robinson lists more than twenty *Sedum* species in "Selection of Plants for Growing on Old Walls, Ruins, or Rocky Slopes."

The only non-plant category in this chapter is devoted to what Robinson calls the "sad subject" of rabbits. His difficulties will sound amusingly familiar to any modern gardener dealing with an over-population of deer. Robinson complains that hungry rabbits "will eat almost anything that can be got" and, although he is eager for an acceptable way to eliminate the rabbits, he settles for compiling a list of plants rabbits are likely to avoid.

The fifth edition's final chapter, XVI, "The Garden of British Wild Flowers and Trees," is significantly revised from Robinson's similarly named chapter in the first edition, and is expanded to include trees. For unknown reasons, Robinson did not include this chapter in interim editions. He may have been ambivalent about describing a garden of British plants in a book promoting the good sense of drawing from the hardy global flora. His preface for the fifth edition clearly envisions the wild garden as a place to naturalize plants from "all northern and temperate regions" that "are hardy and will thrive in our climate as well as native plants." Yet in Chapter XVI he says, "The passion for the exotic is so universal that our own finest plants are never planted," and he goes on to point out a number of superb but horticulturally neglected species indigenous to the British isles.

Robinson's notion of gardening was extremely broad in scope, and perhaps the simple truth is that he could appreciate the beauty and utility to be found

ABOVE LEFT Indigenous to eastern Europe, naturalized *Crocus tommasinianus* blooms in late winter in a Pennsylvania woodland garden. Robinson included crocus "in great variety" among his wild garden recommendations of hardy bulbs for naturalization.

ABOVE RIGHT New leaves of mayapple (*Podophyllum peltatum*) enliven the ground layer in a moist Pennsylvania woodland. Robinson includes this North American species and the Himalayan mayapple (*Podophyllum emodi*) in "Plants Suited for Peat Soil."

LEFT In Oklahoma, locally indigenous *Eryngium leavenworthii* blooms in late summer on dry, rocky soil. Robinson includes this genus in his selections of "Plants Suited for Dry and Gravelly Soil." Part of the pleasure in reading through his recommendations is the inspiration they provide to delve into related but little-known species.

ABOVE LEFT Switchgrass (*Panicum virgatum*) turns color in October with near-black seed heads of *Echinacea* in foreground. Robinson included this *Panicum* in his selections of grasses for naturalization and in "Hardy Plants with fine foliage or graceful habit suitable for Naturalization."

ABOVE RIGHT Common in deciduous woods, glades, and hedgerows throughout the British Isles and also native in northern Europe, the English bluebell was once known as *Scilla nutans*, then *Endymion non-scriptus*, and now *Hyacinthoides non-scripta*. It crosses freely and prolifically with the larger Spanish bluebell (*Hyacinthoides hispanica*), which Robinson and many others introduced to England. Hybrids intermediate in character now dominate many wild populations.

ABOVE Robinson described "living in a world of wood hyacinths." Also known as English bluebell (*Hyacinthoides non-scripta*) this spring-blooming indigenous British species is abundant in the oak and beech woodlands surrounding Gravetye, and in good years it paints the entire forest floor deep blue (photo by Elliott Neep, of a wild population in Oxfordshire).

in the world's diversity, as well as the uniqueness that is best savored by regional specialization. Aren't we still wrestling with the apparent contradiction in these approaches? In any case, Robinson's initial advice to gardeners interested in growing British wildflowers and trees is still a smart strategy for learning the plants of any region: He suggests beginning with a local flora. Robinson never ceased to recognize the relationship between botanical knowledge and creative gardening.

The native range of plants is often obscure in places like Britain, which have long been influenced by human activity. A few of the species Robinson describes in this chapter are unquestionably British natives, but are so wide-ranging they are also indigenous to North American, such as bearberry (*Arctostaphylos uva-ursi*) and marsh-marigold (*Caltha palustris*). Some such as yellow flag (*Iris pseudacorus*) are British natives that have become so extensively naturalized

in North America they are often mistaken for natives there. Others which easily naturalize, such as the wood tulip, *Tulipa sylvestris*, are of doubtful origin and nativity. Robinson was familiar with George Bentham's authoritative *Handbook of the British Flora*, published in 1878, which says this tulip is found

> [i]n fields, pastures, and waste places, in Central and Southern Europe, extending eastward to the Caucasus and northward to southern Scandinavia. Believed to be truly indigenous in some of the eastern counties of England, and occurs, as an introduced plant, in some other localities in England and Scotland.

Despite such uncertainties, the chapter is interesting for Irish immigrant William Robinson's wealth of observations about his adopted country's landscape and flora.

FAR LEFT Wood tulip (*Tulipa sylvestris*) blooms in mid-April in a Pennsylvania woodland garden. Although Robinson included this beautiful, adaptable species in his chapter on British wildflowers, its origin and native range have been obscured by history.

LEFT *Colchicum autumnale*, naturalized in grass under tall trees at Longwood Gardens in Pennsylvania. Called autumn crocus or meadow saffron, this autumn-blooming relative of *Crocus* was known by Robinson from its sometimes abundant occurrence in parts of England, where it is believed to be indigenous.

ABOVE RIGHT *Cornus sanguinea* 'Midwinter Fire' in a December ice storm in a Pennsylvania garden. Robinson devotes more attention to trees and shrubs in his chapter on British plants than anywhere else in *The Wild Garden*. He judged *Cornus sanguinea* to be among the most beautiful of British native shrubs, saying, "[T]he winter effect is bright and good, and the plant fine for association with our handsomer native willows."

RIGHT William Robinson's robust selection of the indigenous British snowflake (*Leucojum aestivum*) blooms in March at Gravetye. Widely distributed from Gravetye, this form was long refered to as 'Gravetye Variety' but is now known as 'Gravetye Giant'. Robinson was very fond of snowflakes and he believed they should "be in any collection of British wild flowers, and with them the Daffodil and the Wood-tulip (*Tulipa sylvestris*)."

THE WILD GARDEN
IN THE
TWENTY-FIRST CENTURY

THE IDEA OF WILD GARDENING is more vital today than ever before. Robinson's historic concept is proving to be eminently modern, providing inspiration for all of us who are interested in combining fine garden design and enlightened environmental stewardship in the creation of livable landscapes and communities. The dynamic nature of wild gardens is a sensible antidote to the increasing density and diminishing biological diversity of many contemporary landscapes. Wild gardens embrace change and encourage spontaneity while holding fast to the underlying values that make landscapes reliably practical and truly sustainable. Wild gardens are full of real intrigue because they are both walkable and watchable.

Wild gardening can be adopted literally anywhere in the world, in landscapes large or small, public or private. Stylish, but not limited to any one style, wild gardening is suited to all sorts of habitats including woodlands, meadows, prairies, seashores, deserts, and urban centers. As Robinson suggested, with a little imagination wild gardening can be fit into appropriate niches in even the most formal of gardens.

This chapter looks at a wide range of gardens and managed landscapes that embody Robinson's wild garden ethics. These examples offer insights into diverse designs, plant palettes, and management strategies suitable for wild gardening in the twenty-first century. Though quite different in appearance, their common feature is that they all include a healthy measure of authentic wildness.

FAR LEFT Naturalized heaths (*Erica* spp.) bloom with *Narcissus* and *Scilla* in late March on the north slope of the West Garden at Gravetye.

GRAVETYE

FOR ANYONE INTERESTED in exploring the legacy and the promise of William Robinson's wild garden concept, Gravetye is an inspiring place to begin. It was Robinson's home, garden, and "field laboratory" for a half century and, remarkably, it survives. Robinson left Gravetye Manor, its gardens and surrounding acres to Great Britain, dedicated to the service of national forestry. The land was to be managed both for timber production and to provide sanctuary for indigenous birds and animals. Operations were to be supported in part by a lease on the Manor, which was not to become a museum or school: It was Robinson's intent that "the trees, woods, and landscapes shall be the only teachers."

Managed since 1935 by the Forestry Commission, Gravetye's fields, forests, and waters have fared well. The gardens nearer the Manor at first went unattended, then received varied amounts of care as the house passed through two residential leases and a period of military occupancy during the Second World War. Gravetye and its gardens began a brilliant new era in 1958 when the house and some thirty acres were leased to a private hotel company led by managing director Peter Herbert. Although clearing the property of weeds and overgrowth took nearly two years, the bones of Robinson's garden and a majority of his plantings had survived.

Guided by the meticulous detail Robinson recorded in *Gravetye Manor, Or Twenty Year's Work round an Old Manor House*, by the principles and concepts in *The Wild Garden*, and with the advice of Will Ingwersen and others who had known Gravetye in Robinson's time, Peter Herbert and his staff brought the garden fully to life. The Manor was opened as a country house hotel, offering fine food and the experience of staying in a sixteenth-century Sussex home surrounded by gardens and a thousand acres accessible by footpaths.

In October 1987, a devastating storm tore through the region, destroying nearly five hundred of Robinson's mature trees. Following a massive clearing operation, the gardens once again survived, though in a sunnier incarnation. Since then new trees have been planted, the forests have regrown, and the herbaceous layers have responded to the additional light with increased vigor and flowering.

Although no garden flourishes without care, even the more formal gardens around the house remain sustainable due to the durable hardiness and self-sufficiency of Robinson's plant palette, and to a management approach that invites a beneficial amount of self-sowing. As Robinson understood well, it usually requires less effort to edit an excess of seedlings than it does to constantly replace plants that are short-lived or poorly adapted.

The resiliency of Robinson's naturalized plantings at Gravetye is proof of the practical value of wild gardening. Peter Herbert recalls that the Alpine Meadow on the south slope below the Manor best survived the long years of neglect, and that bulbs including *Chionodoxa*, *Colchicum*, *Fritillaria*, *Muscari*, and *Narcissus* were

Gravetye Manor, the West Garden,
and the fields, forests, and hedgerows
of the Sussex Weald are visible in
this view south in mid December.

LEFT A hardy mix of geraniums, buttercups, foxgloves, irises, alliums, and ferns populates this section of the West Garden, near the house. The majority of these are truly naturalized, perpetuating themselves by self-sowing and filling open niches in beds and in the crevices of walls.

BELOW Naturalized daffodils arrange themselves in pleasing patterns along a path on the north slope, blooming profusely in early March.

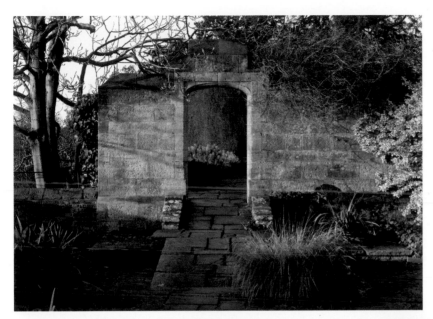

LEFT The walled garden just off the south of the Manor is vibrant with color and texture in late December. Robinson enjoyed the winter landscape, and preferred hardy perennials and vines that remained appealing even in dormancy.

BELOW Crafted of locally grown oak, this post-and-rail fence enclosing a grassy orchard area at Gravetye is part of a beautifully sustainable Sussex tradition that Robinson admired and promoted.

still thriving in the grass when he first arrived. These have continued, and have since been augmented by new plantings. Following Robinson's habit, very little turf is mowed closely: most is allowed to grow tall enough for haying. Naturalized daffodils and primroses (*Primula vulgaris*) still flower along with native wood hyacinths in Warrens Wood and other sections of the estate's managed forests.

The baling technique is modern but the tradition of haying Gravetye's fields continues from Robinson's era. The managed hayfields are more sustainable than closely mowed turf and they offer habitat for birds and other animals.

Glowing in the late afternoon sun at the end of March, these English oaks were bordering the upper pond long before Robinson arrived at Gravetye. Grassy fields full of naturalized bulbs, big trees, and healthy waters were all part of Robinson's broad vision of the wild garden. He deliberately kept the pond margins vegetated to prevent erosion and to enhance habitat for fish and other animals.

Robinson, the prolific writer and publisher, was also a great reader. In much the same way that he employed the impressions of painters to interpret his landscapes, he often used quotations to augment his own words. Robinson's choices often say a lot about his own beliefs and his ethics. The Wordsworth quote that opens the tenth edition (1907) of *The English Flower-Garden and Home*

Grounds ends with the suggestion that gardeners use "good sense in the midst of the realities of things; of birds and beasts, of hills and streams, and trees and flowers, with the changes of night and day, evening and morning, summer and winter, and all their unwearied actions and energies." Robinson surely took this to heart in his stewardship of Gravetye and his plans for its future.

ABOVE Introduced by Robinson, naturalized common primroses (*Primula vulgaris*) still brighten the floor of Warrens Wood in early spring.

RIGHT Daffodils naturalized by Robinson persist among the oaks and beeches of Warrens Wood. This and other woodlands on the Gravetye estate are managed by the Forestry Commission, which was established in 1919 to protect and expand Great Britain's forests and woodlands and to increase their value to society and the environment.

FAR RIGHT Completed in 1900, Robinson's walled kitchen garden still provides fresh fruits and vegetables for Gravetye Manor.

In addition to his wild gardening and his enlightened management of Gravetye's fields, woods, and waters, Robinson introduced other ideas that fit neatly with modern ideas of sustainable practices. In 1898 he began constructing a walled kitchen garden on the hill north of the Manor. The main spring that provides Gravetye's drinking water rises here. Forming a large oval, the wall is built of stone quarried on the estate. More than a century later, the kitchen garden provides the majority of fresh fruits and vegetables in season for Gravetye's table.

Peter Herbert retired in 2004 and responsibility for Gravetye Manor was assumed by Andrew Russell and Mark Raffan, who worked with Mr. Herbert for many years. The team is dedicated to preserving Gravetye Manor and the vibrancy of William Robinson's own wild garden.

WHAT IS WILD?

ON THE SUBJECT OF WILDNESS, William Robinson was clearly a modernist. "There has been some misunderstanding as to the term 'Wild Garden'," he wrote in 1881, "It has nothing to do with the old idea of the 'Wilderness'." More than a century later, we still often confuse wildness and wilderness, and this confusion clouds our vision of what is truly ecological and what is genuinely sustainable.

In recent centuries, "wilderness" has evolved from a fearsome, dangerously wild place to be conquered into a mythic realm where the last best things reside. There's no doubting the romantic appeal of "wilderness" if it evokes a pristine landscape untouched by humans, where plant and animal communities exist in beautiful balance. But if this is the ideal, then we are forced either to exclude ourselves or judge everything we do to be diminishing.

Though "wilderness" is only a distant memory in modern European consciousness, in North America, where remnant "wilderness" even now seems within reach, popular ecological philosophy often focuses on loss. Henry David Thoreau's take on his increasingly populated nineteenth-century New England environment is typical of this perspective. In his journal, he poses his lament as a question: "Is it not a maimed and imperfect nature that I am conversant with?"

Perhaps closer to revolution than evolution, the most recent trend in ecological thinking fully integrates the human community in the environmental model. The welcome news is that this finally outlines an ethical approach that encourages us to take responsibility for our influence. We have the choice and the opportunity to contribute to the greater good.

Environmental historian William Cronon's 1995 essay "The Trouble with Wilderness; or, Getting Back to the Wrong Nature" is an insightful, articulate discussion of "wilderness" and "wildness." Cronon was among the first to liken the landscape to a palimpsest:

This is wild. In autumn, a chestnut oak acorn (*Quercus prinus*) germinates in moss on an island in the middle of the Susquehanna River. This process occurs annually, without any deliberate human intervention, as oaks on the island reproduce themselves. Inviting true wildness into the garden means adopting a design ethic that welcomes the regenerative power of plant populations, and a management ethic that controls wisely and only when necessary.

a surface that has been written on repeatedly, each time the previous writing having been imperfectly erased and therefore remaining partly readable. He suggests the old idea of "wilderness" presents the "false hope of an escape from responsibility, the illusion that we can somehow wipe clean the slate of our past and return to the *tabula rasa* that supposedly existed before we began to leave our marks on the world." Cronon believes "learning to honor the wild—learning to remember and acknowledge the autonomy of the other" will be key to envisioning an "ethical, sustainable, honorable human place" in the global ecology. He says "wildness (as opposed to 'wilderness') can be found anywhere," in "seemingly tame fields and woodlots" and "in the cracks of a Manhattan sidewalk." The notion that wildness is a renewable resource is certainly encouraging. Somehow, William Robinson understood this implicitly when he envisioned free (autonomous) wild things having a place in our gardens.

Robinson's advocacy for a bit more ease and a little less control recognizes that freedom and wildness are

There is order in wildness. Bulblet ferns (*Cystopteris bulbifera*) arrange themselves in a diagonal line following a crevice in a limestone rock face in the Virginia mountains. The ferns are responding to growing conditions suited to their needs. The soil in the crevice is regularly moistened by water running down the rock, yet it drains well and provides good aeration for roots. The limestone creates an alkaline chemistry favored by this fern. Wild gardening derives beauty and utility from fitting plants' growth requirements to existing conditions.

inseparable. The wild garden doesn't abandon design, but it does imply that design devoted to complete control is unsustainable. Robinson valued both "the life we want" and the conservation of resources that results from self-perpetuating, ecologically viable plant populations in the garden. The Robinsonian wild garden is more than naturalistic: its patterns result from the dynamic interaction of the "multiplicity of things and living processes" that we call Nature (Raymond Williams 1980).

Although some plants persist and spread by vegetative means, most depend upon sexual reproduction for their long-term survival. True naturalization therefore depends upon the ability of plants, whether introduced (exotic) or indigenous (native), to complete their

reproductive cycle. Plants' ability to do this depends upon local conditions and on their genetic makeup. Indigenous species are usually synchronized with the local climate; however, changing soil conditions, moisture, sunlight, and temperatures can prevent them from producing viable seed. Introduced species may be able to tolerate growing conditions; however, the growing season may be too short for seed to mature.

Many species, whether indigenous or introduced, require cross-pollination between genetically distinct individuals in order to produce fertile seeds. For this reason, vegetatively propagated identical clones often cannot breed among themselves. Some woody species have separate male and female individuals, and both are required for seed production. Cultivated varieties

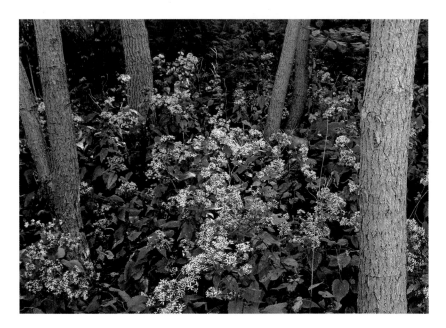

A naturalized population of white wood aster (*Aster divaricatus*) provides a reliable, weed-suppressing, flowering ground cover under a grove of sassafrass trees in a Pennsylvania garden. Dormant stalks are allowed to stand over winter, dispersing seeds that ensure the carpet of asters is continually renewed. Robinson used North American asters for similar purposes. His wild garden planting strategy went beyond naturalistic arrangement, focusing on the true naturalization of plants. Some species will endure many years if allowed to seed freely, but will quickly vanish from the garden if limited to the lifespans of individual plants.

resulting from simple selection typically retain their ability to reproduce by seed; however, cultivars resulting from hybridization, especially between different species, are often sterile. William Robinson grew many plants from seed, and this is still one of the surest strategies for establishing viable populations in the wild garden.

What is a wildflower? Traditionally, and sensibly, it is simply a plant that grows untended. Wildflowers may be found in mountain meadows, in old-growth forests, along rocky coastlines, or in vacant city lots. Wildflowers may be long-established indigenous species or they may be relative newcomers that have naturalized with or without human intervention.

How do wildflowers differ from weeds? This is mostly a matter of perspective. Wildflowers are usually perceived as pretty, but always as innocuous: they do no harm and give no offense. Weeds are unwanted wildflowers. Weeds may be pretty, but their presence is perceived as detrimental to human purpose. An indigenous wildflower in one habitat may be judged an introduced weed in another.

The global flora has been in continual flux throughout the grand scale of history, and all our present ecologies are the result of evolution and migration. Wildness has been essential to the origin and sustenance of today's species, and will remain so for tomorrow's. Wilderness may be no more than a mythic ideal; however, wildness is something tangible, knowable, and valuable.

The morning sun silhouettes Queen Anne's lace (*Daucus carota*) on Montgomery Farm in Texas. Closely related to the cultivated carrot, this plant is a wildflower to some and a weed to others. It is an introduced species that may have originated in Asia but long ago became naturalized in the Americas, Australia, Africa, Europe, and the Mediterranean. It is innocuous in this Texas habitat, growing in a modern balance with a wide range of indigenous grasses and wildflowers.

WOODLAND WILD GARDENS

SUSSEX, ENGLAND, WHERE GRAVETYE is located, has long been known for its fine deciduous forests. Though William Robinson often focused on herbaceous plants and a wide array of wild garden settings, he seems to have had the greatest enthusiasm for woodlands. His 1906 book, *The Garden Beautiful: Home Woods, Home Landscape*, is a clear promotion of woodlands for their intrinsic value and as a place to make wild gardens. In the preface, written from Gravetye, Robinson states, "In the district in which I live there are hundreds of acres of beautiful woods never seen by any but the gamekeeper; woods sheeted with Kingcups, Primroses, and Wood Hyacinths, more beautiful in their effect than any garden." He describes woodlands near to the home as ideal locales to "naturalize good native plants not already to be found there, or the finer woodland plants of other countries." Robinson's writings inspired woodland wild gardens far beyond England, and especially in deciduous forested regions of North America. His vision continues to find ever-greater expression in woodland gardens of all sizes, both public and private.

Gardens inspired by Robinson's ideas are often referred to as "Robinsonian." In North America, there is no greater Robinsonian wild garden than at Winterthur, in northern Delaware. Winterthur is much more than a woodland garden. Like Gravetye, it has forests and fields, ponds and streams, and memorable views between all of these. Also like Gravetye, Winterthur was once a working farm with livestock in the

fields, and both places still have rural railroads at their peripheries. The woods at Winterthur exceed those at Gravetye in height, with oaks, beeches, tulip trees, and hickories forming a canopy over one hundred feet tall.

Winterthur's oldest surviving garden area, the March Bank, is within this canopy. Begun in 1902 by Henry Francis du Pont, it is a spectacular interpretation of Robinson's concepts. Inspired by his 1904 copy of *The Wild Garden*, du Pont experimented with naturalizing thousands of daffodils (*Narcissus*), snowdrops (*Galanthus*), snowflakes (*Leucojum*), *Crocus*, squills (*Hyacinthoides*) and glory-of-the-snow (*Chionodoxa*), beneath the big trees. He continued expanding the palette to include a vast array of naturalized flowering plants and ferns. Many of these were recommended in *The Wild Garden*, including Apennine anemones, hostas, asters, goldenrods, ostrich ferns, and royal ferns. Like Robinson, du Pont mixed indigenous and introduced species adapted to conditions on the site. More than a century later, du Pont's woodland wild garden is very much alive.

Mt. Cuba Center, in Greenville, Delaware, not far from Winterthur, is a woodland wild garden with a regional focus. Unlike Winterthur's cosmopolitan mix, Mt. Cuba's plantings are limited to plants indigenous to the Piedmont (foothill) region of the Appalachian mountains. The property includes diverse woodland growing conditions from sun to shade and moist to dry. The garden is managed to illustrate the display potential of the Piedmont flora, not to replicate

Glory-of-the-snow (*Chionodoxa luciliae*) and other naturalized bulbs paint the woods' floor blue in early April on the March Bank at Winterthur, in northern Delaware. The Bank's south-facing slope is alive with a succession of herbaceous bloom beginning in January with snowdrops, and continuing well into May. Each autumn, as the herbaceous layer is going dormant, a mulching mower is used to shred leaves fallen from canopy trees. This allows the organic material to return to the soil, but makes it easier for bulbs to push up through the leaf layer the following spring.

RIGHT Blue phlox (*Phlox divaricata*) blooms in great drifts in early May on the March Bank along with trilliums, mayapples, Virginia bluebells (*Mertensia virginica*), and English and Spanish wood hyacinths.

FAR RIGHT Great sweeps of ostrich fern (*Matteuccia struthiopteris*) wend their way over the north-facing slope opposite the March Bank at Winterthur. The banks of the small stream at the bottom of the slope provide habitat for naturalized moisture-loving species including sedges, ferns, and hostas. Canopy trees and a variety of indigenous and introduced shrubs self-sow freely. Some are edited to preserve views and design intent, while others remain as essential elements in the garden's regenerative process.

LEFT Seeds ripen on *Eupatorium* species including Joe-pye-weed and white snakeroot below towering tulip trees at Winterthur. Allowing these and other plants to complete their reproductive cycles is necessary to maintaining naturalized populations in the garden, and is a resource-conserving approach to keeping much of the ground covered with vegetation.

BELOW Reminiscent of Gravetye, Winterthur's woods open out to rolling fields and meadows. In keeping with Robinson's tradition, casual mown paths make their way through a taller matrix of introduced and indigenous grasses.

LEFT Indigenous to the Appalachian Piedmont region, great blue lobelia (*Lobelia siphilitica*) grows along a rocky run at Mt. Cuba Center. Growing conditions in this garden site are very similar to those of the lobelia's typical habitat, and the planting has become naturalized.

BELOW Bold masses of golden ragwort (*Senecio aureus*) brighten a moist woodland garden at Mt. Cuba Center. The ragwort is a good example of a plant that might be too vigorous to mix in a formal border, but is ideally suited to the woodland wild garden.

habitats; however, many species are truly naturalized in sites suited to their requirements. In addition
to long-lived perennial species, Mt. Cuba's woodland
gardens include vibrant displays of many ephemeral
plants such as forest phacelia (*Phacelia bipinnatifida*),
a biennial, and short-lived perennials such as bluets
(*Houstonia caerulea*) which persist by self-sowing.

The vitality resulting from true wildness is often
essential to the sustainable management of large
woodland landscapes. This is certainly the situation at the site of Frank Lloyd Wright's masterpiece,
Fallingwater, in Pennsylvania's Laurel Highlands.
Completed in 1938, Fallingwater is surrounded by
the five-thousand acre Bear Run Nature Reserve. The
Western Pennsylvania Conservancy is responsible for
the stewardship of the house and the reserve. Wright's
intent was to design a structure woven into the fabric
of the surrounding woods and waters, and that the

Forest phacelia (*Phacelia bipinnatifida*) mingles with mayapples, on a woodland slope at Mt. Cuba Center. Rarely encountered in cultivation, this biennial species is ideally suited for naturalizing in the woodland wild garden.

LEFT At Fallingwater, rhododendrons, birches, ferns, mosses, and other species mostly indigenous to Pennsylvania's Laurel Highlands region are naturalized all around the house. By allowing plants to self-sow and selectively editing the excess, the Western Pennsylvania Conservancy maintains the site's elemental wildness while conserving maintenance resources.

LEFT BELOW Roots of a sweet birch (*Betula lenta*) flow over rocks exposed along the gravel roadway from the visitor center to the house site at Fallingwater. Polypody and shield ferns inhabit cracks and crevices along with a colorful mix of mosses and lichens. This beautiful assemblage is not the result of deliberate planting, but of allowing indigenous plants to naturalize in habitat resulting from shaping of the land long ago.

This intimate woodland path in a suburban Pennsylvania garden is comprised
almost entirely of naturalized indigenous
species. The space is framed by paw-
paw (*Asimina triloba*), American beech
(*Fagus grandifolia*), and spicebush
(*Lindera benzoin*). The herbaceous layer
is diverse including Christmas ferns
(*Polystichum acrostichoides*), mayapples
(*Podophyllum peltatum*), jack-in-
the-pulpit (*Arisaema triphyllum*),
woodland goldenrods (*Solidago caesia*
and *Solidago flexicaulis*), and sedges
(*Carex grayi* and *Carex laxiculmis*).

LEFT A box turtle finds shady refuge below the Christmas ferns in this garden. These turtles prefer moist woods with thick leaf litter, and eat fruits of woodland plants including mayapple and jack-in-the-pulpit.

BELOW In mid-June, naturalized violets form the groundcover in a wooded edge of the same Pennsylvania garden. Although violets are typically considered weeds in formal designs, their long-lived, free-seeding nature is useful and ecologically valuable in wild gardens, where they contribute to habitat.

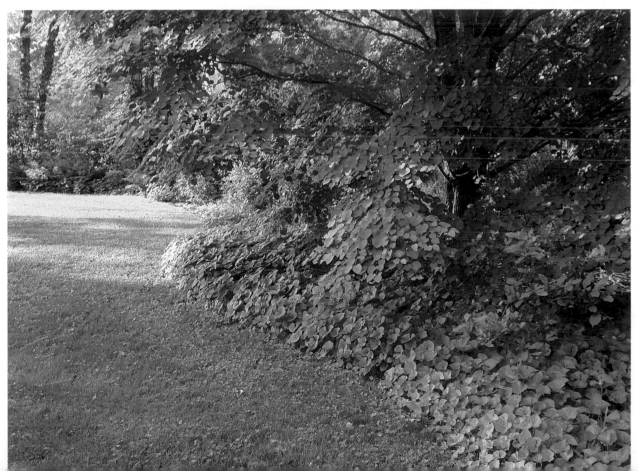

dwelling would forever provide insights into the site's living dynamics. Wright nestled his building among the indigenous vegetation and though his clients, the Kaufmanns, grew some introduced species, there were no traditional gardens skirting the house. In fulfilling its mission to preserve this "harmonious union of man's work with nature," the Conservancy utilizes the property's authentic wildness, employing a mix of planting, preserving, and editing techniques.

Woodland wild gardens employing naturalized plants are also appropriate for smaller residential properties, where they can lower maintenance requirements while increasing year-round interest and habitat diversity. Following Robinson's advice to fit plants to place, rather than amending conditions to accommodate poorly adapted plants, results in labor savings and reduced resource consumption. Naturalized plant populations help suppress weeds and are better able to fill in empty spaces when individual plants fail.

Detail of the previously shown violet groundcover seen here in April. Violets are necessary food for fritillary butterflies. Although the adult butterflies take nectar from milkweeds, thistles, and other summer-blooming plants, the caterpillars feed on violet foliage. Eggs are laid in late summer when violets are going dormant. The larvae hatch in autumn and overwinter in leaf litter. They begin feeding on new violet growth in spring and then they pupate before hatching as butterflies.

WILDNESS IN MEADOW AND PRAIRIE GARDENS

INTEREST IN MEADOW AND PRAIRIE GARDENS has steadily increased since Robinson's time along with the desire for a more sustainable alternative to mowed turf on sunny open landscapes. Although the words *meadow* and *prairie* are often used interchangeably, they are distinct at least in origin.

Meadows are typically grassy open spaces that result from human activity including mowing and clearing. Many meadows were once cleared for crops or pasture use. Other meadows are the result of extreme site characteristics, such as thin rocky soil or waterlogged conditions, that favor the growth of grasses and their close relatives.

True prairies are covered primarily in taller, warm-season grasses mixed with lesser numbers of broad-leaved herbaceous flowering plants (forbs). The classic tall-grass prairies of the North American Midwest are fire-ecologies: they are dependent upon frequent fires to retain their grassy dominance. In the absence of fire or an alternate clearing mechanism, many prairies eventually revert to woodlands.

Although meadows seeded with annuals may

This gravel hill prairie is one of six types of prairie ecosystems that make up the Dixon Prairie garden at the Chicago Botanic Garden in Illinois. The prairie types differ according to underlying soils and moisture levels. This type is drier than most, and features a drought-tolerant mix of lower-growing grasses with asters, coneflowers, goldenrods, and other forbs.

flower colorfully for a year or two, they quickly revert to weedy growth. As Robinson understood, the most sustainable meadow gardens (or prairie gardens) are comprised of locally adapted, hardy perennial grasses and forbs. If established with vigorous species capable of naturalizing, meadow and prairie wild gardens offer low-maintenance alternatives to lawn while contributing meaningfully to habitat for birds and other animals, and to groundwater recharge.

LEFT A great blue heron takes flight from the shoreline of the wet prairie at the Chicago Botanic Garden.

RIGHT Vibrant populations of Joe-pye-weed (*Eupatorium fistulosum*) and New York ironweed (*Vernonia noveboracensis*) bloom in August in a meadow clearing in the Western Pennsylvania Conservancy's Bear Run reserve. Both species are locally indigenous, but have naturalized on the moist slope below the cabin. Maintaining this flowering meadow requires once-annual mowing in late winter or spring and occasional removal of seedling woody plants and undesirable species.

BELOW A spicebush swallowtail takes nectar from an ironweed at Bear Run reserve.

LEFT Blue vervain (*Verbena hastata*) blooms in July in a moist section of the managed meadow at Pennsylvania's Longwood Gardens.

BELOW The managed meadow sits on land once devoted to farming and orchards. The meadow's naturalized mix of regionally indigenous species has been evolving for over thirty years, and is constantly in flux. This broad view in late October reveals patterns of grass and forb populations. Grass paths through the meadow lead to distinct vantage points. The meadow provides habitat for a great diversity of bird life including hawks, owls, hummingbirds, swallows, kingbirds, warblers, meadowlarks, flickers, woodpeckers, orioles, and finches. Over sixty species of birds have been seen in or on the fringes of the meadow, which adjoins an old-growth woodland.

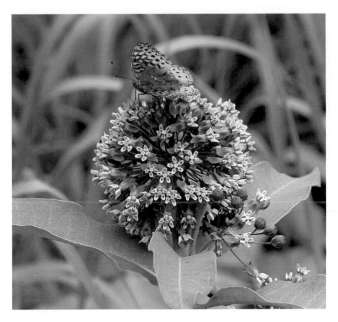

LEFT Common milkweed (*Asclepias syriaca*) flowers in June, attracting bees and a great spangled fritillary butterfly. This is one of four different milkweed species naturalized in Longwood's managed meadow, and all provide edible foliage and nectar for butterflies.

BELOW A wooden bridge and observation deck span the wide natural drainage at the low point of the meadow. Naturalized populations have organized themselves in accord with the meadow's varied hydrology. Moisture-loving species including blue-stemmed asters (*Aster puniceus*), Joe-pye-weed (*Eupatorium fistulosum*), blue vervain (*Verbena hastata*), and soft rush (*Juncus effusus*) occur in great intertwining masses where the ground is most often wet. On drier slopes species such as little bluestem (*Schizachyrium scoparium*), Indian grass (*Sorghastrum nutans*), and various goldenrods (*Solidago* spp.) are more common. The meadow is burned annually, but this is evolving toward a rotational cycle. Longer accumulations of organic matter are more likely to produce fuel fires hot enough to control woody seedlings.

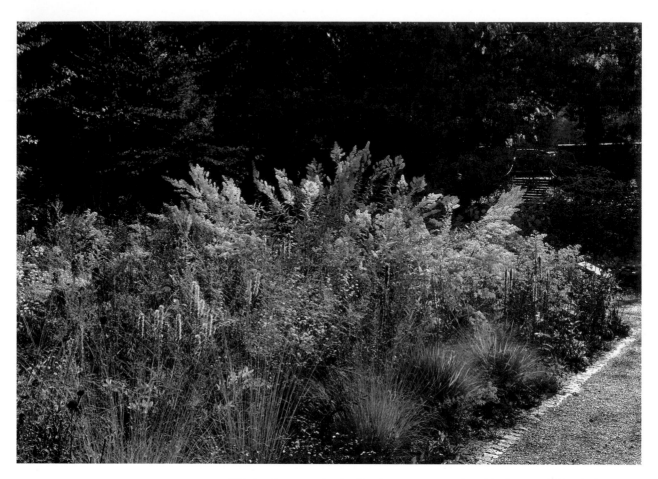

This luminous garden by Cassian Schmidt at Hermannshof in southern Germany is comprised of North American prairie species including showy goldenrod (*Solidago speciosa*), various *Aster* and *Liatris* species, purple lovegrass (*Eragrostis spectabilis*), and prairie dropseed (*Sporobolus heterolepis*). Plantings based upon dynamic, naturalized mixes of North American plants have proved highly sustainable in northern European urban and suburban landscapes.

COASTAL WILD GARDENS

FITTING PLANTS TO PLACE, rather than fitting the place to plants, is at the heart of Robinson's wild garden concept. This idea was inspired by his travels, during which he observed conditions in diverse habitats and noted the plants adapted to them. He was intrigued by plants growing along seashores and coasts, thriving on rocks or in sharply drained sands and gravels, often in the midst of salt spray. In *The Wild Garden*, Robinson describes places near and far, from wintergreens (*Pyrola* spp.) flourishing in moist sandy soils "between the sand-hills on the coast of Lancashire" to *Clematis cirrhosa* growing "in the islands and on the shores of the Mediterranean."

Although coastal regions may not provide conditions suitable for traditional inland gardens, they offer unique potential for wild gardens that recognize opportunity in what might less creatively be viewed as adversity. The New Jersey Pine Barrens is such a place. Situated on the North American Atlantic coastal plain, it is a vast region of deep, droughty sands and gravels juxtaposed with rivers and bogs fed by great fresh-water aquifers. Soil and water conditions are highly acidic, and this has profoundly influenced the local vegetation. Elizabeth White began her wild garden there in 1923. Named "Suningive" and located at Whitesbog, within what is now Brendan T. Byrne State Forest, White's

At Whitesbog in October, multicolored leaves of white fragrant waterlilies, *Nymphaea odorata*, are bright against reflective, tea-colored waters of the New Jersey Pine Barrens. Robinson admired this indigenous waterlily and noted the "dark pools of water" when he glimpsed the Pine Barrens during his 1870 visit to North America. The waters are naturally colored by tannins and other organic materials.

Elizabeth White's early photo of the pond in her wild garden, Suningive. The pond resulted from grading work for the house. In White's words, "The hollow left, when supplied with water from a nearby irrigating ditch, became a pool. Lily seeds came with the water, and by the second summer tiny pads floated on the little pond. The third summer the lilies bloomed. Now they must be thinned each spring to insure open water to mirror sunsets, the moon, and stars." Deliberate and spontaneous seeding introduced many indigenous species to White's wild garden, including two local bog orchids, the grass-pink (*Calopogon tuberosus*) and the rose pogonia (*Pogonia ophioglossoides*).

LEFT Locally indigenous species including Pine Barrens gentian (*Gentiana autumnalis*) are visible in Elizabeth White's photo of a circular space defined by pine rounds at Suningive. This short-lived perennial gentian has a reputation for being difficult to grow, yet it persisted by self-seeding in the wildness of White's garden.

CENTER LEFT Perfectly adapted to the sandy, moist, acid conditions, grass-pink (*Calopogon tuberosus*) found a new home in Elizabeth White's coastal garden.

CENTER RIGHT Pine Barrens gentian (*Gentiana autumnalis*) in mid September.

BOTTOM Shortia (*Shortia galacifolia*) blooms in April at Suningive. Although White devoted her life to the agriculture, culture, and ecology of the New Jersey Pine Barrens, she was a pragmatist, not a purist, regarding plants she grew in her garden. Believing they would thrive in her local conditions, White introduced species from similarly acidic habitats in south-eastern North America, incuding shortia, sourwood (*Oxydendron arboreum*), Carolina rhododendron (*Rhododenron catawbiense*), galax (*Galax aphylla*), fetterbush (*Pieris floribunda*), and yellowroot (*Xanthorhiza simplicissima*). More than a half century later, all of these persist at Suningive, and although many have naturalized, none has spread far beyond White's garden.

house and garden and their ecological context survive as inspiration for modern coastal wild gardening.

Nearly five thousand miles south of Suningive, Chilean landscape architect Juan Grimm's Los Vilos garden is a remarkable modern celebration of coastal wildness. Grimm, who is also an architect, credits the richness and strength of Chile's indigenous flora as providing the principal inspiration for his work. Located on the rocky coast north of Santiago, his garden mixes local Chilean plants with introduced species adapted to the site's dry, sunny, and salty conditions. The house and garden's unifying ethic is to reveal the seasonal events and inexorable changes in a coastal landscape.

FAR LEFT The setting sun illuminates flowering stalks of locally indigenous *Puya venusta* in Juan Grimm's Los Vilos garden. This persistent, naturally occurring population is in constant flux. It is essential to the design of the garden and yet it is truly wild. Grimm (2005) perceives the landscape as "a moment in the cycle of Nature; an infinite succession of scenes in constant movement."

LEFT Perfectly adapted to the sand, sun, and salt, locally indigenous *Alstroemeria pelegrina* grows among rocks in Grimm's garden.

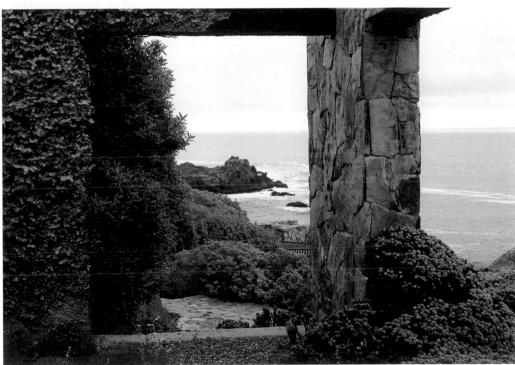

A naturalized mix of indigenous and introduced species helps frame the view from Grimm's wild garden on the coast of Chile.

WILD IN THE CITY

IN MATERIAL HE PREPARED FOR A PROPOSED but never-published 1932 edition of *The Wild Garden*, Robinson wrote,

> As to the origin of my ideas of the Wild Garden, I think they first occurred to me along the banks of the Southern Railway between East Grinstead and West Hoathly. Sometimes when I went though the station I had a pocketful of seeds of some bush or plant which I used to scatter about, usually forgetting all about them afterwards but most certainly they all came up again.

Was Robinson being mischievous, or was he simply taking delight in setting life into motion in an improbable place? Industry was still on the rise in Robinson's time, and he can be forgiven for failing to imagine a world in which crumbling factory landscapes would provide a wealth of new habitats. However, his many references to wildness on old walls, ruins, and along railways point to an enthusiasm for the regenerative power of naturalized plants in derelict urban places.

Traditional ecological concepts of stable "climax" vegetation types are evolving toward more complex models of a global flora continually evolving in

Drawn by a steam locomotive, a Bluebell Railway train travels the old Southern Railway route William Robinson used to commute from Gravetye to London, scattering seeds along the way.

A ruin is now the featured sculptural object in this public space in Cologne, Germany, proving the contemplative power of controlled dereliction. A cosmopolitan mix of plants finds sustenance in the crevices while indigenous reed grass (*Phragmites australis*) flourishes at the margins. Cologne's urban landscape is a great palimpsest, having been continuously re-written since the settlement's founding prior to A.D. 50.

character. With this perspective the cosmopolitan wildness of urban places acquires new meaning and value. Imaginative new city parks and public spaces are providing insights into the successional process in habitats profoundly altered by human activity.

Among the best of these is Nature Park Schöneberger Südgelände in former West Berlin. The site was once a freight railyard, constructed in the 1890s with myriad parallel tracks used to sort and re-organize trains. In the aftermath of World War II, rights for all Berlin railyards were given by the Allies to the East German Reichsbahn, which restricted or eliminated train traffic into West Germany. The Südgelände yard

was essentially abandoned by 1952, and in the ensuing decades the landscape has been reclaimed by successional vegetation. Pioneering grasses and forbs were gradually joined by shrubs and trees, and today the site is increasingly wooded. The wild plants naturalizing between the tracks are a mix of indigenous and introduced species. White-barked European birch (*Betula pendula*) is abundant, as are North American black locust (*Robinia pseudoacacia*) and red oak (*Quercus rubra*).

The park was opened in May 2000, following a masterplan by ÖkoCon & Planland. Professors Ingo Kowarik and Stefan Körner at the Institute of Ecology

Naturalized waterlilies mingle with grasses and other moisture-loving species while vines tumble over walls in this former coal and steel plant in Duisburg, Germany. The vegetation fulfills a healing function, helping to remediate residual soil and groundwater pollution. Abandoned in 1985, the site is now open as a public park: Landschaftspark Duisburg Nord, designed in 1991 by landscape architect Peter Latz.

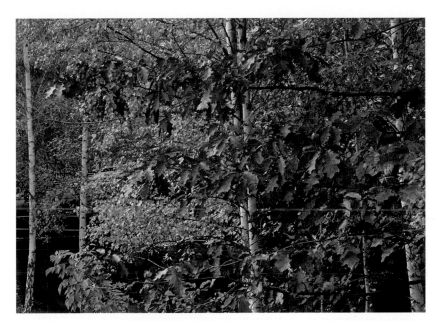

LEFT The naturalized woodland flora at Nature Park Südgelände in Berlin includes abundant North American red oaks.

BELOW Wildness is the defining motif of the Südgelände, which occupies former railyards in Berlin. Cultural geographer and urban planner Karl Ganser is quoted in stainless steel letters over the park's entry, saying "Art is the nearest neighbor to wildness."

in Berlin refer to Südgelände as "new wilderness." In *Wild Urban Woodlands* (2005) Körner summarizes biodiversity in the park, which is currently home to more than three hundred vascular plants, twenty-eight breeding birds, nearly fifty macrofungi, fifty-seven spiders, and more than two hundred bees and wasps. The forty-four acre site also attracts an estimated minimum of fifty thousand visitors per year. Surely William Robinson would appreciate the richness of this new type of wild garden.

Although *The Wild Garden* was published long before ecological science entered popular thought, it clearly recognizes gardens as a blend of environmental and cultural dynamics. Robinson's book remains an inspiration to all of us interested in sustaining an evolving relationship with the global landscape.

LEFT At the Nature Park Südgelände, walkways made by filling tracks with permeable gravel lead gracefully through wild urban woodlands of indigenous white birch and other species from around the globe.

ABOVE A forest plantation or a wild garden? Locally indigenous feather-reed grasses (*Calamagrostis epigejos*) have naturalized between European white birches planted for reforestation at Berlin's margin.

THE WILD GARDEN

Fifth Edition of 1895

Combe in west
country with
Primroses,
Kingcups, and
Daffodils.

THE WILD GARDEN

or

The Naturalization and Natural Grouping
of Hardy Exotic Plants
with a Chapter on the Garden
of British Wild Flowers

FIFTH EDITION

by

WILLIAM ROBINSON

Illustrated by Alfred Parsons

'*Adspice quos submittat humus formosa colores
Ut veniant hederae sponte sua melius*'
PROPERTIUS

John Murray • Albemarle Street
London
M.DCCC.XCV

I WENT TO STAY AT A VERY GRAND AND BEAUTIFUL PLACE in the country where the grounds are said to be laid out with consummate taste. For the first three or four days I was enchanted. It seemed so much better than Nature, that I began to wish the earth had been laid out according to the latest principles of improvement. In three days' time I was tired to death; a Thistle, a heap of dead bushes, anything that wore the appearance of accident and want of intention was quite a relief. I used to escape from the made grounds and walk upon the adjacent goose common, where the cart ruts, gravel pits, bumps, coarse ungentlemanlike Grass, and all the varieties produced by neglect were a thousand times more gratifying.

SYDNEY SMITH

INSCRIBED TO

The Very Reverend

S. REYNOLDS HOLE, D.D.

Dean of Rochester

BY HIS FRIEND

THE AUTHOR

CONTENTS

——◆◆——

LIST OF ILLUSTRATIONS

———••———

PREFACE
to the Second Edition of 1881

————••————

WHEN I BEGAN, SOME YEARS AGO, to urge the cause of the innumerable hardy flowers against the few tender ones, put out in a formal way, the answer frequently was, 'We cannot go back to the mixed border' that is to say, the old way of arranging flowers in borders. Knowing, then, a little of the vast world of plant beauty quite shut out of our gardens by the 'system' in vogue, I was led to consider some ways in which it might be brought to our gardens; and among them was the name and scope of the 'Wild Garden.' I was led to think of the vast numbers of beautiful hardy plants from other countries which might be naturalized, with a very slight amount of trouble, in many situations in our plantations, fields, and woods—a world of delightful plant beauty that we might in these ways make happy around us. We cannot only grow thus a thousandfold more lovely flowers than were seen in flower-gardens, but also many which, by any other plan, have no chance of being seen in gardens.

In this edition, by the aid of drawings, I have tried to tell what the system is;—if I were to write a book for every page that this contains, I could not suggest the many beautiful aspects of vegetation which the Wild Garden may give us.

The illustrations are, with a few exceptions, the work of Mr. Alfred Parsons, and the drawing and engraving have been several years in execution. They are after nature, in places where the ideas expressed in the first small edition of the book had been carried out, or where accident, as in the case of the beautiful group of Myrrh and white Harebells at Cambridge, had

Warrens Wood,
Gravetye 1903, by
Henry G. Moon.

Spiræas, bushy and herbaceous.

given rise to beautiful plant pictures. I cannot too heartily thank him for the skill which he devoted to the drawings, and for his success in showing the motive of the 'Wild Garden.'

There has been some misunderstanding as to the term 'Wild Garden.' It is applied essentially to the placing of perfectly hardy exotic plants under conditions where they will thrive without further care. It has nothing to do with the old idea of the 'Wilderness.' It does not mean the picturesque garden, for a garden may be highly picturesque, and yet in every part the result of ceaseless care.

What it does mean is best explained by the Winter Aconite flowering under a grove of naked trees in February; by the Snowflake, tall and numerous in meadows by the Thames side; by the blue Lupine dyeing an islet with its purple in a Scotch river; and by the blue Apennine Anemone staining an English wood blue before the coming of our Bluebells. Multiply these instances a thousandfold, given by many types of plants, from countries colder than ours, and one may get a just idea of the 'Wild Garden.' Some have thought of it as a garden run wild, or sowing annuals in a muddle; whereas it does not interfere with the regulation flower-garden at all.

I wish it to be kept distinct in the mind from the various sorts of hardy plant cultivation in groups, beds, and borders, in which good gardening and good taste may produce many happy effects; distinct from the rock-garden in its many aspects—all asking for skill and care; from the borders reserved for choice hardy flowers of all kinds; from the hardy sub-tropical garden or that of hardy plants of fine form; from the ordinary type of 'Spring Garden;' and from our own beautiful native flowers, delightful in our woods and fields and hedgerows. In country gardens, where, on the outer fringes of the lawn, in grove, park, copse, or by woodland walks or drives, there is often ample room, fair gardens and new and beautiful pictures may be formed by its means as the swift springs and summers pass.

W. R.
May 28, 1881

PREFACE
to the Fifth Edition of 1895

———◆◆———

THE WILD ROSE HAS GIVEN HER PETALS to the winds for over twenty summers since this book with its solitary wood-cut first saw the light, and if these many years give me any right to judge my own book, I may say that much experience since tells me that the '*Wild Garden*' deserved to live, and that such ideas carried out with some regard to the soil and other things affecting plants in each place, may be fertile in making our open air gardens more artistic and delightful.

The best thing I have learnt from my own wild gardening is that we may grow without care many lovely early bulbs in the turf of meadows (i.e., fields mown for hay) without in the least interfering with the use of the fields. The Blue Anemones, Crocus, Snowdrops, Narcisses, Snowflakes, Grape-Hyacinths, Dog's-tooth Violets, Stars of Bethlehem, Fritillaries, St. Bruno's Lily, Snow-glories, Wild Hyacinths, Scilla, and Wild Tulips best fitted for this early-gardening in the meadow turf, wither before the hay is ready for the scythe, and we do not find a trace of the leaves of many of them at hay time. Many of the plants of the mountains of Central Europe and also of those of what we call the south and east, such as those of Greece and Asia Minor, bloom with me earlier than our own field or woodland flowers. Our feebler sun awakes them in the snowless fields, and so we enjoy many spring flowers while our grass is brown. And if they come so early in the cool and high 'forest range' in Sussex they will be no less early in the warm soils as in Surrey, or in the many valley soils—sheltered as they often are by groves and banks of evergreens. As nearly every

A Golden Rod.

97

country house is set in meadows it is easy to see what a gain this is, not only for its beauty but because it lets us make an end of the repeated digging up of the flower-garden for the sake of a few annual and other spring flowers—themselves to be removed just in the loveliest summer days.

This spring I saw some evidence of what bold wild-gardening may give us in its effects on the beauty of landscape views. The picturesque view from Narrow-water House near Newry, across the park to the bay and the mountains that guard it, was much enhanced during March and the early part of the present spring by the great cloud of Daffodils covering a mound in the foreground. The Daffodils (the double kind so common in Ireland) spread over the mound in clouds, here and there massed close. It was not only good as a picture but as a lesson in the planting in the wild-garden of such flowers—which are often dotted about separately, much as fruit trees are in an orchard, instead of being held together in masses and bold groups, running out here and there into smaller ones.

Many of the reviewers of the book did not take the trouble necessary to see its true motive, and some of them confuse it with the picturesque garden, which may be formed in many costly ways, whereas the idea of the

Columbines and
Geraniums in
meadow-grass.

wild garden is placing plants of other countries, as hardy as our hardiest wild flowers, in places where they will *flourish without further care or cost*. As I first used the word 'wild garden' in this book and in the '*Field*' newspaper, where some of the articles appeared many years ago, I wish to make its aim and meaning clear.

I am happy to be able to illustrate the book with good wood engravings in these days of many 'processes,' often called 'improvements,' in book illustration, but which, so far, are its ruin. The few cuts done in the former edition by such processes have been re-engraved on wood for this. Some of the ideas in the book, such as the beautiful effects one may get in hedgerows and by grass-walks, are not illustrated as I hope they will be in future editions.

As good examples of wild-gardening are likely often to lie out of my own path, and as distinct and unlooked for results will often arise, I should be grateful to all who will tell me of them in the hope of making the book more suggestive in future, as among the ways of escape from the death-note of the pastry-cook's garden there is none more delightful to all who have any grass or fields or woods about them.

W. R.
April 18, 1894

Lilies coming up through carpet of White Arabis.

CHAPTER I
Explanatory

—◆◆—

ABOUT A GENERATION AGO A TASTE BEGAN to be shown for placing numbers of tender plants in the open air in summer, to produce showy masses of colour. The plants were mostly from sub-tropical lands; placed annually in the open air of our summer, and in fresh earth, every year they grew and flowered abundantly until cut down by the first frosts. The showy colour of this system was very attractive, and since its introduction there has been a gradual rooting out of all the old favourites in favour of this 'bedding' system. This was carried to such an extent that it was not uncommon, indeed it was the rule, to find the largest gardens in the country without a single hardy flower, all energies being devoted to the few exotics for the summer decoration. It should be borne in mind that the expense for this system is an annual one; that no matter what may be spent in this way, or how many years may be devoted to perfecting it, the first sharp frost of November announces yet further labours.

Its highest results need hardly be described; they are seen in all our public gardens; our London and many other city parks show them in the shape of beds filled with vast quantities of flowers, covering the ground frequently in a showy way. I will not here enter into the question of the merits of this system; it is enough to state that even on its votaries it is beginning to pall. Some are looking back with regret to the old mixed-border gardens; others are endeavouring to soften the harshness of the bedding system by the introduction of fine-leaved plants, but all are agreed that a mistake has been made in destroying all our old flowers, from Lilies to

Late May's golden light bathes mixed borders in this view north from Gravetye's west entry.

101

Hepaticas, though few have a fair idea of the numbers of beautiful hardy plants which we may gather from every northern and temperate clime to grace our gardens under a more artistic system.

My object in *The Wild Garden* is now to show how we may have more of the varied beauty of hardy flowers than the most ardent admirer of the old style of garden ever dreams of, by naturalizing many beautiful plants of many regions of the earth in our fields, woods, and copses, outer parts of pleasure grounds, and in neglected places in almost every kind of garden.

I allude not to the wood and brake flora of any one country, but to that which finds its home in the vast hill-fields of the whole northern world, and that of the hill-ground that falls in furrowed folds from beneath the hoary heads of all the great mountain chains of the world, whether they rise from hot Indian plains or green European pastures. The Palm and sacred Fig, as well as the Wheat and the Vine, are separated from the stemless plants that cushion under the snow for half the year, by a zone of hardier and not less beautiful life, varied as the breezes that whisper on the mountain sides, and as the rills that seam them. They are the Lilies, and Bluebells, and Foxgloves, and Irises, and Windflowers, and Columbines, and Violets, and Crane's-bills, and countless Pea-flowers, and Moon Daisies, and Brambles, and Cinquefoils, and Evening Primroses, and Clematis, and Honeysuckles, and Michaelmas Daisies, and Wood Hyacinths, and Daffodils, and Bindweeds, and Forget-me-nots, and blue Omphalodes, and Primroses, and Day Lilies, and Asphodels, and St. Bruno's Lilies, and the myriads of plants which form the flora of the northern or temperate regions of vast continents.

It is beyond the power of pen or pencil to picture the beauty of these plants. Innumerable and infinitely varied scenes occur in all northern and temperate regions, at many different elevations, the loveliness of which it is impossible to portray; the essential thing to bear in mind is that the plants that go to form them *are hardy, and will thrive in our climate as well as native plants.*

Large-flowered Meadow Rue; type of plant mostly excluded from the Garden.

Such beauty may be realized in every wood and copse and shrubbery that screens our 'trim gardens.' Naturally our woods and wilds have no little loveliness in spring; we have here and there the Lily of the Valley and Snowdrop, and everywhere the Primrose and Cowslip; the Bluebell and the Foxglove take possession of whole woods; but, with all our treasures in this way, we have no attractions in or near our gardens compared with what it is within our power to create. There are many countries, with winters colder than our own, that have a rich flora; and by choosing the hardiest exotics and planting them without the garden, we may form garden pictures. To some a plant in a free state is more charming than any garden denizen. It is taking care of itself; and, moreover, it is usually surrounded by some degree of graceful wild spray—the green above, and the moss or grass around.

Numbers of plants of the highest order of beauty may be at home in the spaces now devoted to rank grass and weeds, and by wood-walks in our shrubberies.

Among my reasons for thinking wild gardening worth practicing by all who wish our gardens to be more artistic and delightful are the following:—

First, because hundreds of the finest hardy flowers will thrive much better in rough places than ever they did in the old-fashioned border. Even small plants, like the Ivy-leaved Cyclamen, a beautiful plant that we rarely find in perfection in gardens, I have seen perfectly naturalized and spread all over the mossy surface of a thin wood.

Secondly, because they will look infinitely better than they ever did in formal beds, in consequence of fine-leaved plant, fern, and flower, and climber, grass and trailing shrub, relieving each other in delightful ways. Many arrangements will prove far more beautiful than any aspect of the old mixed border, or the ordinary type of modern flower-garden.

Thirdly, because no disagreeable effects result from decay. The raggedness of the old mixed border after the first flush of spring and early summer bloom had passed was intolerable to many, with its bundles of decayed stems tied to sticks. When Lilies are sparsely dotted through

Night effect of
Large Evening
Primrose in the Wild
Garden (Œnothera
Lamarckiana).

masses of shrubs, their flowers are admired more than if they were in isolated showy masses; when they pass out of bloom they are unnoticed amidst the vegetation, and not eyesores, as when in rigid unrelieved tufts in borders, &c. In a semi-wild state the beauty of a fine plant will show when at its height; and when out of bloom it will be followed by other kinds of beauty.

Fourthly, because it will enable us to grow many plants that have never yet obtained a place in our 'trim gardens.' I mean plants which, not so showy as many grown in gardens, are never seen therein. The flowers of many of these are of great beauty, especially when seen in numbers. A tuft of one of these in a border may not be thought worthy of its place, while in some wild glade, as a little colony, grouped naturally, its effect may be exquisite. There are many plants too that, grown in gardens, are no great aid to them—like the Golden Rods, and other plants of the great order Compositæ, which merely overrun the choicer and more beautiful border-flowers when planted amongst them. These coarse plants would be quite at home in copses and woody places, where their blossoms might be seen or gathered in due season, and their vigorous vegetation form a covert welcome to the game-preserver. To these two groups might be added plants like the winter Heliotrope, and many others which, while not without use in the garden, are apt to become a nuisance there. For instance, the Great Japanese Knotworts (Polygonum) are certainly better planted outside of the flower-garden.

Fifthly, because we may in this way settle the question of the spring flower-garden. Many parts of every country garden, and many suburban ones, may be made alive with spring flowers, without interfering at least with the flower-beds near the house. The blue stars of the Apennine Anemone will be enjoyed better when the plant is taking care of itself, than in any conceivable formal arrangement. It is but one of hundreds of sweet spring flowers that will succeed perfectly in our fields, lawns, and woods. And so we may cease the dreadful practice of tearing up the flower-beds and leaving them like new-dug graves twice a year.

Sixthly, because there can be few more agreeable phases of communion

1. In Victorian England, tropical plants were often grown in a "stove" or "stove house," a glass structure with a brick fluelike source of heat that provided the warmer temperature required by such tender plants. Stove houses were also used for propagating over winter months. —Ed.

The Mountain Clematis.

with Nature than naturalizing the natives of countries in which we are infinitely more interested than in those of which greenhouse or stove[1] plants are native. From the Roman ruin—home of many flowers, the mountains and prairies of the New World, the woods and meadows of all the great mountains of Europe; from Greece and Italy and Spain, from the hills of Asia Minor; from the alpine regions of the great continents—in a word, from almost every interesting region the traveller may bring seeds or plants, and establish near his home living souvenirs of the various countries he has visited. If anything we may bring may not seem good enough for the garden autocrat of the day, it may be easy to find a home for it in wood or hedgerow; I am fond of putting the wild species of Clematis and other exotic climbers and flowers in newly-formed hedgebanks.

Moreover, the great merit of permanence belongs to this delightful phase of gardening. Select a rough slope, and embellish it with groups of the hardiest climbing plants,—say the Mountain Clematis from Nepal, the sweet C. Flammula from Southern Europe, 'Virginian Creepers,' various hardy vines, Jasmines, Honeysuckles, and wild Roses and briers. Arranged with some judgment at first, such a colony might be left to take care of itself; time would but add to its attractions.

Some have mistaken the idea of the wild garden as a plan to get rid of all formality near the house; whereas it will restore to its true use the flower-garden, now subjected to two tearings up a year (i.e., in spring and autumn); as may be seen in nearly all public and private gardens, in France as well as in England—new patterns every autumn and every spring—no rest or peace anywhere. In the beautiful summer of 1893, the flower-beds in the public gardens of Paris were quite bare of all flowers in June, before the wretched winter-nursed flowers had been set out in their patterns. If such things must be done in the name of flower gardening, it were many times better to carry them out in a place apart, rather than expose the foreground of a beautiful house or landscape to such disfigurement. Spring flowers are easily grown in multitudes away from the house, and, therefore, for their sakes the system of digging up the flower-beds twice a year need not be carried out. Wild gardening should go hand in hand with the thorough cultivation of the essential beds of the flower-garden around the house, and to their being filled with plants quite different from those we entrust to the crowded chances of turf or hedgerow:—to rare or tender plants or choice garden flowers like the Tea Rose and Carnation—plants which often depend for their beauty on their double states, and for which rich soil and care and often protection are essential.

Blue-flowered Composite plant; fine foliage and habit; type of noble plants excluded from gardens (Mulgedium Plumieri).

CHAPTER II
Example from Hardy Bulbs in Grass of Lawns or Meadows

———•◦•———

WE WILL NOW SEE WHAT MAY BE DONE with one type of vegetation—hardy bulbs like Daffodils and plants dying down after flowering early in the year, like the Winter Aconite and the Blood-root (Sanguinaria). How many of us enjoy the beauty which hardy Spring flowers of these orders might give us? How many get beyond the conventionalities of the flower-garden, with its patchings, and taking up, and drying, and playing with our beautiful Spring Bulbs? Garden adornment with early bulbs is merely in its infancy; at present we merely place a few of the showiest in geometrical lines. The little done leads to such poor results, that many people, alive to the charms of a garden too, scarcely notice Spring-flowering Bulbs at all, regarding them as things which require endless care, and as interfering with the 'bedding-out.' And this is likely to be the case so long as the most effective of all modes of arranging them is unused.

Look, for instance, at the wide and bare belts of grass that wind in and around the shrubberies in nearly every country place; frequently, they never display a particle of plant-beauty, and are merely places to be roughly mown now and then. But if planted here and there with the Snowdrop, the blue Anemone, Crocus, Scilla, and Winter Aconite, they would in spring surpass in charms the gayest of 'spring gardens.' Cushioned among the grass, the flowers would unfold prettier than they can in the regulation sticky earth of a border; in the grass of spring, their natural

Naturalized daffodils bloom in great drifts in early March under a dove tree, *Davidia involucrata*, planted by Robinson on the slope above Gravetye's West Garden.

bed, they would look far better than they ever do on the brown earth of a garden. Once carefully planted, they—while an annual source of the greatest interest—occasion no trouble whatever.

Their leaves die down so early in spring that they would not interfere with the mowing of the grass, and we should not attempt to mow the grass in such places till the season of vernal flowers had passed. Surely it is enough to have a portion of lawn as smooth as a carpet at all times, without shaving off the 'long and pleasant grass' of the other parts of the grounds. It would indeed be worth while to leave many parts of the grass unmown for the sake of growing many beautiful plants in it. If in a spot where a wide carpet of grass spreads out in the sheltered bay of a plantation, there be dotted the blue Apennine Anemone, any Snowdrops, the Snowflake, Crocuses in variety, Scillas, Grape-Hyacinths, many Narcissi, the Wood Anemone, and any other Spring flowers liking the soil, we should have a picture of vernal beauty, the flowers relieved by grass, and the whole devoid of man's weakness for tracing wallpaper patterns where

Star of Bethlehem
in Grass.

everything should be varied and changeful. In such a garden it might be clear that the artist had caught the true meaning of Nature in her grouping, without sacrificing anything of value in the garden.

Mowing the grass once a fortnight in pleasure grounds, as now practised, is a costly mistake. We want shaven carpets of grass here and there, but what nonsense it is to shave it as often as foolish men shave their faces! There are indeed places where they boast of mowing forty acres! Who would not rather see the waving grass with countless flowers than a close surface without a blossom? Think of the labour wasted in this ridiculous work of cutting the heads off flowers and grass. Let much of the grass grow till fit to cut for hay, and we may enjoy in it a world of lovely flowers that will blossom and perfect their growth before hay time; some who have carried out the ideas of this book have waving lawns of feathery grass where they used to shave the grass every ten days; a cloud of flowers where a daisy was not let peep.

It is not only to places in which shrubberies, and plantations, and belts of grass in the rougher parts of the pleasure ground, and moss-bordered walks occur that these remarks apply. The suburban garden, with its single fringe of planting, may show like beauty, to some extent. It may have the Solomon's Seal arching forth from a shady recess, behind tufts of many Daffodils, while in every case there may be fringes of strong and hardy flowers in the spring sun.

The prettiest results are only attainable where the grass need not be mown till nearly the time the meadows are mown. Then we may have gardens of Narcissi, such as no one dreamt of years ago; such as no one ever thought possible in a garden. In grass not mown at all we may even enjoy many of the Lilies, and all the lovelier and more stately bulbous flowers of the meadows and mountain lawns of Europe, Asia, and America.

On a stretch of good grass which need not be mown, and on fairly good soil in any part of our country, beauty may be enjoyed such as has hitherto only gladdened the heart of the rare wanderer on the high mountain lawns and copses, in May when the earth children laugh in multitudes on their mother's breast.

All planting in the grass should be in natural groups or prettily fringed colonies, growing to and fro as they like after planting. Lessons in this grouping are to be had in woods, copses, heaths, and meadows, by those who look about them as they go. At first many will find it difficult to get out of formal masses, but that may be got over by studying natural groupings of wild flowers. Once established, the plants soon begin to group themselves in pretty ways.

As further showing what may be done with the hardy bulbs, not only outside the flower-garden but even in what forms part of the farm, I print here a paper read by me before the Royal Horticultural Society in 1891.

EARLY FLOWERING BULBS IN MEADOW GRASS

Having during the past five years planted several hundred thousand bulbs and roots in meadow grass, the results may, perhaps, be suggestive to others. An advantage of this method is the delightfully artistic arrangements of which it permits. It is also a deliverance of flower-beds from the poor thing known as spring bedding. This system of 'bedding,' which began in France, and is there still seen in all its bareness, spread to many of our gardens; it consisted of putting out in formal masses a few biennial plants, such as the Wood Forget-me-not and Silene. This necessitated a complete change in the contents of the beds every year, or, rather, twice a year, and therefore prevented their being given to the nobler kinds of flower gardening. It is easy to have all the flower-beds proper devoted to precious and enduring plants, such as Tea Roses, Carnations, and the plants that require good and constant culture and time for development, by the aid of the wild garden.

We begin with the blue **Apennine Anemone**: of this I planted several thousand roots in grass. Not having any beds or borders near the house where I wanted it, I put it in meadows around the house in light broken groups and masses. It flowers and increases every year without the slightest attention; and, being early in growth as compared with grass, disappears before the meadow grass has to be cut in summer. This is an important point, and shows what may be done with many beautiful spring flowers. One has the pleasure of seeing them year by year flowering in their seasons, and giving delightful effects, as these Anemones did this year, both in groups in the open sunny fields, and also clustering thickly round the base of old Elm-trees on their margin. Among the blue Anemone, here and there, stood groups of Narcissus, and in cases where the Anemones and Daffodils flowered together the effect was often beautiful. This Anemone is hardy, and always grows freely in grass, and never deteriorates.

In Greece this year I saw on the mountains acres of the blue **Greek Anemone**, and think it is equally as hardy and as free as the Italian one, and quite as useful for naturalization in the grass. The simplicity of the culture of plants like this, which thrive in meadow grass, and the foliage of which withers before the grass need be mown for hay, makes them a most important group, as so much meadow grass comes near most country houses. A very great number of the spring flowers of the northern world may be treated in this manner, and give us beautiful spring gardens.

The most important group of all these early flowers is the **Narcissus**. Five years ago I planted many thousands in the grass. I never doubted that I should succeed with them, but I did not know I should succeed nearly so well. They have thriven admirably, bloomed well and regularly, the flowers are large and handsome, and, to my surprise, have not diminished in size in open, rich, heavy bottoms, along hedgerows, in quite open loamy fields, in every position I have tried them. They are delightful when seen near at hand, and also effective in the picture. The leaves ripen, disappear before mowing time comes, and do not in any way interfere with farming. The harrowing and rolling of the fields in the spring are a little against the foliage, and probably a better result could be obtained with the finer Narcissus by wood-walks and open copses, which abound in so many English country places.

With the great group of forms of the common English, Irish, and Scotch Daffodils I have had good results; they thrive better and the flowers are handsomer than in the wild plant—not uncommon in Sussex. The little Tenby Daffodil is very sturdy and pretty, and never fails us. The only one that has failed is the Bayonne Daffodil.

A very delightful feature of the Narcissus meadow gardening is the way great groups follow each other in the fields. When the Star Narcissi begin to fade a little in their beauty the Poet's follow, and as I write this paper we have the most beautiful picture I have ever seen in cultivation. Five years ago I cleared a little valley of various fences, and so opened a pretty view. Through the meadow runs a streamlet. We grouped the Poet's Narcissus near it, and through a grove of Oaks on a rising side of the field. We have had some beauty every year since; but this year, the plants having become established, or very happy for some other reason, the whole thing was a picture such as one might see in an Alpine valley! The flowers were large and beautiful when seen near at hand, and the effect in the distance delightful. This may, perhaps, serve to show that this kind of work will bring gardening into a line with art, and that the artist need not be for ever divorced from the garden by geometrical patterns which cannot possibly interest anybody accustomed to drawing beautiful forms and scenes.

I need say no more to show the good qualities of this group of plants for wild gardening, many places having much greater advantages than mine for showing their beauty in the rich stretches of grass by pleasure-ground walks. Various kinds of places may be adorned by Narcissi in this way—meadows, woods, copses, wood-walks, and drives through ornamental woodland and pleasure grounds, where the grass need not be mown until late in the summer.

Dog's-tooth Violet.—This beautiful and delicate-looking plant surprises me by the free way it grows in grass in several places where I have planted it, varying a good deal, according to the soil, in its size, but never failing to interest by its beautiful leaves and flowers. It withers rather early, and is a perfect plant for meadow culture.

Last autumn I made a trial of the **Grape-Hyacinth** (Muscari), and was delighted with the result this spring, with the pretty clouds of blue, quite distinct in the grass.

Snowdrops in various forms are indispensable, and do fairly well, though they vary very much in the way they thrive on different soils. They look much better in the grass than in bare earth.

Among the flowers in the meadow grass there is nothing more beautiful than the varieties of **Snake's-head** (Fritillaria). It is the very type of plant for this work, and the white and pretty purple flowers are admired by all who see them in the early grass.

The **Crocus**, from its early brilliancy, is indispensable, and the hardier forms are able to take care of themselves. In all this kind of work, if we could get the wild types of plant it would be all the better, because such beauty as they possess is certainly never the result of cultivation. When we buy bulbs highly cultivated we may expect some reduction in the size of the flower when it assumes a semi-wild state; but nobody who cares for the form and beauty of the flowers will mind this reduction. Flowers from bulbs planted several years are somewhat smaller than the newly planted kinds, but certainly no less beautiful. While we have proof enough that Crocuses grow well in meadow grass on a large scale, they seem particularly suitable for growing under groves of trees, their growth coming before the trees spread forth their leaves. In many country places outside the garden proper there are many spaces under trees often possessed by Gout-weed and other weeds which should be given to the Crocus and like early flowers.

Tulips.—I have tried only one wild Tulip, the Wood Tulip (T. sylvestris), sent me from Touraine to the extent of a thousand roots, and I do not think we have lost any; they bloom gracefully every year. The shortness of bloom which Tulips show should lead one to try the wild kinds in grass. Their broad, fragile leaves are apt to be injured by the harrow. They are better tried in copses or drives through woods, where they are free from this injury.

Stars of Bethlehem (Ornithogalum).—The starry trusses of the common old border kind are quite different in effect from our other early flowers, and very pretty. In this genus there is much difference in habit, the greenish, drooping-flowered kinds, like O. nutans, giving quite a different

The association of exotic and British wild flowers in the Wild Garden. The Bell-flowered Scilla, naturalized with our own Wood Hyacinth.

effect from that of the common white border kind. There is no difficulty about growing these in grass.

The **Snowflakes** (Leucojum) do admirably, the early one being a more precious flower than the Snowdrop, useful to gather, and brightly effective very early. The later ones are also graceful things, free and handsome in rich grass.

Living in a world of Wood Hyacinths, there was less need to try the **Scillas** than the non-British flowers, which give us new aspects of flower life; but so far the results have been good with the Spanish Scilla and the new **Scilla-like plants** (Chionodoxa), which are early and disappear early.

To this sort of flower gardening, which extends so much the interest in flower life, the bulb merchants might do great good by offering such bulbs and roots as these at lowest possible rates by the thousand. It would pay cultivators to grow such roots in quantity for the public, as it now pays Lincolnshire farmers to grow the Snowdrop for the trade in that popular flower. The whole success of wild gardening depends on arranging bold, natural groups with a free hand.

Portion of field of Poet's Narcissus in bloom. Late variety, planted six
years; soil cool loam. Meadow mown every year; plants never degenerating,
but improving yearly, and showing much difference as to size and
height according to rainfall. No preparation of the soil given, only
turning up the sod, placing the bulbs beneath and replacing the turf.

CHAPTER III
Example from the
Forget-me-not Family

———•◦•———

I WILL NOW TRY TO SHOW what may be done with one type of northern plants—the Forget-me-nots, one not so rich as others in plants for the wild garden. Through considering it, however, we may be able to form some idea of what we may do by choosing from all the plants that grow in the meadows and mountain woods of Europe, Asia, and America.

The Forget-me-not family embraces a number of coarse weeds, but if it had only the common Forget-me-not, would have some claims on us; but what lovely exotic plants there are in this order that would afford delight if met with creeping about along our wood and shrubbery walks! Nature, say some, is sparing of her deep true blues; but there are obscure plants in this order that possess the deepest and most delicate of blues, and which will thrive in the wild garden.

The creeping Omphalodes verna even surpasses the Forget-me-not in the depth and beauty of its blue, and runs about quite freely in any shrubbery or open wood, or even in turf in moist soil not very frequently mown. Besides, in the garden border, it would be a not very agreeable object when once the sweet spring bloom had passed; whereas, in lanes, woods, or copses, the low plants are not noticed when out of flower, but live modestly till returning spring jewels them with the charm of fine colour.

Another plant of the order is so useful for this purpose, that if a root or two of it be planted in any shrubbery, it will soon run about, exterminate

Looking south from the West Garden in late May. As in Robinson's time, many of Gravetye's borders are filled with a mix of naturalized herbaceous plants, shrubs, and vines.

the weeds, and prove quite a lesson in wild gardening. I allude to the Caucasian Comfrey (Symphytum caucasicum), which grows about twenty inches high, and bears quantities of the loveliest blue pendulous flowers. It, like many others, does well in a grove, or shrubbery, filling in the naked spaces between the trees, and has a quick growth but never becomes weedy. As if to contrast with it, there is the deep crimson Bohemian Comfrey (S. bohemicum), which is sometimes startling from the depth of its vivid colouring; and the White Comfrey (S. orientale), quite a vigorous-growing kind, blooming in spring.

These Comfreys, indeed, are admirable plants for rough places—the tall ones thriving in a ditch, and flowering better than they do in the garden in prim borders. There are about twenty species, mostly from Southern and Central Europe, Asia, and Siberia.

I should perhaps omit the British Forget-me-nots, wishing now chiefly to show what we may do with exotics quite as hardy as our own wildings, but where a British plant is not wild within the district in which we live, it may be brought into the wild garden with good effect. When I went to Gravetye Manor there was not a trace of the common Water Forget-me-not there, in either of the two lakes or in the woodland streams that fed them. We had of course to get so good a plant for the garden to carpet moist beds; it grows very rapidly, and when the plants were thick the

Caucasian Comfrey
in Shrubbery.

boys took baskets of them and threw them into the streamlets and round the margin of the ponds so that in a year we had delightful groups of the Forget-me-not by the water in many places, and as the ponds and streams of the place flow into the Medway River, no doubt seeds and plants were carried far down its banks. Also, as there was none of our beautiful Wood Forget-me-not in the place, I sowed some in freshly sown turf and had the pleasure of seeing it bloom for many years. Thus we may not only introduce hardy exotic plants, but some fair flowers of our own country. How many garden waters do not show some of our handsomest native water-plants, as the Flowering Rush, great Buttercup, and Bog-bean?

We have another Forget-me-not, not British, which surpasses them all—the early Myosotis dissitiflora. This is like a patch of the bluest sky, before our own Forget-me-not has opened, and is admirable for banks in a wood or for moist stony slopes. In carting away the soil to put in the foundations of an addition to Gravetye house, many loads of rubbish were thrown in a heap in Warrens Wood, where a year afterwards I came upon some beautiful tufts of this which had planted themselves from bits thrown out with the rubbish.

For rocky places and sandy banks we have the spreading Gromwell (Lithospermum prostratum) of a fine gentian-blue.

Good plants are the Lungworts (Pulmonaria), and often destroyed through exposure on bare dug and often dry borders. The old Pulmonaria (Mertensia virginica) is one of the loveliest of spring flowers. It is rare in gardens; if placed in a moist place near a stream, or in a peat or free sandy bottom, it will live; whereas it frequently dies in a garden. The newer and more easily grown Mertensia sibirica is a lovely plant, taller and loving a marshy place. These two plants alone would repay a trial in the wild garden and may show that for cultivation alone (apart from art, or arrangement) the wild-garden idea is sometimes worth carrying out.

Among annual flowers we have Borage, a few seeds of which scattered over fresh ground soon germinate and form pretty patches. The Cretan Borage is a curious old perennial, seldom seen in gardens; for its growth is robust and its habit coarse. It is, however, a good plant for a rough place where the ample room which it wants may be spared and where it may take care of itself, showing among the hardiest of the early spring flowers.

Thus, though I say little of the Alkanet (Anchusa) tribe, several of which could be found worth a place with our own British Evergreen Alkanet, it will be seen that a garden of beauty may be reaped from the Forget-me-not tribe alone. Any one could settle the matter to his satisfaction in a couple of years with these plants alone, in a shrubbery, ditch, lane, or copse, always provided that he takes care to adapt each kind to the position and the soil. For instance, the Giant Comfrey will grow six feet high in rich or moist soil in a ditch, and therefore, once fairly started, might be

The Cretan Borage (Borago Cretica); example of perennial too vigorous for flower-beds.

trusted to take care of itself. The Caucasian Comfrey, on the other hand, grows from eighteen inches to two feet high, and is at home in the spaces in a copse or shrubbery. The creeping Forget-me-not (Omphalodes verna) is a little plant that creeps about in grass not over a span high, or forms a carpet of its own—these differences must be thought of, as without knowing something of the habits and stature of plants, mistakes will be made.

These Borageworts, as rich in blue as the gentians, are often poor rusty things in exposed sunny borders, and much in the way when out of flower, whereas in shady lanes, copses, or shrubberies, in hedgerow-banks, or ditches, we only notice them in their beauty.

CHAPTER IV
Example from the
Globe Flower Order

———•◆•———

THE BUTTERCUP ORDER OF PLANTS embraces many widely diverse in aspect from the common kinds that burnish our meadows. In it, for the wild garden, is the sweet-scented Virgin's Bower (Clematis flammula), a native of the south of Europe, but as hardy in all parts of Britain as our native Clematis. And as the Hawthorn sweetens the air of spring, so will this add fragrance to the autumnal months. It is never more beautiful than when crawling over some low tree or shrubs, and I have planted it in newly formed hedgerows. An open glade in a wood, or on shrubby banks near, would be charming for it, while in the pleasure ground it may be used as a creeper over old stumps or trees.

The Hair Bell Virgin's Bower (Clematis campaniflora), and the beautiful white Indian Clematis montana grandiflora, a native of Nepal, are as beautiful, and many others of the family are worthy of a place, rambling over old trees, bushes, hedgerows, or tangling over banks. These single wild species of Clematis are more graceful than the large hybrid kinds now common; they are very hardy and free.

In genial seashore districts a beautiful pale kind, common in Algeria, and in the islands and on the shores of the Mediterranean (Clematis cirrhosa), will be found charming—nearly evergreen, and flowering very early in spring—even in winter in some places and in mild years.

Next in this order we come to the Windflowers, or Anemones, and

Grasses and other hardy perennials spill over borders at Gravetye in late May.

more beautiful flowers do not adorn this world of flowers. Have we a bit of rich grass land not mown? If so, the beautiful Alpine Anemones (A. alpina and A. sulphurea) may be grown there, though they are rare and 'slow' to establish. Any sunny bushy bank or slope to adorn with charming early flowers? For this we have Anemone blanda, a lovely Greek kind; place it in open bare spots, as it is dwarf, and it will perhaps at Christmas, and onward through the spring, open its large blue starry flowers. The common Poppy Anemone (A. coronaria) will be happiest in open, bare, sandy or rocky places in loam; and the showy scarlet Anemone will do best in rich but not heavy soil.

Of other Anemones, hardy, free, and beautiful to run free in our shrubberies and pleasure grounds, the Japan Anemone, its white varieties, and the Snowdrop Windflower (A. sylvestris), are among the best of the exotic species. The Japan Anemones grow so strongly that they will thrive even among stiff brushwood, brambles, &c.; and scattered along the low, tangled margins of shrubberies.

Group of Globe flowers (Trollius) in moist places; type of nobler Northern flowers little cultivated in gardens.

Few plants are more lovely in the wild garden than the White Japan Anemone and the various other tall Anemones of the same country. The wild garden is a home for numerous plants, to which people often begrudge room in their borders, such as the Golden Rods, Michaelmas Daisies, Compass plants, and a host of others, which are beautiful for a season only, or perhaps too rampant for what are called choice borders and beds. This Anemone is one of the most beautiful of garden flowers, and one which is as well suited for the wild garden as the coarsest. Partial shade seems to suit it; and in any case the effect of the large white flowers is, if anything, more beautiful in half-shady places. The flowers, too, are more lasting here than where they are fully exposed.

As for the Apennine Anemone (the white as well as the blue forms), it is one of the prettiest flowers of any clime, and should be in every garden, in the borders, and scattered in woods and shrubberies. I have planted many thousands of it in various soils, and it never fails, though it shows a great

The White Japan
Anemone in the
Wild Garden.

difference in growth and freedom of bloom, according to the soil, being much larger for example on warm free Irish limestone soils than on cool soils in Sussex. But it is so well worth growing everywhere that for it alone it would be worth while to form a wild garden!

Near to it is the also beautiful blue Windflower of the Greek hills, in effect like the blue Apennine Windflower, but more varied in size and colour in the south, and in some of its forms earlier in bloom in spring. This might perhaps not have the same love for the grass as the Italian blue Anemone, but if not it would be easy to naturalize in bare or stony places. The yellow A. ranunculoides, a doubtful native, found in one or two spots in England, but not really British, is strange and charming but flowers well only on chalk.

The large Hungarian Hepatica (Anemone angulosa) grows freely among low shrubs and in half-shady spots, and we all know how readily the old Hepatica grows on garden soils of fair quality. There are many forms of the common Hepatica (Anemone Hepatica) grown in gardens, and all the colours of the species should be represented in every collection of spring flowers, where the soil is favourable to these plants, but Hepaticas are often evergreen plants, and being very dwarf ask for more care in naturalizing them than is needed for vigorous plants of the same order, some of which will hold their own among the coarsest weeds.

There are many of the Ranunculi, not natives of Britain, that would grow as freely as our native kinds. Many may remember the pretty button-like white flowers of the Fair Maids of France (Ranunculus aconitifolius fl. pl.), in the old mixed border. This, and the wild form from which it comes—a frequent plant in Alpine meadows—may also be enjoyed in our wild garden. Quite distinct from all these, and of charming beauty, is R. amplexicaulis, with flowers of pure white, and simple leaves of a glaucous green and graceful form; a hardy and pretty plant on almost any soil. This is one of the elegant exotic forms of a family well represented in the golden type in our meadows, and therefore valuable as giving us a distinct form.

Anemones in the Riviera.

Of the Globe Flowers (Trollius), there are various kinds apart from the native one, all rich in colour and good in form. These are among the noblest wild-garden plants—quite hardy, free of growth in the heaviest of soil and wettest of climates, a lovely type of early summer flower, and one distinct from any usually seen in our fields or gardens; for these handsome Glove Flowers are among the many flowers that for years have found no place in the garden proper. They are lovely in groups or colonies, in cool grassy places, where many other plants would perish, but where they will get on well, even among docks or the coarsest native plants. I put them in wet hollows at Gravetye that no man could clear of weeds and had the pleasure of seeing their handsome flowers come instead.

The Winter Aconite (Eranthis hyemalis) should be naturalized quite under the branches of deciduous trees, will come up and flower when the trees are naked, will have its foliage developed before the leaves come on the trees, and be afterwards hidden from sight. Thus masses of this earliest flower may be grown without sacrifice of space, and will be noticed only when bearing a bloom on every little stem. On heavy soils it is not so free or bright as on free and limestone ones.

That fine old plant, the Christmas Rose (Helleborus niger), likes partial shade better than full exposure, and should be used abundantly, giving it rather snug and warm positions, so that its flowers may be encouraged to open well and fully. Any other kinds may also be used. Recently many kinds of Helleborus have been added to our gardens; and although all of them are not conspicuous as the Christmas Rose, yet they are of remarkable beauty of foliage and habit as well as of blossom, and they flower in the spring. These, too, show the advantage of the wild garden as regards cultivation. They will *do better in any bushy places, or copses or in mutually-sheltering groups on warm banks and slopes, even in hedge-banks, old quarries, or rough mounds, than in the ordinary garden border.* Of the difference in the effect in the two cases it is needless to speak.

Some of the Monkshoods are handsome, but they are

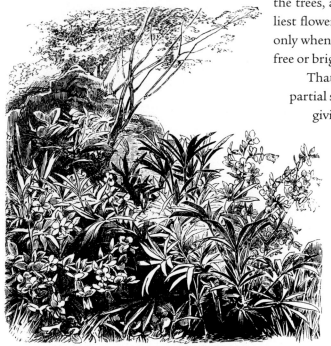

The Green Hellebore in the Wild Garden.

virulent poisons; and, bearing in mind what fatal accidents have arisen from their use, they are better not used at all in the garden proper. Amongst tall and vigorous herbaceous plants few are more suitable for rough places. They are robust enough to grow anywhere in shady or half-shady spots; and their tall spikes of blue flowers are very beautiful. An illustration in the chapter on the plants suited for the wild garden shows the common Aconite in a Somersetshire valley in company with the Butterbur and the Hemlock.[1] The larger rich blue kinds, and the blue and white one, are showy grown in deep soils, in which they attain a great height. When out of flower, like many other stately perennials, they were often stiff and ugly in the old borders and beds; in the wild garden their stately forms when flower-time is gone, no longer tied into bundles or cut in by the knife, will group finely with other vigorous herbaceous vegetation.

The Delphiniums, or tall perennial Larkspurs, are amongst the most beautiful of all flowers. They embrace almost every shade of blue, and, being usually of a tall and strong type, will make way among vigorous weeds, unlike many things for which we have to recommend an open space, or a wood with nothing but a carpet of moss under the trees.

One of the prettiest effects which I have seen was a colony of tall Larkspurs. Portions of old roots had been chopped off by the men when a bed of these plants was dug in the autumn, and the refuse thrown into a near plantation, far in among the shrubs and trees. Here they grew in half-open spaces, so far removed from the margin that they were not dug and were not seen. When I saw the Larkspurs in flower they were more beautiful than they are in borders or beds, not growing in such close stiff tufts, but mingling with and relieved by the trees above and the shrubs around. This case points out that one might make wild gardens from the mere parings and thinnings of the beds and borders in autumn in any place where there is a collection of good hardy plants.

The engraving on the next page represents one of the most beautiful effects obtained in his wild garden by an acquaintance of mine who began when he knew very little of plants and their favoured haunts, and

1. See page 223. —Ed.

Tall Perennial Larkspurs, naturalized in Shrubbery (1878).

succeeded well in a not very favourable site. Herbaceous Pæonies are amongst the most free, vigorous, and hardy of perennial plants, and in free good soil with them alone most novel and beautiful effects may be carried out in most places where there is room. Even in small gardens, a group or two outside the margin of a shrubbery would be good. The effect of the blooms amongst the long grass is finer than any they present in borders, and when out of flower they are not in the way. It is almost needless to speak here of the great variety of forms now obtainable amongst these Herbaceous Pæonies, the fine double forms of which deserve the best cultivation in beds and borders—the hardy free-growing wild kinds will often come in for the wild garden. My friend's Pæonies formed a group that could be seen from a distance; when I saw them they were surrounded by long and waving grass. I cannot give any idea of the fine effect.

The blue alpine Clematis-like Atragene alpina is one of my favourite flowers—seldom seen out of a botanical garden. It likes to trail over old

Double Crimson Pæonies in grass at Crowsley Park.

stumps or through bushes, or over rocky banks. Speaking of such plants as this, one would like to draw a sharp distinction between them and the various weedy and indistinct subjects that are now creeping into cultivation owing to the revival of interest in hardy plants. Many of these have some botanical interest, but they can be only useless in the garden. Our chief danger now is getting into cultivation plants that are neither very distinct nor very beautiful, while perhaps we neglect many of the really fine kinds. This Atragene is a precious plant for low bush and bank wild gardening.

Among plants which one rarely sees in a flower-garden are the Meadow Rues; yet there is a quiet beauty about them. As some will grow often in a hedgerow or lane or byway, or in a copse, or under the shrubs, in places usually abandoned to common weeds, there is no reason why they should not be rescued from the oblivion of the botanic garden.

CHAPTER V

Plants Chiefly Fitted
for the Wild Garden

——•◆•——

A GOOD REASON FOR ONE FORM of the wild garden is that it offers us a way of growing a number of exotic plants not suited for garden culture in the old sense. Many of these plants have much beauty when in flower, and at other seasons, but they are so vigorous in growth that they overrun all their more delicate neighbours. Many, too, are so coarse that they are unfit for choice borders, and after flowering they leave a blank or a mass of unsightly stems. These plants are not pretty in gardens, and are a main cause of the neglect of hardy flowers; yet beautiful at certain stages.

A tall Harebell, stiffly tied up in a garden border, is at best of times an unsightly object; but the same plant growing amongst the long grass in a thin wood is lovely. The Golden Rods and Michaelmas Daisies used to overrun the old mixed border, and were with it abolished. But these seen together in a New England wood in autumn are a picture. So also there are numerous exotic plants of which the individual flowers may not be so striking, but which, grown in colonies, afford beautiful aspects of vegetation.

When I first wrote this book, not one of these plants was in cultivation outside botanic gardens. It was even considered by the best friends of hardy flowers a mistake to recommend them, for they knew that it was the mastery of these weedy vigorous plants that made people give up hardy flowers for the glare of bedding plants. The wild garden then, in

The public footpath connecting Gravetye with the village of West Hoathly wends its way through a hedgerow in late May.

Type of erect Compositæ
for the Wild Garden.

the case of these particular plants, opens up to us a new world of infinite beauty. In it every plant vigorous enough not to require the care of the cultivator or a choice place in the mixed border will find a home. Of such plants there are numbers in every northern country. The taller Yarrows, the stately Aconites, the vigorous, and at certain seasons handsome, Althæas, Angelica with its fine foliage, the herbaceous kinds of Aralia with fine foliage from the American woods, also the Wormwood family (Artemisia), the stronger kinds of American Cotton-weed (Asclepias), certain vigorous Asparagus, Starworts in great variety, Betonica, pretty, and with delicate flowers, but hardly fit for the mixed border, various vigorous Grasses, showy Buphthalmums, handsome Bindweeds, too free in a garden, the stout Campanulas, exotic Thistles, numerous Centaureas, somewhat too coarse for the garden; and among other hardy plants, the following are chiefly suitable for the wild garden:

Crambe	Helenium	Rhaponticum
Digitalis	Helianthus	Rheum
Dipsacus	Heracleum	Rudbeckia
Doronicum	Inula	Scolymus
Echinops	Lavatera	Silphium
Elymus	Ligularia	Solidago
Epilobium	Mulgedium	Symphytum
Eupatorium	Onopordon	Veratrum
Ferula	Phytolacca	Verbascum
Funkia	Polygonum	Vernonia
Galega		

Giant Cow Parsnip. Type of Great Siberian
herbaceous vegetation. For rough places only.

The Giant Scabious
(eight feet high)
(Cephalaria procera).
Tall herbaceous
plant, best fitted for
the Wild Garden.

CHAPTER VI
Ditches, Shady Lanes, Copses, and Hedgerows

—◆◆—

MEN SEEK SUNNY SPOTS for their gardens, so that they would scarcely perhaps care for these for a garden! Yet there are ditches, and shady nooks in every district, that may be made more beautiful than many a 'flower-garden.' But what would grow in them? Many of the beautiful wood plants of the north—things that do not care for sunny hillsides or meadows, but take shelter in woods, are happy deep between rocks, or in caves beneath the great boulders on many a mountain gorge, and garland the flanks of rock that guard the rivers on their way through the hills. And as these dark walls, ruined by ceaseless flow of the torrent, are often beautiful, so may we adorn the shady dykes and lanes. For while the nymph-gardener of the ravine may depend on the stray grains of seeds brought in the moss by the robin when building her nest, or on the mercy of the hurrying wave, we may place side by side the snowy white wood Lily (Trillium grandiflorum), whose home is in the shady American woods, the Twin-flower of Northern Europe, and find both thrive on the same spot.

In North America in the woods and near them I often saw the wet ditches filled with noble ferns. And not only may we be assured that numbers of the most beautiful plants of other countries will thrive in deep ditches and in like positions, but also that not a few of them, such as the white wood Lily, will thrive much better in them than in the open garden, the results widely differing according to the nature of the soil and

Woods in Summer, undated, by Henry G. Moon.

other things, the action of which is not always easy to understand. The Trillium has a flower as fair as any white lily, but, in consequence of being a shade-loving plant, it often perishes in a dry garden border, while in a shady moist dyke it will thrive as in its native woods; and, if in moist, free soil, prove as fair as anything seen in our stoves.

Our wild flowers take possession of the hedges that seam the land, often draping them with such inimitable grace that half the conservatories in the country, with their small red pots, are poor compared with a few yards' length of the blossomy hedgerow verdure. Wild Roses, Purple Vetch, Honeysuckle, and Virgin's Bower clamber above smaller, but not less pretty, wildings, and, throwing veils of graceful life over the hedgerow, remind us of the plant-life in the thickets of low shrubs on the Alpine meadows.

Next to the most beautiful aspects of Alpine flowers, there are few things in plant-life more lovely than the delicate tracery of low-climbing things wedded to the shrubs in all northern and temperate regions. Often perishing like grass, they are safe in the earth's bosom in winter; in spring, finding the bushes once more enjoyable, they rush over them as children from school over a meadow of cowslips. Over bush, over brake, on mountain or lowland copse, holding on with delicate grasp, they engrave themselves on the mind as the type of graceful plant-life.

Besides climbing Pea-flowers and Convolvuli, of which the stems perish in winter, we have the great tribes of wild vines, noble in foliage, the many Honeysuckles, from coral red to pale yellow, all beautiful; and the Clematidæ, varied, and lovely, some with small flowers borne in showers like drops from a fountain jet, and often sweet as Hawthorn blossoms.

This climbing vegetation may be trained and tortured into forms in gardens, but never will its beauty be seen until we entrust to it the garlanding of shrub, and copse, or hedgerow, fringes of plantation, or groups of shrubs and trees. All that need be done is to put in a few tufts of a kind, and leave them alone, adapting the plant to the spot and soil. The large Hungarian Bindweed would be best in rough places, out of the pale of the garden, so that its roots might spread where they could do no harm,

Foliage of Teazle, on hedge-bank in spring.

while a fragile Clematis might grow over a tree and star its green with fair flowers. In a wood we see a Honeysuckle clambering up through an old Hawthorn tree, and then struggling with it as to which should give most bloom—but in gardens not yet.

Some may say that this cannot be done in the garden, but it can be; because, for gardens we can select plants from so many countries, and adapt them to our particular wants and soils. We can effect contrasts, in which nature is often poor in one place, owing to the few plants that naturally inhabit one spot of ground. Foolish old 'laws' laid down by landscape-gardeners perpetuate the notion that a garden is a 'work of art, and therefore we must not attempt in it to imitate nature!' true gardening differing from all other arts in this that it gives us the living things themselves, and not merely representations of them in paint or stone or wood.

Where there are bare slopes, an excellent effect may be obtained by planting the stouter climbers, such as the Vines, Mountain Clematis, and Honeysuckles, in groups on the grass, away from shrubs or low trees; while, when the banks are precipitous or the rocks crop forth, we may allow a curtain of climbers to fall over them.

Endless charming combinations may be made in this way in many spots near country houses. The following are among the climbing and clinging hardy plants most suitable for garlanding copses, hedges, and thickets:—Everlasting Peas (many kinds), the Honeysuckles, Clematis (wild species mainly), the common Jasmine, Brambles, Vines (American and the common varieties), single Roses, Virginian Creepers (Ampelopsis), the large Bindweed (Calystegia dahurica), Aristolochia Sipho and A. tomentosa, and several of the perennial Tropæolums (T. pentaphyllum, T. speciosum, and T. tuberosum). The hardy Smilax and the Canadian Moonseed, too, are very handsome, and suitable for this kind of gardening.

Among the plants that are suitable for hedgerows and lanes, &c. are—Acanthus, Viola, both the sweet varieties and some of the large scentless kinds, Periwinkles, Speedwells, Globe Flowers, Trilliums, Plume Ferns (Struthiopteris), and many other kinds, the Lily of the Valley and its many varieties and allies, the Canadian Blood-root, Winter Greens (Pyrola),

The large white Bindweed. Type of nobler climbing plants, with annual stems. For hedgerows and shrubberies.

Solomon's Seal, and allied exotic species, May Apple, Orobus in variety, many Narcissi, the common Myrrh, the perennial Lupin, hardy common Lilies, Snowflakes, Everlasting Peas and allied plants, admirable for scrambling through low hedges and over bushes, Windflowers, the taller and stronger kinds in lanes and hedgerows, the various Christmas Roses that will repay for shelter, the European and hardier kinds of Gladiolus, such as G. segetum and G. Colvillei, the taller and more vigorous Crane's-bills (Geranium), the Snake's-head (Fritillaria) in variety, wild Strawberries of any variety or species, Giant Fennels, Dog's-tooth Violets in spots bare in spring, the Winter Aconite, the May-Flower, for sandy poor soil under trees, Toothworts (Dentaria), the 'coloured' forms of Primroses, 'Bunch' Primroses, Ox-lips, Polyanthus, the hardy European Cyclamens, Crocuses in places under trees not bearing leaves in spring, the yellow and pink Coronilla (C. montana and C. varia), many of the taller Harebells, Starworts (Aster), the Monkshoods which people fear in gardens; the different species of Allium often not welcome in gardens, some of which are beautiful, as, the White Provence kind and the old yellow garden Allium (A. Moly). With the above almost exclusively exotic things and our own wild flowers and ferns, beautiful colonies may be made.

When I first wrote *The Wild Garden*, it was to encourage the gardener to put some beautiful life in his garden grass, shrubberies, and half-waste places—if ashamed of that beautiful life among his Perilla and dark Beet and Alternanthera. But now I want the fields to be gardens too, since at Gravetye I found I could do so much in the meadows mown for hay. The wild garden I see now need not stop at the pleasure-ground fence. Among the ways one may enjoy it most is in the making of living fences.

In our country the system of keeping stock in the open air, instead of in sheds, makes a fence a necessity as all know to their cost, who have to look after a country place or farm of any size. But we live in mechanical days, when many think that among the blessings and fine discoveries of the age is that of making a gridiron fence! and so we see some of the fairest landscapes disfigured by a network of iron fencing. And when a man throws away beautiful living fences and gives us miles of ugly iron in the

The Nootka Bramble. Type of free-growing flowering shrub. For copses and shrubbery.

foreground of a fair landscape, I think of the Devil setting up as an econo-
mist. Artistic, too, no doubt some of these improvers think themselves!

IRON FENCES AND OUR LANDSCAPES

The iron fence bids fair to ruin the beauty of the English landscape, unless
men see its ugliness and its drawbacks as a fence, its great cost, and the
further cost of tinkering and daubing it with tar or paint. With bullocks
on one or both sides of an iron fence, its fragility as a fence is soon seen. It
is no use as a shelter, nor as a protection, as it only forms a ladder for all
who want to get over with ease. As a boundary fence it means the loss of
all privacy. Estates of much natural beauty have their charms stolen away
by iron fences. Used to fence the pleasure ground or by drives, the effect is
bad to any one who knows how much more beautiful live fences are. There
is nothing an iron fence does that an 'old fashioned' one will not do better, while it always looks well with its Ivy, Ferns, Primroses, and varied life.

The Yellow
Allium (A. Moly),
naturalized

The bad opinion of the old-fashioned fence arose from its being so often neglected, and injured by trees until no longer effective.

It is not only the tradesman emerging from the city who fancies there is no fence so perfect as an iron one. Such an idea would be excusable in mechanics, and many others who have not studied the question of fences from the point of safety, endurance, and beauty, and who fear the expense and trouble of forming a living fence. But I regret to see the plague of iron fencing in some of the finest country places and marring the foreground of good views.

NO FENCE SO GOOD AS A LIVE ONE ON A BANK

One objection to the live fence is its weakness at first, and the need of protecting it when small, but these difficulties are not insurmountable. It is usual to plant Quick[1] small, and then protect it with elaborate fencing on either side—wearisome work, for which there is no need if people would take the trouble to get plants strong enough to form a good fence to begin with. With stout Quick, and a mixture of Holly, or other strong bushes, a good fence can be made at once without protection being needed. In every country place it would be easy to have a few lines of young and vigorous Quick put out in fields in lines a yard or so apart, where they might get stout, and be ready for fencing at any time. Where there are underwoods with Quick growing in them, it is often easy to grub up bushes of it, cut them down half way, and plant them in a fence, always on a bank.

I have done this with success and without losing a bush, but should prefer to have a few lines of stout grown Quick ready to take up at any time. Most fences should be on banks with 'dicks'[2] where the ground requires them, because the bank itself forms a fence against lambs and small animals, and the added soil that goes to make the bank gives much better growth. Three years ago I formed a fence of this sort, every bush of which was gathered in the underwood near; the line of Quick was so strong that there was no need to fence them. To prevent, however, any chance of cattle rushing through, a thin Larch pole was run through along and just

1. Quick = hawthorn (*Cratægus*). —Ed.

2. Robinson's meaning here is unclear, and the word is not found elsewhere in a landscape or garden context. One possibility is that is is a misspelling of 'dyke', a term Robinson does use elsewhere. —Ed.

below the top of the fence, supported by the bushes, and no animal has since passed the fence or injured it. The waste slender tops of Larch lying in a wood near were used. This fence will be good for as many years as it is wanted, will form a shelter as well as a fence, and will not want any attention for many years to come. It should be clearly understood that in the formation of this fence we had not even the cost of the ordinary 'stake and heather' protection commonly used in re-making rough fences. The tough bushes did it all themselves, the sod bank helping them in all ways. Consider this as compared with the costly galvanized or iron fence, with its dangers, ugliness, and coldness!

By far the best fence for farm and general work is the living fence—the most satisfactory and least expensive in the long run, and the most beautiful in its effect upon the landscape and for its varied life. I mean the living fence that is not too trim, and annual trimming is not necessary. Small, 'skinny' Quick fences are not so handsome as rough ones. The constant clipping of fences is needless in many grazing and woody districts. In good arable farms it may be desirable, but in most districts where fields are large the fence should also be a shelter—a bold, free-growing screen, with Bramble, wild Rose, Ferns, Ivy, and other scrambling things that like to live in it.

I have many such fences that do not want attention for years at a time—on banks, as they always should be. They are better furnished at the bottom than some of the constantly clipped hedges. To plant on a bank may in some very dry soils, and where there is a low rainfall, be a mistake, but the bank itself doubles at least the depth of the soil, and the protection of the bank and its little dick is a great gain to fencing, by allowing Briers and wild Roses to fill in the bottom of the hedge, and preventing small animals from making tracks through. My fences round woods are only re-made when the underwood is cut, say every ten years, and that is sufficient. The mass of wood behind and the strong growth in the fence itself are such that no animal makes an attempt on them. The only source of weakness in such places is hedge trees, and they should be removed.

A hedge can be kept in good order for generations by cutting and laying it every ten or dozen years, and the owner of such a fence deserves to suf-fer if he does not take care that this is done when the time comes round. The labour for it is enormously less than the cost of forming and tarring the iron fence and keeping it in repair.

BUSHES TO USE AND AVOID IN FENCES

To use bad fencing plants is folly, the money is thrown away, and the work never done. I have planted some thousands of Quick this season, in lines three feet apart, for the sake of getting strong bushes to make fences, and some Cockspur Thorn, of which I saw an excellent fence in France in 1892. I am not so sure about the Cherry Plum, which grows well in some places, but is not so tough as a Thorn, and in some cold soils, where the Quick is all we want, the Cherry Plum will not thrive. A few Sloe bushes may be used, but they are not so tough as Quick. A few seedling common Hollies not over three feet high are good, and, where there are not many rabbits to bark it, nothing is more successful than Holly.

Hollies grow under trees better than any other fence plant. From the protection they give to stock, it is surprising that they are not more largely grown for shelter in stock-raising districts, and not clipped but grown naturally. One very often sees beautiful, almost natural fences of Holly and Quick in the forest districts of the south of England, and among Holly hedges well formed in better land, those at Woolverstone, in Suffolk, are excellent. Except, however, in open woodless districts where rabbits are few, Hollies are sure to be barked when rabbit food is scarce. I have planted several thousands within a few years, and none are intact that are not protected by wiring. Sweet Brier, Dog Rose, and cut-leaved Bramble are very good to mix, and beautiful too in a rough, wild-looking hedge.

It is as necessary to avoid bad fencing plants as to select and grow good ones. The worst is the common Privet, the ghost of what a fence plant should be. Its rapid growth deceives, and it is often used with a danger-ous sharp-pointed iron fence outside as a guard, and perhaps, at the same time, to be the death of some animal. Privet is a rapid grower, or seems so at first; it is never so strong a grower in the end as Quick, Holly, or wild Rose. The quicker the Privet grows the worse it is, and the plant should never be seen in a fence.

Laurel is a soft useless fence plant, apt to be killed in cold districts and in valleys. Spruce is sometimes used in hedgerows, and is most unfitted for them for many reasons. The common Elder is always a source of weakness in a fence, and should never be planted or allowed to live in a fence.

OAK AND OTHER NOT UGLY FENCING

Where there are beautiful views, people who enjoy the landscape will do well *not* to mar them with iron fencing. In some cases good views are kept by a sunk fence, and to prevent this from looking hard or deceptive in any way I throw a garland of wild Roses along the top of the wall, which marks the position of the fence, and always looks well. The groups of wild Roses I set out in a colony along the sunk fence made at Gravetye are charming at all seasons.

In many other cases, along important drives perhaps commanding interesting views, a finer thing by far than any iron fencing is the strong split Oak post-and-rail fence. There are many estates where Oak is abundant, and where the men split it up into stout heartwood posts and rails. This is not necessarily a dear fence, and it is a very beautiful and efficient one if well done. In colour it is perfect, improving as it gets older. Such a visible tangible fence will last for many years, and might come in the foreground of a picture by Corot or Turner. A few Sweet Briers or wild Roses stuck in the post-holes often turn out very pretty.

For dividing lines in stockyards, too, nothing is so good and safe as a split Oak fence. Where good effects are thought of, nothing is more important than good post-and-rail fences in certain places on the farm, where we want to keep animals back without hiding the view, and where shelter is not required. Oak park fencing is pretty, and in many cases efficient, but too expensive to be done on a large scale for field work. Nor should I rank it as high as a good live fence, because of its cost, repairs, and the quickness with which it is often destroyed when old.

THE FENCE AS A SHELTER

Apart from the ugliness of the iron fencing, its giving no shelter whatever is one of its worst points, as a good live fence gives excellent shelter for sheep and other animals. The prim, neat little hedge is not so good as a shelter, but better than an iron fence. A well-grown fence, cut down and re-made after a lapse of say ten years, gives good shelter.

There are many such shelter fences, with Holly and Thorn allowed to grow at will, with an interlacing of Ivy, all seated on a good bank. Such lines as these across the direction of the strong winds could not fail to be helpful for stock in exposed fields. We have plenty of materials to form such fences as hardy and enduring as the bank itself. We might even have them evergreen if we used the Holly largely.

The shelter of a good line of naturally-grown Holly on the north side of a high field in an exposed district would be equal to that of a shed. There would be no great difficulty in establishing such Holly fences in open farming districts where rabbits do not abound, but it is not so easy in wooded districts. Seedling plants, not large (i.e., one foot to three feet high), are the best to use. It is a good plan to buy some very small seedling Hollies, and let them get strong in a nursery, so as to be able to get a few when mending or making fences.

The more ordinary materials, too, with an occasional Holly intermixed, give very efficient shelter indeed. The Ivy runs through such fences and makes them very pretty, tying them together with its graceful lace work, and its growth seldom chokes the Quick or other plants.

THE FENCE BEAUTIFUL

So far this about the true British fence is to lead to what I want to emphasise—that the best and safest live fence may be beautiful as well as enduring and effective. If my reader will go so far as to form the right fence, then he has it in his power to make a very beautiful one, and to prove that use and beauty are one even in a fence. Wild rough fences in many countries are often pretty with Ivy, Clematis, Thorn, Fern, wild Rose, Honeysuckle, Brier and Sloe, but the trim clipped fence made of one sort of bush or tree only is stupidly ugly. We may make fences for miles, for ever beautiful yet always varied as one goes along. But to do this one must never deviate from the best fencing plants as a centre to the fence—Quick, Holly, and Cockspur Thorn, and while keeping to this central idea of the resisting and enduring bushes, add what beauty we can, and that is much! And as this is the wild garden, its main idea may well be kept in view; for though we may make a fence of beautiful native plants, fences in pretty positions near the house may be made more beautiful and interesting by adding perfectly hardy plants of other countries. It gives us a means of varying fences which is often surprising, and we may tie them together with graceful climbers which are not of our own country, though none surpass our Honeysuckle wreathed over a fence.

I use Sweet Brier largely, and have for several years planted thousands in fence making. As this plant is not native in all parts of our country, it may be considered as worth introducing as any exotic! The odour from the early days of spring fills the field, and then there are the summer flowers, and the bright Hips for autumn and winter days. Its advantages are that cattle do not eat it, and that the flower or fruit-laden branches swing careless into the field, when Hazel and other things would be eaten back to the stump. The shoots are so fiercely armed with spines that cattle respect it, and it is a fine aid in live fence making.

In building our fence some young Sweet Briers should be put alongside the bank, while Quick and the essential fencing plants that we may prefer for the spot go on the top. The same thing applies to the wild Roses, the common Dog Rose of England being excellent. Other Roses will be found useful, such as the Japanese and the Needle Rose (R. acicularis). Different kinds of Bramble too are excellent, and often beautiful in flower, fruit, and leaf. There is great variety among our Brambles, and not a few foreign ones are worth introducing, if we can get them. Anyone who notices English landscape beauty in spring will know how much we gain from Crab and Sloe, and May Blossoms in the fence. More beautiful things we cannot have, but it is wise to add to them as we can in various ways.

Various bushes often abundant in gardens may be introduced here and there. I have used some of the dwarf Japan Crabs and Apples, the common Medlar, the Quince, the Japan Pear, which in some places comes so easily from seed, sowing the seeds on banks as well as planting. The beautiful 'Pyracantha' is a dwarf evergreen shrub, which I look forward to as an excellent evergreen fence plant.

It is not only this kind of shrub we may use, for beautiful climbers, such as the wild species of Clematis, which are often easily raised from seed; or small plants may be got for a few pence from English or continental nurseries. I speak of such kinds as the Virgin's Bower (C. Viticella), C. Flammula, C. montana, C. graveolens, C. campanulata, and other wild kinds, many of them yet to be introduced. The gardeners are not always alive to their charms, and if we get them at all, we may sometimes have to put them in newly-made fences, in which they do and look well. The large Bindweed and other climbers may also be used in these free fences. Our common Ivy is a delightful plant in fences, and some of the less common and more graceful kinds (when plentiful in gardens) may be used.

The same is true of many hardy climbers. It is not only shrubs and climbers we may add to our fences, but hardy flowers of the more vigorous kinds, which indeed often thrive well in hedge-banks. I have planted in them bulbs of Narcissus, Tulip, Violets, Wild Strawberries, Starworts, Moon Daisies, and various vigorous plants which grow perhaps too well in the garden. They do not add to the strength of the fence, but when large rough fences are made they often adorn it, whereas the shrubs above mentioned, Wild Roses and Briers, tie the fence together, and add security as well to its beauty.

In certain parts of Kent, on the hills, we see a very picturesque fence, of unclipped Yew, creeping in dark single files across the hills, here and there bearing garlands of wild Clematis. A fence suggested by this may often be useful in gardens, and be improved upon. I mean an unclipped fence of native Evergreens, not planted close, and among them, at intervals, flowering shrubs. Where Yew is used for this, such a fence should not be put in open fields, but in country places there is often occasion for such a free dividing line, to separate orchards and other enclosures from roads or woods. Such a fence I made to protect the west side of the new orchard at Gravetye, running from the moat up the hill, using Yew in this case, as there was no grazing on either side; between the Yews were planted Medlar, Sloe, Quince, Wild Rose, Sweet Brier, Wild Raspberry, and, here and there, Virgin's Bower and other Clematises, and the large Bindweed, which could do no harm there. This fence is meant to be a good shelter as well as a division, and such fences should not be clipped if their shelter is to be thought of. They are also much more beautiful unclipped, and where planted on the cold sides of orchards or fields are valuable for the warmth and shelter they give. The Holly in such positions, carrying garlands of Wild Rose, is very beautiful.

CHAPTER VII
Climbers for Trees and Bushes

———•◦•———

THE NUMEROUS HARDY CLIMBERS are rarely seen to advantage, owing to their being stiffly trained against walls, and many of them have gone out of cultivation for this reason. One of the happiest ways of enjoying them is that of training them in free ways over trees; in this way many beautiful effects may be secured. In some low trees a graceful creeper may garland their heads; in tall ones the stem only. Some vigorous climbers in time ascend tall trees, and there are few more beautiful than a veil of Clematis montana over a tall tree. Many lovely kinds may be grown, apart from the popular climbers, and there are graceful wild Clematises which have never come into gardens. The same may be said of the Honeysuckles, wild Vines, and various other families. Much of the northern tree world is garlanded with creepers, which we may grow in similar ways, and also on rough banks and in hedgerows. The trees in our pleasure grounds, however, have the first claim.

Some time ago I saw a Weeping Willow, on the margin of a lake, its trunk clothed with Virginian Creeper, and the effect in autumn, when the sun shone through the drooping branches of the Willow—whose leaves were just becoming tinged with gold—upon the crimson of the creeper-covered trunk was very fine. The Hop is a very effective plant for draping trees, but the shoots should be thinned out in spring and not more than three or four allowed to climb up to the tree. When the leader emerges

Wisteria blooms in late May in Gravetye's West Garden.

153

from the top of the bush, and throws its long, graceful wreaths of Hops over the dark green foliage, the contrast is most effective. The Wistaria is a host in itself, and should be freely planted against Pines and other trees, also by itself on banks and in the open; its use on houses is too limited for the noblest of hardy flowering climbers. I have planted many against Pines and other trees in plantations.

A correspondent, who has added largely to the charms of a place in Suffolk by means of the wild garden, writes as follows:—

Large White Clematis on Yew tree at Great Tew (C. montana grandiflora).

'Some time ago I discovered and had removed from the woods to the pleasure grounds a robust Holly, which had been taken entire possession of by a wild Honeysuckle, which, originating at the root of the tree, had scrambled up through the branches to the top, and there, extending itself in all directions, had formed a large head and hung in festoons all round. The Holly had endured the subjection for many years, and still seemed to put forth sufficient shoots and leaves annually to ensure a steady support to its companion.'

Climbing shrub (Celastrus), isolated on the grass; way of growing woody Climbers away from walls or other supports

The Honeysuckle in question is an example of what might be done with such handsome climbers. The climbing Honeysuckles are now as numerous as delightful, and require very little encouragement to garland a plantation, and flourish in hedgerow or on bank without care.

Mr. Hovey, in a letter from Boston, Mass., wrote me as follows, on certain interesting aspects of tree drapery:—

A Liane in the North. Aristolochia and Deciduous Cypress.

'Some years ago we planted three or four rows of climbers in nursery rows, about one hundred feet long; these consisted of the Virginian Creeper, the Moonseed (Menispermum), Periploca græca, and Celastrus scandens; subsequently, it happened that four rows of Arbor-vitæs were planted on one side, and about the same number of rows of Smoke trees, Philadelphus, and Dogwood (Cornus florida) on the other. For three or four years many of these climbers were taken up annually until rather too old to remove, and year by year the Arbor-vitæs and shrubs were thinned until what were too large to transplant remained. The land was not wanted then, and the few scattered trees and climbers grew on until the climbers had fairly taken possession of the trees, and they are now too beautiful to disturb! Some of the Arbor-vitæ are overrun with the Moonseed (Menispermum), whose large leaves overlap one another like slates on a roof. Over others, the leaves of the Periploca scramble, and also the Celastrus, and on still others the deep green leaves of the Ampelopsis completely festoon the tree; from among the tops of the Sumach the feathery tendrils of the Ampelopsis, and, just now, its deep blue berries, hold full sway. The Apios tuberosa is indigenous, and springs up everywhere as soon as our land is neglected. This also has overrun several trees, and coils up and wreathes each outstretching branch with its little bunches of fragrant brownish flowers. One Hemlock Spruce has every branch loaded with the Apios and profuse with blossoms. When such strong climbers as Bignonia and Wistaria take possession of a shrub they generally injure it; but the very slender stems

of Menispermum and Apios die entirely to the ground after the
first sharp frost, and the slender stems of the others do not appear
to arrest the growth of the Arbor-vitæ.'

But the noblest kind of climbers forming drapery for trees is not so
often seen as some of the general favourites mentioned above. A neglected
group are the wild Vines, plants of the highest beauty, which, if allowed to
spring through the tall trees, which they would quickly do, would soon
charm by their bold grace. With these might be associated certain free
growing species of Ampelopsis. In the garden of MM. Van Eden, at Haar-
lem, I was surprised to see a Liane, in the shape of Aristolochia Sipho
or Dutchman's Pipe, which had grown high into a fine old deciduous
Cypress. When I saw it early in spring the leaves had not appeared on
either the tree or its companion, and the effect of the old rope-like stems
was very picturesque. The Aristolochia ascends to a height of over thirty-
five feet on the tree, which was a superb one.

CHAPTER VIII
Shrubbery, Plantation, and Wood

——◆◆——

IT MUST NOT BE THOUGHT that the wild garden can be formed only in places where there is some extent of rough pleasure ground. Pretty results may be had from it in even small gardens, on the fringes of shrubberies and plantations, and on open spaces between shrubs, where we may have plant-beauty instead of garden-graveyards—the dug shrubbery borders seen in gardens, public or private. Every shrubbery that is so needlessly dug over every winter may be full of beauty. The custom of digging shrubbery borders prevails now in almost every garden, and there is no worse custom! When winter is once come, almost every gardener, with the best intentions, prepares to make war upon the roots of everything in his shrubbery. The practice is to trim and to mutilate the shrubs and to dig all over the ground that is full of feeding roots. Choice shrubs are disturbed, herbaceous plants are disrooted, bulbs are injured, the roots as well as the tops of shrubs are mutilated, and a miserable aspect is given to the borders; while the only 'improvement' that comes of the process is the darkening of the surface of the upturned earth!

Illustrations of these bad practices are seen by the mile in our London parks in winter. Walk through any of them at that season and observe the borders around masses of shrubs. Instead of finding the earth covered with vegetation close to the margin and each shrub grown into a fair example of its kind, we find a wide expanse of dug ground, and the shrubs

Tawny meadow grasses alternate with hedgerows and forest patches in this late July view from Gravetye across the Sussex Weald.

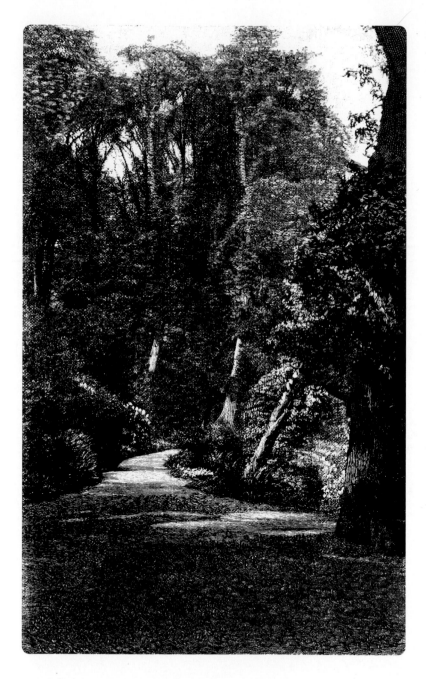

Woodland Walk
at Belvoir.

upon it with an air of having recently suffered from a whirlwind, that led to the removal of mutilated branches. Rough pruners go before the diggers and trim in the shrubs for them, so that nothing may be in the way; and then come the diggers, plunging their spades deeply about plants, shrubs or trees. The first shower that occurs after this digging exposes a whole network of torn-up roots. The same thing occurs everywhere—in botanic gardens as well as in our large West-end parks, and year after year the brutal process is repeated.

While such evil practice is the rule, we cannot have a fresh carpet of beautiful living things in a plantation. What secrets one might have in the hidden parts of these now dug shrubberies—in the half-shady spots where little colonies of rare exotic wildings might thrive! All the labour that produces these ugly dug borders is worse than thrown away, and the shrubs would even do better if left alone.

If no annual digging is to be done, nobody will grudge a thorough preparation of the ground at first. Then the planting should be so done as to defeat the digger, and this could best be done by covering the whole surface with groups of free-growing hardy plants and of dwarf Evergreens. Happily, there is quite enough of these to be had suitable for every soil. Light, moist, peaty or sandy soils, where such things as the sweet-scented Daphne Cneorum would spread forth its neat bushes, would be better than a stiff soil; but for every soil good plants might be found. The dwarf Evergreen Sun Roses (Helianthemum), Evergreen Candytuft (Iberis), Purple Rock Cress (Aubrietia), Arabis, Alyssum, dwarf shrubs, little conifers like the creeping Cedar and the Savin, and Lavender in the spreading groups and colonies would help well. All these should spread out into wide groups covering the margin and helping to cut off the stiff line which usually borders a shrubbery, and the margin should be varied also as regards the height of the plants.

In one spot we might have a wide-spreading colony of the prostrate Savin bush with graceful evergreen branchlets; in another the dwarf Cotoneasters might form the front, relieved in their turn by Scotch or pretty Wild Roses of dwarf stature; and herbs, dwarf evergreen or grey shrubs, and stout herbaceous plants, in colonies between the trees.

In forming a garden plantation of evergreen or other trees, the best way is not to plant in the far too thickly set way that is usual, but rather openly, and then cover all the space between the trees with groups of easily increased hardy flowers. This was done at Gravetye, in the belt of evergreen trees I planted west of the house, using among other plants Compass plants, Starworts (Aster), Lavender, Moon Daisies, Geraniums (hardy spreading kinds), Jerusalem Sage (Phlomis), Fuchsia, scarlet Bee Balm (Monarda), Evening Primrose, Sea Lyme Grass (Elymus), Alum root (Heuchera), Stenactis speciosa, Prairie Sunflowers, Rheum Emodi, Globe Thistle, and Golden Yarrow. The effects were the best we had, the plants giving little trouble after planting, but, on the other hand, saving us trouble. Before we planted in this way weeds were a constant trouble, but the vigorous colonies of plants wanted all the good of the ground for themselves, and took care of the weeds for us! Certainly it was very much less trouble than an ordinary mixed border; there was no staking of any kind, and the stems were not cut down till late in spring; they looked very pretty in colour in winter. This, like every other plan, must be changed in the course of years; when the trees meet there will be less need of the plants, but it is a system that can be easily suited to the circumstances as they arise.

All that the well-covered shrubbery would require would be an occasional weeding or thinning, and in the case of the choicer plants, a little top-dressing with fine soil. In suitable soils such dwarf plants as Forget-me-nots, Violets, and Primroses might be scattered, so as to give the borders interest even at the dullest seasons; but in large and new plantations and shrubberies *the best plants are those that give bold effects and are very hard to kill.*

In beds of choice shrubs, the same plan on a small scale will do, but in this case rare plants might often be planted, and that is flower gardening. But the theme of this book is the planting of things that will take care of themselves once fairly started, and we only come into the shrubberies to save them from ugliness and dreariness by a modification of the same plan, which to succeed must be done in a bold and simple way. To do it well, one should have a few nursery beds of hardy flowers, or frequently divide and make groups of those that grow and increase rapidly. The rule should be—never show the naked earth: clothe it. It need hardly be said that this argument against digging applies to two or three beds of shrubs and to places where the 'shrubbery' is little larger than the dining-room, as much as to the large country seat, public park, and botanic garden.

One of the prettiest plant pictures I have ever seen was in a shrubbery forming a belt round a botanic garden. In the inner and hidden parts, probably from want of labour, the digging had not been done for years. Some roots of the common Myrrh (Myrrhis odorata), thrown out of the garden in digging, had rooted by accident and spread into a little colony. Among the tufts of Myrrh some tall white Harebells came, also thrown out of the flower-beds in the garden to get rid of them, and the effect of these, standing above the spreading foliage of the Myrrh in the shade of the trees, was very beautiful. The front of the shrubbery in which this picture was found was as stiff and hideous as usual—raw earth, full

A beautiful accident. A colony of Myrrhis odorata, in shrubbery not dug, with white Harebells here and there.

of mutilated roots, and shrubs cut in for the convenience and the taste of the diggers. This was in the shrubbery surrounding the botanic garden at Cambridge, where Mr. Parsons made a sketch of it here engraved on wood.

There are some advantages, too, in leaving the leaves to nourish the ground and protect it. Here is a note from a friend inquiring about what he thinks difficulties, and an answer to it:—

> 'You draw a pretty picture of what a shrubbery border should be and how it should be kept in winter. There should be no digging, and the fallen leaves should be left. I fully agree, except as to the leaves. Theoretically, it seems quite right to allow the leaves to lie and decay amidst the surrounding plants, but in practice it does not answer. There are, for instance, in most gardens such things as slugs and snails. These delight in a leafy covering, and, protected from frost by the shelter, will prey upon the perennial green leafage and the starting crowns of the herbaceous plants, and do an immense amount of mischief. Then there are usually in gardens in winter, especially in hard weather, blackbirds and thrushes, which in their efforts to obtain food set all notions of tidiness at defiance. The first storm that came would whirl the disturbed leaves all over the place.'

How do the swarming plants of the woods and copses of the world exist in spite of the slugs? In the garden we may please ourselves as to leaves, and besides all gardens are frequently enriched by soil and other things, but not one leaf would I ever allow to be removed from a clump of shrubs or trees on lawn or pleasure ground, and I should prefer the leaves all over the place to dug borders. In a plantation of choice trees, their branches resting on the ground, with low shrubs and hardy plants like, say, Starworts between, there are impediments to the leaves rushing about in the way mentioned. Our annual digging, mutilation, raking away of leaves, and exposing on bare earthy borders plants that in Nature shelter each other, and are shielded from hard frost and heat by layers of fallen leaves, which gradually sink into light soil for the young roots, are practices that must be given up by all who look into the needs of our hardy garden flora. In my plantation ten thousand stems of Starworts and other plants all the winter standing brown in their place, keep hold of all the leaves that may get among them!

WOODS

Woods vary so much in their character and the plants growing beneath the trees, that we may for ever see different effects, and a thousand things may be suggested to us by woods. In Pine woods in mountain districts we may see sheets of Ferns and even Alpine flowers in them, and our own southern Pine woods in Surrey and Hants often spring out of gardens of lovely Heaths. In the same parish we find woods so close with oaks and underwood, that only tall and stout flowers like wood Angelica, showy Ragwort, large wood Grasses and Foxglove, French Willow and Bracken will grow—these, too, if one goes into the wood and looks at them, often giving us pictures. But this little book cannot tell us the lessons to be learnt about flowers in the woods of the world, whether in those set out by man for his use, or in the great and more stately woods of the earth mother, as, say, in those of the mountains of California, a garden woodland with lovely Evergreens set below great Pine trees, and on the ground lace-work of delicate Ferns and a thousand flowers.

Here is a letter from an observer of what goes on in the woods of New England.

'I go into the woods in the spring-time, and find them carpeted with Dog's-tooth Violets, Wood Anemones, blue and purple Hepaticas, Spring Beauty, Trillium, Blood-root, Star-flowers, Solomon's Seal, Gold Thread, trailing Arbutus, and a host of pretty little flowers, all bright, arising from their bed of decaying grass and tree leaves, and many of them in perfection, too, before a tree has spread a leaf; nourished and sheltered by their tree friends. When their petals drop and their leaves are mature, the trees expand their leafy canopy and save the little nurslings from a scorching sun. And early as the earliest, too, the outskirts of the woods and meadows are painted blue and white with hosts of Violets and speckled everywhere with Bluets, or little Innocents, as the children call them. Woodsias, tiny Aspleniums, and other Ferns are unfolding their fronds along the chinks among the stones; the common Polypody is reaching over blocks and boulders, and even the exposed rocks, with their rough and Lichen-bearded faces, are beautiful. Every nook and cranny among them, and every little mat of earth upon them, is chequered with the flowery print of the Canada Columbine, the Virginia Saxifrage, and the grey Corydalis. What can be prettier than the Partridge Berry (Mitchella repens), the Twin-flower (Linnæa borealis)—does well with us—Creeping Winter Green (Gaultheria procumbens), Bearberry (Arctostaphylos Uva-Ursi), Cowberry (Vaccinium Vitis-idæa), dwarf Cornel (Cornus canadensis), Fringed Polygala (P. paucifolia), the common Pipsissewa (Chimaphila umbellata), with its shining deep green leaves, the Spotted Pipsissewa (C. maculata), the sombre-hued Pyrola and Galax, and that bright Club Moss (Lycopodium lucidulum)?

'One day last spring, when strolling through the Medford Wood, I came upon an open meadow with a high bank—cleared timber land—on one side. Adown this bank in a rocky bed came a little stream of water, bordered on both sides with patches of Blood-root, with large blossoms, clasped erect in their own leaf-vases and sparkling in the sun, while the sward and other vegetation around were yet dormant. True, near by in the hollow, the malodorous Skunk Cabbage was rank in leaf and flower, and the Indian Poke was rushing out its plaited, broadly oval leaves, and away in the streamlet as few Marsh Marigolds glittered on the water. But the Blood-root is neither an aquatic nor a bog plant, but most at home in the leaf-mould beds of rich woodlands.

'Hereabouts, a little wild flower (Erythronium Americanum),

more commonly known as Dog's-tooth Violet, is a charming plant, with variegated handsome leaves and comely flowers in earliest spring. In low copses, in rich deposits of vegetable mould, it grows around here in the utmost profusion. In one place by the side of a wood is a sort of ditch, which is filled with water in winter, but is dry in summer, wherein is collected a mass of leaf-soil. Here the Yellow Dog's-tooth Violet runs riot, and forms the densest kind of matted sod, all bespeckled with yellow blossoms before a tree has spread a leaf. When Blackberry bushes get a growing and sprawling everywhere, the trees expand their leafy shade, and grass and weeds grow up and cover the surface of the earth, it is all too late for evil, the early flower's mission for a year is ended; it has blossomed and retired.'—W. Falconer.

THE WOOD WILD GARDEN

Longleat is one of the first places in which the idea of the wild garden in English woods was ably carried out by the late forester, Mr. Berry. With such a fine variety of surface and soil, the place offers many positions in which the plants of other countries as cold as our own could be so planted that they would take care of themselves in the woods. A forester's duties make it difficult for him to carry out such an idea, and even to know the plants that are likely to succeed is in itself a knowledge which every planter does not possess; however, the idea was clearly understood and carried out well, so far as possible in the face of rabbits, which are the great destroyers of almost all ground vegetation.

To get the necessary quantities of plants, a little nursery in which could be raised numbers of the more vigorous perennials, bulbs, and climbers was required. If the wild garden is to be carried out on the old dotting principle of the herbaceous border, its charming effects cannot be realized. To do it rightly we must group and mass as Nature does. Though we may enjoy a single flower or tuft here and there, the true way is to make pretty colonies of plants, one or two kinds prevailing in a spot; in that way we may secure distinct effects in each place, and better means of meeting the wants of a plant, inasmuch as dealing with a colony we can easily see the result of putting the plants in any soil or place.

Among the plants used are vigorous hardy climbers on old trees, Thorn and other bushes of little value—Japanese and other Honeysuckles, Virginian Creepers, Clematis, Wistarias and others. A part of the arboretum is devoted to these plants, and forms a wild garden, where the Poet's Narcissus may be found among Sweet Briers, Lilacs and many kinds of fragrant shrubs and stout perennials. While carrying out wild gardening, pure and simple—that is to say, the naturalization of foreign hardy plants—beautiful native kinds were also planted when not naturally wild in the neighbourhood. Thus the Lily of the Valley has been brought in quantities and planted wide along the drives, and so have the Meadow Saffrons and the Snowflakes and Daffodils. To group and scatter these in a natural and pretty way has required care, the tendency of the men being, almost in spite of themselves, to plant in stiff and set or too regular masses.

Few things are more delightful to anybody who cares about hardy plants than naturalizing the Lily of the Valley in woody places about a country house. It is in every garden, and very often so crowded and so starved that it seldom flowers well. A bare garden border is not so suitable for it as a thin wood or little openings in a copse, where it enjoys enough light. And by planting it in various positions and soils, we may secure an important difference as to bloom. On a cool northern slope it blooms ten days later than on a warm garden border. Recently different varieties of Lily of the Valley have been collected, and are cultivated. This fact should be noted by any who would, in places where the Lily of the Valley does not grow wild, desire to establish it.

There are advantages in plantation culture for many hardy plants— the shelter, shade, and soil affording for some things conditions more suitable than garden borders. The warmth of the wood, too, is an advantage, and the fallen leaves help to protect the plants in all ways. In a hot country, plants that love cool places could be grown in a wood, while they would perish if exposed. Mr. G. F. Wilson has made himself a remarkably interesting wild garden in a wood, from which he sent me in the autumn of 1880 flowering stems of the American Swamp Lily (L. superbum) eleven feet high. These Lilies grow in a woody bottom where rich dark soil has gathered, and where there is shelter and shade.

Mr. Wilson sends me (August, 1893) a list of the things that did best in his wood wild garden. Lilium auratum (many thousands), and some of its varieties such as platyphyllum and rubro-vittatum; Lilium superbum (many), L. pardalinum and varieties, L. Szovitzianum, L. giganteum, L. cordifolium, L. Leichtlinii, and others in smaller quantities. Iris Kæmpferi, raised in most part from seed, in different parts of the garden from five thousand to six thousand clumps, Iris sibirica and I. orientalis in large quantities, and other Irises in smaller numbers. Most of the plants liking heath soil such as heaths, Andromeda, Ledum, Gaultheria procumbens, Linnæa borealis, Pyrola, Shortia galacifolia, Galax aphylla, Xerophyllum asphodeloides, Gentians—Gentianella (G. acaulis), Gentiana septemfida in large quantities, G. asclepiadea blue and white, hundreds of clumps, a

The Lily of the Valley in copse.

number of other Gentians in smaller quantities, and many Hypericums. 'Rhododendrons grow so freely in our wood that we planted an acre with seedlings which were crowding their parents.'

'Though the wood comprises but a few acres, there is a wide range of soil and aspect in it. The wood is chiefly of Oaks; beneath them is a great depth of leaf soil—a soil in which many plants will thrive if the exposure is right for them. A better place for shade-loving plants could not well be found. Outside the wood is a wide stretch of sloping treeless ground fully exposed, consisting of a good loam, and between it and the wood is a low-lying portion through which runs a little stream; in another place is a deep bog where one might sink knee-deep in soft mud, and where Calthas and such plants thrive.

'Lilies abound everywhere in the wood, and may be counted by the thousand under various conditions of soil and aspect. For Lilium auratum, total shade is worse than full exposure, particularly if the season be a wet one. The healthiest plants are well sheltered and have a partial shade. Here North American Lilies of the superbum and pardalinum types may be seen probably finer than in their native haunts. The tall stems of the Swamp Lily rise up midst brushwood and carry huge heads of flowers that make the slender stems bow with every breath of wind. Never till now had we seen large colonies of Lilies of the dahuricum and elegans type, the effect of which was charming. Just at the bottom of the slope, in a deep loam, where they were fully exposed, they were the finest, some of the stems being four feet and five feet high, and loaded with blossoms. Higher up were masses of Lilium monadelphum and its varieties, called severally Szovitzianum, Loddigesianum, and colchicum, all uncommonly fine, the stems tall and stout, and carrying huge heads of flowers. In this spot the soil is a deep loam, neither too light nor too heavy, but of such character as just to suit this Lily as well as all the Martagons, the old white L. candidum, L. testaceum, and, in fact, all the European kinds.

'Besides Lilies may be noticed here—other interesting results—gigantic tufts of Funkias in the shadiest part of the wood, for, as a rule, they like sun. It is clear they are not fastidious in this respect, for finer tufts we have not seen; those who would relieve the monotony of woodland walks might plant by the margins tufts of F. Sieboldii, F. ovata and F. subcordata, avoiding the small-growing kinds, especially those with variegated foliage. One of the greatest successes has been with the charming little Epigæa repens or May-Flower of the N. American woods. Here it forms quite a carpet, amidst the fallen leaves, and under these conditions pretty Linnæa borealis also grows.'—*Garden*.

A great many beautiful plants haunt the woods, we cannot change their nature easily: and even if we grow them well in open places, their bloom will not be so enduring as in the wood. The secret of wild gardening is adapting plants to the soil. The Solomon's Seal is typical of certain wild garden plants that do not go off early, like Daffodils and Crocus, and therefore require a different position—the friendly shelter of wood or copse.

In my district there was not a bit of it wild, and it was important to secure so beautiful a thing in large groups, without giving any of the flower-garden to it—I mean places where we wanted to grow our Roses and Carnations, and the many things on which the beauty of the flower-garden depends throughout our summer. So I put it pretty freely under a plantation of Hollies, right out of the garden, in a place never disturbed, and there it takes care of itself, and flowers abundantly without any kind of attention. A prettier thing could hardly be seen in masses. At about the same time roots of it were scattered in the Moat shaw where there were large oaks overhead, and the usual underwood. They have done pretty well every year since, but each year they get stronger, and this year we have been surprised at their beauty, especially in the lower and richer parts of the copse, where they found a depth of washed-down soil near a small stream. It is delightful to creep through the undergrowth and see their beautiful forms a yard high or more fully blown and very much prettier than in a mass in the pleasure garden, because they grow separately, and one gets the full value of the arching and bell-laden stem growing out of sheets of Bluebells. No manure or attention has even been given beyond planting—taking a basket of roots, making a few holes in the copse here and there at not too regular intervals and letting the plants along ever since.

In districts where Solomon's Seal grows in the woods there is no need to plant it, but there are many places where it does not; and where there are no woods it is sure to make a charming feature in the shrubbery. I remember, at Angers, seeing some forms of it tall, and natives of central France—at least, I was told so by M. Boreau, the then director of the Angers garden. There is also a tall American kind, which would be very charming if naturalized in similar places. In the same wood with Solomon's Seal I have also been planting Narcissus Stella, which naturalized in this way, and blooming at the same time, has made the pretty copse a charming spring garden. Solomon's Seal in masses shows good colour of the leaves in autumn.

In the hot days of May, 1893, in walking from Compiègne to Pierre-fonds, in the Forest of Compiègne, we passed by many acres of Lily of the Valley in bloom under trees. It was one of the few things that retained its delightful freshness in the greatest drought within living memory. As people so often ask for plants suitable for growing in bare places under trees, they might try the Lily of the Valley. It is so common in gardens, and gets so thick when planted in rich ground, that many can spare some for trial. It is a mistake to suppose that it requires rich ground. The attempt to grow Grass in shady and half-shady places is often a failure, and it is well to know of some plants that will grow in such situations. The Lily of the Valley is one of the things that will form a carpet and require no attention. It would be pretty to vary its mass here and there with groups of hardy Ferns, Solomon's Seal, and Woodruff.

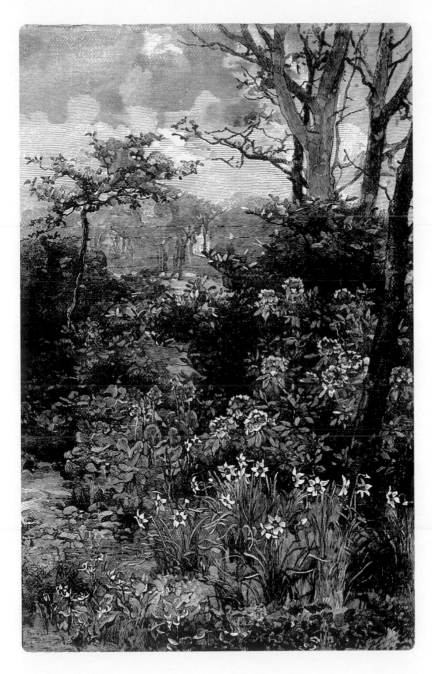

Colonies of Poet's
Narcissus and Broad-
leaved Saxifrage.

CHAPTER IX
Woodland Drives and Grass Walks

———•◦•———

IN THE LARGER COUNTRY PLACES the often noble opportunities for beautiful woodland drives are not always seized, sometimes because people have the primitive and wholly inartistic idea that the proper way to make a drive is to plant two or four lines of trees along it. These are often set far too close, and as they are rarely thinned in time, the whole ends in a gloomy tunnel without air, light, or shade. Even where the avenue is not the 'leading feature,' drives through woods and parks are too narrow.

Fine airy effects might be got by breadths of low covert or fern beside drives, and these drives should take the line of easiest grade, and the best for views where possible. There is no reason why drives should not pass under trees here and there, but, generally, a better effect is got by keeping the groups and fine trees a little off the drive, and having bold groups of hardy shrubs and carpets of plants as a foreground to the woodland picture.

Here and there, as at Penrhyn, are some beautiful glades of wild Fern coming near the drives, and there is a lovely example at Powys of what our native plants do in the foreground of a really picturesque drive. But by a little forethought we may easily get finer things in this way from Thorns, Foxglove, or Willow Herb, wide sheets of large Ferns with breaks of Wild Roses, large rambling colonies of Sweet Brier, lovely fields of native Heaths, double Furze as well as the single kind, Broom on poor banks

Allium 'Purple Sensation' blooms with bearded iris in late May in Gravetye's West Garden against the new green hues of fields and forests to the south.

175

and Partridge Berry in half-shady places—a host of beautiful things that would spread about and give excellent covert as well as pretty effects.

Of regularly formed roads—those made of gravel, flint, or other stone—there are three times too many in most country seats. It is wise economy to reduce these to the real needs of the place. All places are the uglier for being beset with gate lodges, which are usually ugly in themselves and lead to needless cutting up of beautiful ground, the increase of gates, and the springing up of the iron fiend in every direction. As the artistic and true way is to reduce as much as possible these needless drives often made for mere show, or to save five minutes, let those we keep be as good in grade and view as we can make them, and have as many picturesque charms as we may give them.

We never have enough of Grass walks and drives. When we want a way merely for our own convenience, by far the best is a Grass drive or walk through pretty woodland scenery, over park, hill, or by stream or river. A delightful privilege which English gardens have, more than others, is that of having Grass walks of the finest texture and verdure. At Holwood, in the late Lord Derby's time, it was pleasant to see the number and the delightful charm of the Grass walks there. Around our houses we must have good firm walks; but once free of the house and regular gardens, one may break into the graceful Grass walks without injury to anything. Some prefer gravel walks in winter, but the gravel walk is not always much drier than a well-made Grass walk; however, as we use our gardens most in summer, it does not matter so much. Even on heavy soils Grass walks may be delightful the greater part of the year, and on dry soils we need not fear the wet.

It is not only the effect of Grass walks that is in their favour—they are a great economy. They can be cleaned with one-fourth of the labour which the gravel walks take. Once free of the garden, it is rather in the rougher parts of the pleasure ground and about the park that Grass walks are made with the best results. The line of ground should be studied both for ease in walking and mowing, and for the sake of the best views. Nothing in gardening rewards us so well as well-thought-out Grass walks and drives. If, as they should be, the gravel walks about the house are reduced to the strictly necessary dimensions, it is surprising how much the wearisome trouble of hoeing is done away with. The toilsome labour of ripping up walks, raking, and hoeing, seen in so many gardens, need not, happily, go on. It only makes matters worse by softening the walks, for the hoeing is a serious labour in the hot days and is absolutely unnecessary.

Having our Grass drive or Grass walk, what shall we place beside it? Our British plants are as fair as any others, and we may see as beautiful groups of fern, heather, thorn, and bramble as are given by the flora of any country. Still, those who care for the plants of other countries have by the Grass walk a charming opportunity of adding other pretty things to our own wild flowers.

There is much difference in districts as to their wild flowers and the effects from native plants. Some places may be full of beautiful things— others have very few. What a place has in this way depends upon the cultivation and the quality of the land, and other conditions which need not be gone into; it is enough to know that these differences exist. Where the natural vegetation is poor, there is all the greater need for adding beautiful things of easy naturalization.

Our Wood Anemone is pretty in the fields and groves in spring, but the blue Apennine Anemone, which is quite hardy, gives us a wholly distinct and charming colour, and this is true of other things. The high mountain plants of the Alps of Europe, to whose flora many early flowers belong, give us the precious gift of earliness; crocus, narcissus, and scilla, all come before our own early flowers awake, while nearly all are as hardy as our own native flowers.

Then there are many hardy climbers which, if we planted them among trees, would be quite as beautiful as any native climbers, of which the number is too small. The Indian Mountain Clematis is hardy, and as easy to establish as our native Clematis, while it is more beautiful, and there are other beautiful plants one may add to our own, though, generally, it will be safer to trust to our native flora by drives. The prettiest brake of shrubs I ever saw was an immense group of the common Barberry at Compton Winyates, laden with berries weeping down with glowing colour.

Much may be done in the direction of Grass walks to take them not only where the views and landscape charm us, but also where the native flora shows itself best. Very often our common ferns in the west country and in moist districts make themselves great ferneries which ought to be seen. The idea that the fernery can only be made with heaps of old stone or other rubbish is too absurd to be worth disputing. The plants rarely grow naturally in that way, and the most vigorous and effective of ferns, which make evergreen covert and give such cool and beautiful effects, certainly do not. There are also numbers of fine hardy North American and other ferns tempting us to naturalize them, but for all artistic ends our native ferns are sufficient.

Still those who have ever seen the fine North American hardy ferns in their own country, sometimes in more severe climates than that of our own country, will often be tempted to naturalize the more vigorous kinds—success in which will depend on the positions chosen for them.

CHAPTER X
The Brook-side, Water and Bog Gardens

———•◦•———

IN THE WATER, AT LEAST, PLANTS DO NOT TROUBLE us for attention. If we take the trouble to establish them the rest is easy, and therefore those living near lake or stream may find much interest in adorning them with beautiful flower life of our own and other lands. The richness of our own country in handsome water-plants is not known to many even of those who know our wild flowers—until perhaps they row up a back-water of the Thames, where the water-plants are often superb, or see the great size and variety of those by the Norfolk Broads.

Nearly all landscape gardeners seem to have put a higher value on the pond than on the brook as an ornament to the garden; but many pictures might be formed by a brook on its way through glade or meadow. No such beauty comes through the pond, which gives us water in repose—imprisoned water; while the brook ripples between mossy rocks or flower-fringed banks, its margin, too, giving an excellent place for hardy flowers. Hitherto we have only used in such places water or bog plants, but the improvement of the brook-side will be most readily effected by planting the banks also with vigorous hardy flowers, making it a wild garden, in fact.

Many of our finest herbaceous plants, from Iris to Meadow Sweet, thrive in the moist soil; many hardy flowers, also, that do not in nature prefer such soil, exist in health in it. Plants on the bank would have this

Late May view east across the West Garden to Gravetye Manor.

merit over water-plants, that we could fix them, whereas water-plants are apt to spread too much and often one kind exterminates the rest. The plants, of course, should be such as would grow freely among Grass and take care of themselves. If distinct groups were encouraged, the effect would be all the better. The common way of repeating a plant at intervals

Solomon's Seal and Herb
Paris, in copse by streamlet.

would spoil all: groups of free hardy things, different in each place, as one passed, would be best; Day Lilies; Iris, many; Gunnera; Starwort; American swamp Lilies in peaty soil; the deep rose variety of the Loosestrife Golden Rods; the taller and stouter Bell-flowers (Campanula); the Compass plants (Silphium); Monkshoods; the free-flowering Yuccas; the hardiest flame-flowers (Tritoma); the stouter kinds of Yarrow (Achillea); the perennial Lupin; the red and other Meadow Sweets as well as our own wild kind—these are some of many types of hardy flowers which would grow freely near the water-side apart wholly from the plants that naturally frequent the water. With these hardy plants too, a variety of the nobler hardy ferns would thrive, as the Struthiopteris; and the Royal Fern would also come in well here.

Colony of hardy exotic Flowers, naturalized by brook-side.

We will now consider the plants that naturally belong to the water. Water-plants of northern and temperate regions add much to the beauty of a garden if well chosen. A great deal of variety may be added to the margins, and here and there to the surface, or water, by means of hardy aquatics. Usually we see the same monotonous vegetation all round the margin if the soil be rich; in some cases, where the bottom is of gravel, there is little or no vegetation, but an unbroken ugly line of washed earth between wind and water. In others, water-plants thicken till they become an eyesore—not only submerged weeds, but such as the Water Lilies when matted together. A plant or group of plants of the Water Lily, with its fine leaves and flowers, is beautiful; but when it runs over a piece of water and water-fowl cannot make way through it, then even this fine plant loses its charms. No garden water, however, should be without a few groups of the Water Lily. Where the bottom is not rich enough, earth might be gathered in certain spots for the growth of the Nymphæa, and thus grown it would not spread much.

In the summer of 1893, at Middleton Hall, Tamworth, I saw the finest example I remember of its beauty, not only in growth and large flowers, but in effect over a lake—in masses and sheets divided by open water—an enormous sheet of Water Lilies, and the picture, in association with a pretty old manor house, was lovely. The flowers were very large, and of two forms—one with a bronzy-green outer division of the flower, and a flush of delicate pink inside; the other, a smaller form, pure white with dark green outer divisions; so we have at least two forms of our native Water Lily, and there may be others.

In the numerous waters which have to be occasionally cleared of sediment in gardens and parks, instead of throwing all the mud on to the land, it would be better to put some of it in masses near the margins of lakes in which Water Lilies and other vigorous plants might grow, and from which they would not wander far. It is one way and the best of keeping rambling water-plants in groups, instead of spread all over the water.

The yellow Water Lily (Nuphar lutea), though not so beautiful as the preceding, is worth a place; then there is the large N. advena, a native of

North America, which pushes its leaves boldly above the water, and is bold in habit. The American white Water Lily (Nymphæa odorata) is a noble species, and there are other species, while our gardens have lately been enriched with a series of noble hybrids of these plants, soft yellow, rose, and of other good colours. When these are increased the hardiest of them will be good to add to our water-gardens.

A very pretty effect is that of a sheet of Villarsia belting round the margin of a lake near a woody recess, and before it, in deeper water, a group of Water Lilies. The Villarsia is a pretty little water-plant, with Nymphæa leaves and golden flowers, which give a beautiful effect under a bright sun. It is not very common in Britain, though, where found, generally very plentiful.

Not rare—growing, in fact, in nearly all districts of Britain—but beautiful and singular, is the Buckbean or Bog-bean (Menyanthes trifoliata), with flowers fringed on the inside with white filaments, and the found buds blushing on the top with rose. It will grow in a bog or any moist place, in or by the margin of water. For grace, no water-side plant surpasses Equisetum Telmateia, which, in deep soil, in shady places near water, often grows several feet high, the long, close-set, slender branches depending from each whorl in a singularly graceful manner. It will grow on the margins of lakes and streams, especially among water-side bushes, or in boggy spots in the shade, and will run by thousands through the worst and stiffest soil.

As a picturesque plant on the margins of water, few are finer than the great Water Dock (Rumex Hydrolapathum); its fine leaves of a lurid red in the autumn—a grand 'foliage' plant, and, unlike many water-plants, not spreading much. This plant, like many others named here, needs no care after planting, and thus is a true wild-garden plant. The Cat's-tail (Typha) must not be forgotten: the narrow-leaved one (T. angustifolia) is more graceful than the common one (T. latifolia).

Carex pendula is excellent for the margins of water, its elegant drooping spikes being quite distinct in their way. It is common in England, more so than Carex Pseudo-cyperus, which grows well in a foot or two of

Cyperus longus.

water or on the margin of a muddy pond. Carex paniculata forms a thick stem, often three or four feet high, somewhat like a tree Fern, with luxuriant masses of drooping leaves, and on that account is transferred to moist places in gardens, and cultivated by some, though generally these large specimens soon perish.

Scirpus lacustris (the Bulrush) is too good a plant to be left out, as its stems, sometimes attaining a height of more than seven feet and even eight feet, look very imposing; and Cyperus longus is also a fine plant, reminding one of the Papyrus when in flower. It is found in some of the southern counties of England. Poa aquatica might also be used. Cladium Mariscus is another distinct water-side plant which is worth a place.

If one chose to name the plants that grow in British and European waters, a long list might be made, but plants having no distinct character or no beauty of flower would be useless; it is only by a selection of the best plants that gardening of this kind can charm us.

Those who enjoy the Flowering Rush (Butomus umbellatus) in blossom are not likely to omit it now. It is a native of the greater part of Europe

The Cape Pond Weed in an English ditch in winter.

and Asia, and of the central and southern parts of England and Ireland. Plant it not far from the margin, and it likes rich muddy soil.

The Arrow-head (Sagittaria), frequent in England and Ireland, but not in Scotland, might be associated with this; and there is a finer double exotic kind, which is really a handsome plant, its flowers resembling, but larger than, those of the old white double Rocket. This used to be grown in abundance in the pleasure gardens at Rye House, Broxbourne, where it filled a wide ditch, and was very handsome in flower. It forms large egg-shaped tubers, and in searching for these, ducks destroy the plants occasionally.

Calla palustris is a beautiful bog plant, and nothing gives a better effect creeping over rich, soft, boggy ground. It will also grow by the side of water. Calla æthiopica (the beautiful Lily of the Nile) is hardy in the south if planted rather deep. Pontederia cordata is a stout and hardy water-herb, with erect habit, and blue flowers. The Sweet-flag will be associated with the Water Iris (I. Pseudacorus), and a number of exotic Irises will thrive in wet ground, such as I. sibirica, I. ochroleuca, I. graminea, and others.

The Cape Pond Flower (Aponogeton distachyon) is a native of the Cape of Good Hope, a singularly pretty plant, which is hardy in our climate, and, from its sweetness and curious beauty, a good plant to have. It frequently succeeds in water not choked by weeds, and wherever there are springs that tend to keep the water a little warmer than usual it seems to thrive in any part of the country.

The Water Ranunculuses, which sheet over our pools in spring and early summer with such silvery beauty, are not worth an attempt at cultivation, so rambling are they; and the same applies to not a few other things of interest. As beautiful as any plant is the Water Violet (Hottonia palustris). It occurs most frequently in the eastern and central districts of England and Ireland, and is charming in ditches. A companion for the Marsh Marigold (Caltha) and its varieties is the very large and showy Ranunculus Lingua, which grows in rich ground to a height of three feet or more.

If with our water-garden we combine the wild-garden herbaceous plants—I mean the handsomer of the hardy flowers that love moist or

Day Lily by margin of water.

heavy soil—some of the loveliest effects in gardens will be ours. The margins of lakes and streams are happily not upturned by the spade in winter; and hereabouts, just away from the water-line, many a vigorous and hardy flower (among the thousands now in our gardens) may be grown and will afterwards take care of itself. The Globe Flowers form beautiful effects in such positions, and would endure as long as the Grass. Near the various Irises that love the water-side might be planted those that thrive in moist ground. The singular Californian Saxifraga peltata is a noble plant for the water-side.

It would require a very long list to enumerate all the plants that would grow near the margins of water, apart from the true water-plants; given a strip of ground beside a stream or lake, a garden of the most delightful kind may be formed of them. The juxtaposition of plants inhabiting different situations—water-plants, water-side plants, and land-plants thriving in moist ground—would prevent what would, in many cases, be so undesirable—a general admixture of the whole, and greatly add to the effect, which is very fine indeed where both the surface of the water and the banks are gay with flowers.

Marsh Marigold and
Iris in early spring.

An interesting point in favour of the wild garden *is the succession of effects* which it may afford, and which are shown by the illustrations on these pages, both showing a succession of life on the same spot of ground.

The bog garden is a home for the numerous children of the wild that will not thrive on our harsh, bare, and dry garden borders, but must be cushioned on moss, or grown in moist peat soil. Many beautiful plants, like the Wind Gentian and Creeping Harebell, grow on our own bogs and marshes, much as these are now encroached upon. But even those who see the beauty of the plants of our own bogs have, as a rule, but a feeble notion of the multitude of charming plants, natives of northern and temperate countries, whose home is the open marsh or the boggy wood.

In our own country, we have been so long encroaching upon the bogs that some of us come to regard these as exceptional tracts all over the world. But in new countries in northern climes, one soon learns what a vast extent of the world's surface was at one time covered with bogs. In North America day after day, even from the railroads, one sees the vivid spikes of the Cardinal-flower springing from the wet peaty hollows. Far

The same spot as in opposite sketch, with aftergrowth of Iris, Meadow Sweet, and Bindweed.

under the shady woods stretch the black bog pools, the ground between being so shaky that you move a few steps with difficulty. One wonders how the trees exist with their roots in such a bath. And where the forest vegetation disappears the American Pitcher-plant (Sarracenia), Golden Club (Orontium), Water Arum (Calla palustris), and a host of other handsome and interesting bog plants cover the ground for hundreds of acres, with perhaps an occasional slender bush of the swamp Magnolia (M. glauca) among them.

In some parts of Canada, where the painfully straight roads are often made through woody swamps, and where the few poor 'houses' offer little to cheer the traveller, he will, if a lover of plants, find conservatories of beauty in the ditches and pools of dark water beside the roads, fringed with a profusion of stately ferns, and often filled with masses of the pretty Arrow-head.

Southwards and seawards, the bog flowers become tropical in size and brilliancy, as in the splendid herbaceous Hibiscus, while far north, and west and south along the mountains, the beautiful Mocassin flower (Cypripedium spectabile) grows the queen of the peat waste. Then in California, all along the Sierras, there are a number of delicate little annual

Partridge Berry
(Gaultheria).

plants growing in small mountain bogs long after the plains have become parched, and flowers have quite gone from them.

But who shall tell of the beauty of the flowers of the marsh-lands of this globe of ours, from those of the vast bog wastes of America, to those of the breezy uplands of the high Alps, far above the woods, where the mountain bogs teem with Nature's most brilliant flowers, joyous in the sun? No one worthily; for many mountain-swamp regions are as yet as little known to us as those of the Himalaya, with their giant Primroses and many strange flowers. One thing, however, we may gather from our small experiences—that many plants commonly termed 'alpine,' and found on high mountains, are true bog plants. This must be clear to anyone who has seen our pretty Bird's-eye Primrose in the oozing mountain bogs of Westmoreland, or the Bavarian Gentian in the spongy soil by alpine rivulets, or the Gentianella (Gentiana acaulis) in the snow water.

Bogs are not often found near our gardens nowadays, but, wherever they are, there are many handsome flowers from other countries that will thrive in them as freely as in their native wastes, and among these the strange and beautiful Pitcher-plants of the bogs of North-Eastern America which are hardy here too.

CHAPTER XI
Wild Gardening on Walls, Rocks,[1] or Ruins

———••———

THERE ARE HUNDREDS OF MOUNTAIN and rock-plants which thrive better on an old wall, a ruin, a sunk fence, a sloping bank of stone, with earth behind, or a 'dry' wall than they do in the most carefully prepared border! Many an alpine plant, which may have perished in its place in the garden, thrives on an old wall near at hand, as, for example, the pretty Pyrenean Erinus, the silvery Saxifrages of the Alps, Pinks like the Cheddar Pink, established on the walls at Oxford, many Stonecrops, Houseleeks, the Purple Rock Cress and Arabis.

In the gardens at Great Tew, in Oxfordshire, the charming Balearic Sandwort, which usually roots over the moist surface of stones, planted itself high up on a wall in a small recess, where half a brick had been displaced. It is suggestive, as so many things are, of the many plants that may be grown on walls.

A mossy old wall, or ruin, gives a home for many rock-plants which no specially-prepared situation equals; but even on well-preserved walls we can establish rock-plants which year after year will repay us for their planting or sowing. Those who have observed how dwarf plants grow on the mountains, or on stony ground, must have seen in what hard places many flourish, fine tufts sometimes springing from a chink in an arid rock or boulder. They are often stunted in these conditions, but always more enduring than when growing on the ground.

1. The rocks meant here are natural ones—not the absurdities too often made in gardens.

A venerable mulberry drapes over the stone wall of Robinson's kitchen garden in late March.

Now, numbers of alpine plants perish if planted in the ordinary soil of our gardens, and even do so where much pains are taken to grow them. This results from over-moisture at the root in winter, the plants being made more susceptible of injury by our moist green winters inducing them to make a lingering growth. But by placing many of these fragile plants where their roots have a dry if poor soil they remain in perfect health. Many plants from latitudes a little farther south than our own, and from alpine regions, show on walls and rocks a dwarf, sturdy growth, which enables them to endure a winter quite different from that of their native countries.

In many parts of the country there are few opportunities for this gardening; but in various districts, such as the Wye and other valleys, there are miles of rock and rough wall-surface, where the scattering of a few seeds of Arabis, Aubrietia, Erinus, Acanthus, Saxifraga, Viola, Stonecrops, and Houseleeks, would give rise to a garden of rock blossoms that would need no care from the gardener. Growing such fine alpine plants as the true Saxifraga longifolia of the Pyrenees on the surface of a rough wall is quite easy.

Arenaria Balearica, self-planted on wall at Great Tew.

Cheddar Pink, Saxifrage, and Ferns, on cottage wall at Mells, Somerset.

A few seeds of the Cheddar Pink, for example, sown in a mossy or earthy chink, or even covered with a dust of fine soil, would soon take root; and the plant would live for years in a dwarf and perfectly healthful state. The seedling roots vigorously into the chinks, and gets a hold which it rarely relaxes. The names of some of the plants that will grow on walls will be found at the end of this chapter.

The Yellow Fumitory
(Corydalis lutea) on wall.

In forming dry or rough walls to support banks we may easily plant many kinds of rock-plants so that they will grow well thereon, but that work belongs rather to the planting of a rock-garden, whereas the whole aim of this book is to take advantage of surfaces already at hand for us.

SOME OF THE FAMILIES
OF ROCK AND ALPINE PLANTS
FOR WALLS, ROCKS, AND RUINS IN BRITAIN

Achillea	Coronilla	Lychnis (rock and
Alyssum	Corydalis	mountain kinds)
Antirrhinum	Dianthus	Saxifraga
Arabis	Draba	Sedum
Arenaria	Erinus	Sempervivum
Aubrietia	Erodium	Silene
Campanula	Gypsophila	Thymus
(mountain kinds)	Helianthemum	Tunica
Centranthus	Hutchinsia	Veronica (rock and
Cheiranthus	Iberis	mountain kinds)

Purple Rock Cress (Mountains of Greece).

CHAPTER XII
Wild and Other Roses in the Wild Garden

———— •• ————

PEOPLE WHO SHAKE THEIR HEADS about naturalizing plants in grass, and say it cannot be done, will hardly say we cannot enjoy the Wild Roses of Europe and Northern Asia in any rough place. These do not want our assistance to trail over the mountains and adorn the river-bed rocks down to the shore. If the soil of the hillside and the stony waste is enough for them, surely the rich fields of lowland England, and its hedgerows, and the good soil which is found near most country houses will nourish Wild Roses as well as the mountains and heaths. Our own Wild Roses—we know what they do in the midlands, the west country and on the hills, but not many have a just idea how many beautiful Wild Roses there are in the world that are as hardy as our Sweet Brier. If at present many Wild Roses cannot be had at nurseries, there are some interesting kinds that can be, and there is scarcely a country of Europe or Asia that one goes into, in which the seeds of beautiful Wild Roses may not be gathered, and they are easy to raise.

It will not do to put Wild Roses in the flower-garden, where we want choice cultivated flowers; but there are ways in which any Wild Rose we bring or gather might be delightfully used (i.e., in the shrubbery, and in forming fences and also in beds in the rougher parts of pleasure grounds). It is a very common thing to see the sunk fence, which has been made in so many places, without any plant life upon it, though some is needed for

Giant feather grass, *Stipa gigantea,* is heavily budded in late May in this view south from Gravetye's West Garden. Robinson recommended this grass for naturalizing.

marking the drop and to some extent garlanding the brow of the fence. In my own garden, where I made a sunk fence, we planted groups of various Wild Roses from one end to the other—bold running groups five to seven feet wide, and few things have given us so good a return; they do not grow high, they garland the sunk fence and add to its effect from both sides and give pretty effects of flower and fruit. I use the Sweet Brier, the American Glossy Rose, the Japan Rose, Scotch Rose, Carolina, and the Russian Wild Rose, and any Wild Roses that are plentiful and grow freely, and take care of themselves.

How may we get a slight idea of the riches of the world in Wild Roses? I thought I had some notion of it myself till I went to Lyons last September (1892) to get Tea Roses for my garden. These roses of garden origin are the loveliest things raised or grown by man: sweet with all the delicate fragrance of the morning air on down or Surrey heath, having the colours of the cloud, and all that is loveliest in form of bud and bloom. But these precious roses are things of cultivation only. Without the good gardener's spade and knife they would soon become a tangle with less meaning and beauty than the Wild Brier. Their size and beauty are not to be had without good cultivation, and nothing can so well show us the difference between the wild garden and the flower-garden than these fairest garden roses and the Wild Roses of the hills, growing in the same place in quite different ways.

Having got my garden roses a friend happened to say that the Wild Yellow Rose, that has given us the Austrian Yellow Rose, was wild in the region, and I bought a flora of the country to see something about its Wild Roses.[1] In it the Wild Roses are grouped as shown below, and the numbers given represent the species in each section. And this, it will be noted, is only in one region of France.

1. *Étude des Fleurs.* Renfermant la Flora du bassin moyen du Rhone et de la Loire. Par L'Abbé Cariot. Lyon, 1889.

SECTIONS	SPECIES	SECTIONS	SPECIES
I. Systylæ	5	VI. Montanæ	14
II. Gallicanæ	24	VII. Caninæ	46
III. Pimpinellifoliæ	12	VIII. Rubiginosæ	33
IV. Alpinæ	9	IX. Tomentosæ	24
V. Sabiniæ	5	X. Pomiferæ	8

Wild Rose growing on a
Pollard Ash in Orchardleigh
Park, Somerset.

Here in one district of France, exposed to the alp wind and frost, we have nearly two hundred kinds of Wild Rose: it shows how rich the northern world is in rose beauty—at least to all to whom the earth-born loveliness of the leaf, bud, blossom, and fruit of the Wild Rose is visible. And these roses want no budding, pruning, or learned cultivation of any kind; but let no one suppose I wish them to take the place of our lovely Tea Roses in the flower-garden. There are, at least in my own garden, places for both.

The Rev. H. N. Ellacombe writes as to old garden Roses among bushes:—

'I have here a large Box bush, in the centre of which there has been for many years an Ayrshire Rose. The long branches covered with flowers, and resting on the deep green cushion, have a very beautiful effect. Other Roses may be used in the same way. The Musk Rose of Shakespeare and Bacon would be particularly well suited for this, and would climb up to a great height. Rosa scandens or sempervirens, Rosa multiflora, and perhaps some others, might be grown in the same way; and it would be worth while to experiment with other garden forms, such as Aimée Vibert, purple Boursault, &c. If grown against a tree of thin foliage, such as a Robinia, they would grow quicker and flower sooner; but this is not necessary, for even if grown near a thick-foliaged tree they will soon bring their branches to the outside for the light. But besides climbing Roses, there is another way in which Roses may be combined with trees to great advantage, viz. by planting some of the taller-growing bushes in rough grassy places. These would grow from six feet to ten feet high, and would flower well in such a position. For such a purpose the old Dutch Apple Rose (Rosa villosa var. pomifera) would be very suitable, and so would R. cinnamomea, R. fraxinifolia, R. gallica, R. rubifolia, and the common monthly China.'

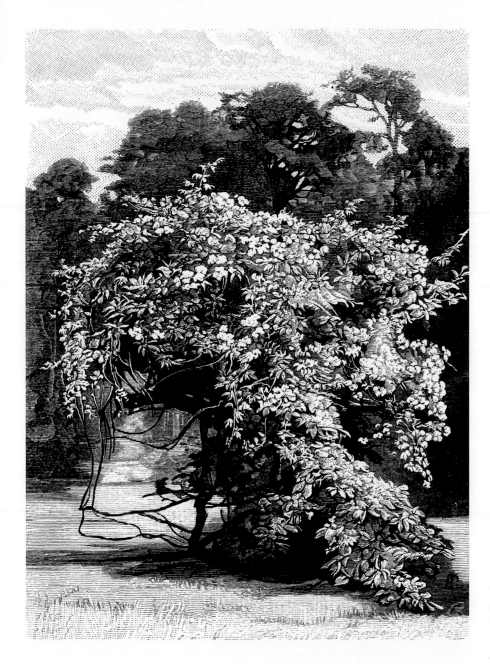

White Climbing Rose
scrambling over old
Catalpa Tree.

Mr. Greenwood Pim writes, referring to the above note:—

'I have two large Hawthorns—round-headed standards—growing close together, so that their edges touch, forming, as it were, two gentle hills with a valley between, and sloping down to within about six feet of the lawn. Of these one is Cratægus Crus-galli; the other C. tanacetifolia. Behind, and partly through these, climbs a very old Noisette Rose—all that now remains of an arched trellis—producing a vast number of bunches of white flowers, six or eight together, and about one and a half or two inches across. The old gnarled stem of the Rose is scarcely noticeable amongst those of the Thorns till it reaches the top of them, whence it descends between the trees in a regular torrent of blossom, in addition to occupying the topmost boughs of the Cockspur Thorn. A smaller plant of the same Rose has recently been trained up a large Arbor-vitæ and has its stem clothed with Ivy. It is now festooned with snowy flowers hanging down from and against the dark green of the Arbor-vitæ and Ivy.'

A correspondent says:—

'We have a collection of Roses, but one of the most attractive is an old double white Ayrshire Rose, growing in a group of common Laurel. We cannot tell how old the plant may be, but it has probably been in its present situation for thirty years, struggling to keep its place among the tall Laurels, sometimes sending out a shoot of white flowers on this side and sometimes on that side of the clump, and then scrambling up to the tops of the tallest limbs and draping them with its blossoms throughout June and July. Nearly three years ago the Laurels were cut down to within six feet of the ground, leaving the straggling limbs of the Rose amongst them, and since then it has thriven amazingly, and now seems to gain the mastery, the plant being now over seventy feet round. Within this space the plant forms an irregular undulating mound, in all parts so densely covered with Roses that not so much as a hand's breadth is left vacant anywhere, and the Laurel branches are quite hidden, and in fact are now dying, smothered by the Rose. The plant has been a perfect sheet of bloom for a month or more, and there are thousands of buds yet to expand, and hundreds of bunches of buds had been cut just at the opening stage—when they are neater and whiter than a Gardenia—to send away. Except against walls, there is no need to prune climbing Roses. Left to themselves, they give the best bloom in deep, strong soil, and with a fair amount of light on all sides.'

Climbing Rose on grass.

CHAPTER XIII
Some Results

———•◆•———

DETAILS OF A FEW OF THE RESULTS OBTAINED, where the system has been tried, in addition to those already given of Longleat, may be not without interest. How much a wild garden intelligently made may effect for a country seat is shown at Crowsley in Oxfordshire. It is one of the first-formed wild gardens existing, and in May was full of charms. No garden yields its beauty so early in the year, or over a more prolonged season, than the wild garden, as is abundantly evidenced here. The maker of this wild garden had no inviting site with which to deal; no great variety of surface, no variety of soil for plants of widely different habitats to be grown; he had only a neglected plantation, with a poor gravelly soil and little variety of surface beyond a few gravel banks thrown up long before. The garden is on each side of a Grass drive, with scattered trees on the one hand and rather shady ground on the other. The most beautiful aspect at the end of May after an ungenial spring, which had not allowed the Pæonies to unfold, was that of the German Irises, with their great Orchid-like blossoms seen everywhere through the wood, clear above the Grass and other herbage—stately flowers that, like the Daffodils, fear no weather, yet with hues that cannot be surpassed by tropical flowers. If this wild garden should teach only effective ways of using the many beautiful Irises in our garden flora, it would do good service. The Irises are perfectly at home in the plantation and among the Grass and wild flowers. When they go out

Nepeta blooms in a great billowy sweep in late August in the West Garden, in the same space where *Allium* flowered in May.

Crane's-bill, wild, in grass.

of flower, they will not be in the way as in a 'mixed' border, but rest in the grass till awakened in spring.

In the wild garden the fairest of our own wild flowers may be happily grouped with like plants from other countries. Here the sturdy Bell-flowered Scilla (S. campanulata) grows wild with our Wood Hyacinth; the white and pink forms also of the last-named look beautiful here associated with the common well-known form. The earlier kinds of Scilla are past; they are nice for the wild garden, especially S. bifolia, which thrives freely in woods. The Lily of the Valley did not inhabit the wood before; it was pleasant to thin out some of its matted tufts in the garden and carry them to the wild garden, where they are now in bloom. The Solomon's Seal, which is often charming on the fringes of shrubberies, is here arching high over the Woodruff and other woodland flowers, among which it seems a giant, showing fine form with every leaf, and stem, and blossom. The vigour and grace shown by this plant in rich soil are delightful. The greater Celandine (Chelidonium majus) and its double form are very pretty here with their tufts of golden flowers, taking care of themselves. The same may be said of the Honesty, the common Columbine, and Allium Moly, an old plant, which is one of the many at home in the wild garden, and better left out of the garden proper. The myriads of Crocus leaves dying off without the indignity of being cut off or tied into bundles as is common in gardens, the dense growth of Aconite and Snowdrop leaves, of coloured and common Primroses and Cowslips, suggest the beauty of this wild garden earlier in spring. The yet unfolded buds on the many groups of Pæonies, promise noble effects early in June; so do the colonies of the splendid Eastern Poppy (Papaver orientale) and the Lilies, and Sweet Williams, and Lupins, which will show their blossoms above or among the summer Grass in due time. The most brilliant effect I have ever seen in any garden was in a corner of this wild garden in summer, when many great oriental Poppies stood in ranks with the Lupins and Columbines, all growing close together in long grass in a green bay of the plantation.

Among the best of the Borageworts here, are the Caucasian Comfrey (Symphytum caucasicum), an admirable wood or copse plant, and red-purple or Bohemian Comfrey (S. bohemicum), which is very handsome. And what lovely effects from the Forget-me-nots—the Wood Forget-me-not, and the Early Forget-me-not (Myosotis dissitiflora)—are seen here! where their soft clouds of blue in the Grass are much prettier than when set in the brown earth in a prim border. Here the pushing of the delicate Grass blades through the blue mass, and the way in which the fringes of the tufts mingle with the other plants, are very beautiful.

Some gravel banks are covered with Stonecrops, Saxifrages, and the like, which would, as a rule, have a poor chance in Grass. Some of the prettiest

Autumn Crocuses
in the Wild Garden.

effects of this wild garden result from the way in which dead trees have been adorned. Some of the smaller branches are lopped off, and one or more climbers planted at the base of the tree. Here a Clematis, a climbing Rose, a fine Ivy, a wild Vine, or a Virginian Creeper, has all it requires, a firm support on which it may arrange itself after its own natural habit, without being mutilated; it gives no trouble to the planter, and has fresh ground free to itself.

Even when an old tree falls and tosses up a mass of soil and roots the planter is ready with some handsome Bramble or wild Vine to scramble over the stem. Ferns are at home here in the shady corners; all the strong hardy kinds may be so grown, and they look better among the flowers than in the 'hardy Fernery' so called. Even more graceful than the Ferns, and in some cases more useful, because they send up their plume-like leaves very early in the year, are the Giant Fennels (Ferula), which grow well here, and hold their own easily among the strongest plants. The common Fennel is also here, but it seeds so freely that it becomes a weed and overruns plants of greater value.

Such plants as Heracleum, Willow Herb, and many others, which not only win, but destroy all their fellows, in the struggle for life, should be planted only in outlying positions, islands, hedges, and small bits of isolated wood or copse, where their effects might be seen in due season, and where they might ramble without destroying. Rabbits—dreaded vermin in the wild garden—are kept out here effectually by means of wire fencing. The presence of these pests prevents all success in the wild garden.

To succeed with the wild garden, one should have a good collection of hardy flowers from which it can be supplied. Here one has been formed, consisting of about eleven hundred species, mostly arranged in borders. From these, from time to time, over-vigorous and over-abundant kinds may be taken to the wild garden. In a large collection one often finds kinds fit for freedom. The many plants good in all positions may increase in these borders till plentiful enough for planting out in some quantity in the wild garden. The wild garden here has been wholly formed by the

Tiger Lilies in Wild Garden at Great Tew.

owner, who planted with his own hands the plants that now adorn it throughout the year.

Tew Park will long be interesting, from the fact that it was there J. C. Loudon practised agriculture before he began writing the works that were such a marked addition to the garden literature of England. The Grove there is a plantation of fine trees, bordering a wide sweep of grass that varies in width. This grove, unlike much of the rest of the ground, does not vary in surface, or varies but little, so that one of the greatest aids is absent. Originally this now pleasant grove was a dense wood, with Gout-weed mainly on the ground, and troublesome flies in the air.

A few years ago the formation of a wild garden was determined upon, and the first operation was the thinning of the wood; light and moving air were let into it, and overcrowded trees removed. It was found, after deeply digging the ground, and sowing the Wood Forget-me-not, that Gout-weed rapidly disappeared. The effect of broad sheets of this Wood Forget-me-not (Myosotis sylvatica) beyond, and seen above, the long waving Grass, gradually receding under the trees, was very beautiful; now (June) its beauty is not so marked as earlier, when, the plants being more compact, the colour was fuller; but one charm of the wild garden is that the very changes of plants from what may be thought their most perfect state of blossom, may be itself a new pleasure instead of a warning that we must cut them down or replace them.

Not to mow is almost a necessity in the wild garden, and as there is often in large gardens much more mown surface than is necessary, many will not regret it. Here the Grass is left unmown in many places. Of course it may be cut when ripe, and most of the spring flowers have past and their leaves are out of danger. Even in parts where no flowers are planted the Grass is left till long enough to cut as meadow. Except where wanted as a carpet, Grass may often be allowed to grow even in the pleasure ground; quite as good an effect is afforded by unmown as by mown Grass—indeed, better when the long Grass is full of flowers. Three-fourths of the most lovely flowers of cold and temperate regions are companions of the

Grass—like Grasses in hardiness, like Grasses in summer life and winter rest, like Grasses in stature.

Whatever plants may seem best to associate together in gardens, an immense number—more than two thousand species of those now culti-vated—would thrive to perfection among our meadow Grasses, as they do on the Grassy breast of the mountain in many northern lands. Some, like the tall Irises or Columbines, will show their heads clear above the deli-cate bloom of the Grass; others, like the Cerastiums, will open their cups below it. The varieties of Columbine in the Grass were perhaps the pret-tiest flowers at the time of my visit. The white, purplish, and delicately-coloured forms of this charming old plant, just seen above the tops of the long Grass, growing singly, in little groups, or in colonies, formed a June

Large-flowered Clematis.

garden of themselves. Established among the Grass, they will henceforward, like it, take care of themselves. The rosy, heart-shaped blooms of the Dielytra spectabilis are seen at some distance through the Grass, and, so grown, furnish a bright and pretty effect. Tree Pæonies succeed, and their great heads of flower quite light up this charming wilderness. Plants of the Goat's Beard Spiræa (S. Aruncus) are very stately and graceful, even now, before they flower, being quite six feet high.

In the wild garden, apart from the naturalization of free-growing exotics, the establishment of rare British flowers is one of the most interesting occupations; and here, under a Pine tree, the modest, trailing Linnæa borealis of the northern Fir-woods is beginning to spread. The Foxglove was not originally found in the neighbourhood; now the ordinary kind and various other forms of this fine wild flower adorn the woods. In this way also the Lily of the Valley has been planted and is spreading rapidly.

Many climbing Roses and various other climbers have been planted at the bases of trees and stumps. A White Indian Clematis here, first trained on a wall, sent up some of its shoots through a tree close at hand, and now the long shoots hang from the tree full of flowers.

The large plumes of the nobler hardy Ferns are seen here and there through the trees and Grass, and they are better here among the Grass and flowers, half shaded by trees, than in the 'hardy Fernery.' The wild garden of the future will be also the true home of all the larger hardy Ferns. The rivals of the Ferns in beauty of foliage, the Ferulas, and other hardy plants with beautifully cut foliage, have also their homes in the wild garden. The Welsh Poppy thrives, as might be expected, admirably here, its rich yellow cups just showing above the meadow.

In another part of the grounds there is a high walk quite away from trees, open and dry, with banks on each side—a sun-walk, with Scotch Roses, Brooms, Sun Roses, Rock Roses, and things that love the sun, like the plants of the hot and rocky hillsides of the Mediterranean shores. Spanish Broom, Lavenders, Rosemary, Thyme, and Balm, are among the plants that thrive as well on a sunny sandy bank in England as in Italy or Greece.

Sun roses (Cistus) and other exotic hardy plants among heather, on sandy slope in Surrey.

True taste in the garden is, unhappily, much rarer than many people suppose. No amount of expense, rich collections, good cultivation, large gardens, and plenty of glass will suffice. A garden of a few acres showing a real love of the beautiful in Nature, as it can be illustrated in gardens, is rare; and when it is seen it is often rather the result of accident than of design. This is partly owing to the fact that the kind of knowledge one wants in order to form a really beautiful garden is very uncommon. No man can do so with few materials. It is necessary to have some knowledge of the wealth of beauty which the world contains for our gardens; and yet this knowledge must not have a leaning, or at any rate but a very partial leaning, towards the Dryasdust.[1] The disposition to 'dry' everything, to concern oneself entirely with nomenclature and classification, is not the gardening spirit—it is the *life* we want.

The garden of the late Mr. Hewittson, at Weybridge, had some of the most delightful garden scenes. Below the house, on the slope over the water of Oatlands Park, and below the usual lawn beds and trees, there is a piece of heathy ground—charming beyond any power of the pencil to show. The ground was partially clad with common Heaths with little green paths through them, and naturalized in the warm sandy soil were the Sun Roses which are shown in the foreground of the engraving. Here and there among the Heaths, creeping about in a perfectly natural-looking fashion, too, was the Gentian-blue Lithospermum prostratum. Among these groups were the large Evening Primroses and Peruvian Lily (Alstrœmeria), the whole relieved by bold masses of flowering shrubs, so grouped as not to show a trace of formality. All this was done without in the least detracting from the most perfect keeping. The garden is more free from offensive geometrical-twirling, barren expanse of gravelled surface, and all kinds of puerilities—old-fashioned and new-fangled—than any garden I have seen for years.

The following, from a correspondent, shows what may be done with few advantages as to space or situation:—

1. Dryasdust (dry as dust) refers to someone who presents historical information in thorough but dry detail minus any human interest. The term was created by Sir Walter Scott. —Ed.

'We have a dell with a small stream of spring water running through it. When I first came to Brockhurst I found this stream carried underground by a tile culvert, and the valley sides covered with Rhododendrons, the soil between carefully raked and kept free from weeds, so that it was only during springtime that flowers relieved the sombre effect of this primness. After five years this has all been changed into what I think you would call a wild garden, and we have cheerfulness and beauty all the year round.

'In the first place the brooklet was brought to the surface, and its course fringed with marsh plants, such as Marsh Marigolds, Forget-me-nots, Celandines, Irises, Primroses, and Ranunculuses, together with Osmundas, Hart's-tongues, and other Ferns. Many large-grow-ing Carex and large Rushes are also here. Little flats were formed and filled with peat, in which Cypripediums, Trilliums, Orchises, Solomon's Seal, and many rare bog plants find a home. In the valley

Woodruff and Ivy.

we have planted bulbs by thousands—Crocuses, Snowdrops, Daffodils, and Narcissi. The Rhododendrons were thinned and interspersed with Azaleas, and other handsome-foliaged shrubs, to give
brightness to the spring flowering, and rich colour to the foliage
in autumn. In the spaces between we introduced Wild Hyacinths
everywhere, and in patches among these the Red Campion, together
with every other pretty wild flower we could obtain—Forget-me-
nots, Globe Flowers, Columbines, Anemones, Primroses, Cowslips,
Polyanthuses, Campanulas, Golden Rods, &c.

'We have also planted bulbs very extensively, and as they have
been allowed to grow on undisturbed we have now large patches of
Daffodils, Narcissi, and other spring flowers in great beauty. When
we trim the garden all the spare plants are brought here, where they
form a reserve, and it is thus gradually getting stocked, and all the
bare ground covered with foliage and flowers. Lastly, for autumn
blooming we raised large quantities of Foxgloves in every colour,
and the larger Campanulas, and these were pricked out everywhere,
so that we have, to close the year, a glorious show of Foxglove
flowers worth all the trouble.

'A wild garden of this sort is a very useful reserve ground, where
many a plant survives after it has been lost in the borders. The
Lily of the Valley and Sweet Violet also flourish here, creeping
over heaps of stones, and flower more freely than they do in more
open situations. Visitors often say that the dell beats all the rest
of the garden for beauty, and it certainly gives less trouble in the
attainment.'—Wm. Brockbank, Brockhurst, Didsbury (in *Garden*).

Snowdrops by streamlet.

CHAPTER XIV
Hardy Exotic Flowering Plants for the Wild Garden

—◆◆—

WHEREVER THERE IS ROOM, plants for the wild garden should be at first grown in nursery beds to ensure a good supply. The many nursery collections of hardy plants being now more numerous than they were a few years ago, getting the plants is not so difficult as it once was. The sources of supply are these nurseries; seed houses, which publish lists of hardy plant seeds—many kinds may be easily raised from seed; botanic gardens, in which many plants are grown that hitherto have not found a place in our flower gardens; orchards and cottage gardens in pleasant country places may supply plants from time to time; and those who travel may bring home seeds or roots of plants they meet with in cool or mountain regions. Bulb and seed-merchants should offer hardy bulbs in large quantities for wild gardening, and at nearly wholesale rates. Few plants, vigorous and hardy in the British Islands without any attention after planting, are included here:—

Bear's Breech, *Acanthus.*—Vigorous perennials with handsome foliage, mostly from Southern Europe. Long cast out of gardens, they are now receiving more attention, and in no position will they look better than planted here and there on the margin of a shrubbery, where the leaves of the Acanthus contrast well with those of the ordinary shrubs or herbaceous vegetation. Hardy in all soils, they flower most freely in free loamy ground. Not varying very much in character, all obtainable hardy

Lichens on heavily budded branches of azaleas add to the rich hues of Gravetye's West Garden on a rainy day in late March.

species would group well together. The most vigorous kind at present in cultivation is the one called A. latifolius, which is almost evergreen, and a fine plant when well established. Few plants are more fitted for adorning rough and stony places, as they grow and increase without care, and are, for foliage or bloom, unsurpassed by any of the numerous plants that have been so long neglected because they have not been available in 'flower gardening.'

Monkshood, *Aconitum.*—Tall, handsome perennials, with very poisonous roots, which make it dangerous to plant them in or near gardens. Being vigorous they spread freely, and hold their own amongst herbaceous plants and weeds. Masses of them seen in flower in half-shady places in rich soil give a fine effect. There are many species, nearly all of equal value for the wild garden. Coming from the plains and mountains of Siberia and Northern Europe and America, they are among the hardiest of plants. Spreading groups of Aconites in bloom in open spaces in shrubberies has a finer effect than when the plants are tied into bundles in trim borders. The old blue-and-white kind is charming, and attains stately dimensions in good soil. The species grow in any soil, but on cold heavy ones are often somewhat stunted in growth.

Bugle, *Ajuga.*—Not a very numerous family as represented in gardens, but some of the species are valuable for the wild garden, notably Ajuga genevensis, which thrives freely in ordinary soils in open and half-shady places among dwarf vegetation, and affords beautiful tufts and carpets of blue. It spreads rapidly and is hardy everywhere. The plants mostly come from the cool uplands and hills of the temperate regions of Europe and Asia.

Yarrow, *Achillea.*—A numerous family of hardy plants spread through Northern Asia, Italy, Greece and Turkey, Hungary, but more in Southern than in Central or Northern Europe. In the Alps and Pyrenees numerous species are found. The Golden Yarrows (A. Eupatorium and A. Filipendula) are stately herbaceous plants, with handsome corymbs of yellow flowers attaining a height of three feet or four feet; growing freely in any soil, they are well worthy of naturalization. Various other kinds would

The Monkshood,
naturalized.

grow quite as well in plantations and rough places as the common Yarrow. The vigorous white-flowered kinds are fine for shrubberies, where their many white heads of flowers give a pleasing effect under the trees in summer. With few exceptions these plants have never been grown out of botanic gardens, many of them being thought too coarse for the mixed border. They are, nevertheless, remarkably beautiful both in flower and foliage, and many effects never before seen in gardens may be obtained by massing them under trees in open shrubberies or copses, as a rule allowing one species to establish itself in each place and assume an easy and broken boundary.

Allium.—Plants scattered in abundance throughout the northern temperate and alpine regions of Europe and Asia and also America. Some are so beautiful as to claim a place in gardens notwithstanding their

Large White Achilleas, spread into wide masses under shade of trees in shrubbery.

disagreeable odour. It is only in the wild garden, however, that this family finds a fitting home. One of the prettiest effects to produce in the wild garden would be that of the beautiful white Narcissus-like Allium of the south of Europe (A. neapolitanum). The sheets of this in the Lemon orchards of Provence will be remembered by many travellers. It would thrive in warm and sandy soils, and there is an allied species (A. ciliatum) which does well in any soil, gives a similar effect, and produces myriads of star-like white flowers. Singular effects may be produced from species less showy and more curious and vigorous, as, for example, the old yellow A. Moly.

Alstrœmeria.—All who care for hardy flowers must admire Alstrœmeria aurantiaca, especially spreading into healthy masses, and when there is a great variety in the height of the flowering stems. A valuable quality of the plant is, that it spreads freely in any light soil, and is quite hardy. For dry places between shrubs, for dry or sandy banks (either planted or bare), or heathy places, this plant is admirable. I have noticed it thriving in the

The White Narcissus-like Allium, in the orchards of Provence; type of family receiving little place in gardens which may be beautiful for a season in wild places.

shade of fir trees. It is interesting as being a South American plant, thriving in warm soils, but often slow and dwarf on cold soils.

Marsh Mallow, *Althæa.*—These are plants rarely seen out of botanic gardens, and yet, from their vigour and showy flowers, may be effective in the wild garden. The common Hollyhock is an Althæa, and in its single form is typical of the vigorous habit and good showy flowers of other rampant species, such as A. ficifolia. A group of these plants would be effective near a wood-walk, no flower-garden being large enough for their extraordinary vigour.

Alyssum.—In spring every single little shoot of the wide tufts and flakes of these plants sends up a little fountain of small golden flowers. For bare, stony, or rocky banks, and for poor sandy ground, and ruins, they are admirable. Alyssum Wiersbecki and A. saxatile are strong enough to take care of themselves on the margins of shrubberies, &c., where the vegetation is not very coarse, but are best for rocky or stony places, or old ruins, and thrive freely on cottage garden walls in some districts. There are many species, natives of Germany, Russia, France, Italy, Hungary, and Dalmatia; Asia, principally Siberia, the Altai Mountains, Georgia, Persia, and the entire basin of the Caspian, is rich in them.

Windflower, *Anemone.*—A numerous race of dwarf herbs that contribute much to the most beautiful effects of the mountain, wood, and pasture vegetation of all northern and temperate climes. The flowers vary from intense scarlet to the softest blue; many of the exotic kinds would thrive as well in our woodlands and meadows as they do in their own. There is hardly a position they may not adorn—warm, sunny, bare banks, on which the Grecian A. blanda might open its large blue flowers in winter; the tangled copse, where the Japan Windflower and its varieties might make a bold show in autumn; and the grove, where the Apennine Windflower would contrast charmingly with the Wood Anemone so abundantly scattered in our own woods. The Hepaticas should be considered as belonging to the same genus, not forgetting the Hungarian one, A. angulosa. The Hepaticas thrive best and are seen best in half-woody places, where the spring sun may cheer them by passing through the branches, which afterwards become leafy and shade them from the scorching heats of summer.

St. Bruno's Lily, *Anthericum.*—One of the most lovely effects in the Alpine meadows of Europe is that of the delicate white flowers of the St. Bruno's Lily in the Grass in early summer, looking like miniature white Lilies. All who have seen it would no doubt like to enjoy the same on their Grassy meadows. The large-flowered or major variety might be tried with advantage in this way, and the smaller-flowered kinds, A. Liliago and its varieties, are pretty. They are not so likely to find favour in gardens as the larger kind, and therefore the wild garden is the home for them, and in it many will admire their graceful habit and numerous flowers. The kinds best worth growing are natives of the Alpine meadows of Europe.

Alkanet, *Anchusa.*—Tall herbaceous plants, with numerous flowers of a fine blue, admirable for dotting about in open places in sunny glades in woods or copses. They mostly come from Southern Europe and Western Asia. Anchusa italica and A. capensis are among the most useful. The English A. sempervirens, rare in some districts, is an excellent wild garden plant.

Snapdragon, *Antirrhinum.*—The common Snapdragon and its beautifully spotted varieties are easily naturalized on old walls and ruins by sowing the seed in mossy chinks. Antirrhinum Asarinum, A. rupestre, and A. molle do well treated in the same way. Probably many other species would be found good in like places. About two dozen species are known, but comparatively few of these are in cultivation. They mostly come from the shores of the Mediterranean.

Columbine, *Aquilegia.*—Favourite herbaceous plants, generally of various shades of blue and purple, white, and sometimes bright orange. The varieties of the common kind (A. vulgaris), which are very numerous, are those most likely to be naturalized. In bare places in elevated and moist districts some of the beautiful Rocky Mountain kinds would be worth a trial. In places where wild gardens have been formed the effect of Columbines in the Grass has been beautiful—the flowers group themselves in all sorts of pretty ways, showing just above the long Grass. The tall

Siberian Columbine
in rocky place.

and handsome A. chrysantha of Western America is the most hardy and enduring of the American kinds. The Columbines are a northern and alpine family, most abundant in Siberia.

Wall Cress, *Arabis.*—Dwarf mountain plants, often producing myriads of white flowers, suitable for sandy or rocky ground, where the vegetation is very dwarf. With them may be associated Cardamine trifolia and Thlaspi latifolium, which resemble Arabis in habit and flowers. All these are suited for association with the purple Aubrietia or yellow Alyssum, and in bare and rocky or gravelly places, and old walls.

Sandwort, *Arenaria.*—Of these little plants there are certain kinds that are vigorous and useful, such as A. montana and A. graminifolia. The small alpine species are charming for rocky places, and as for the little creeping A. balearica, moist rocks or stones suffice for its support. It covers such surfaces with a close carpet of green, dotted with numerous star-like flowers. Some of the smaller species, such as A. cæspitosa, better known as Spergula pilifera, might be grown in gravel and sandy places. In certain positions in large gardens it would be an improvement to allow the very walks or drives to become covered with very dwarf plants— plants which could be walked upon with little injury. The surface would be dry enough, being drained below, and would be more agreeable to the feet.

Asphodel, *Asphodelus.*—The Asphodels are among the plants that have never been popular, the habit of the species being somewhat coarse and the flowering period not long; and yet they are of a distinct order of beauty, which well deserves to be seen in open spaces in shrubberies. The plants are mostly natives of the countries round the Mediterranean, and thrive freely in ordinary soils.

Lords and Ladies, *Arum.*—Mostly a tropical and sub-tropical family, some plants of which grow as far north as Southern Europe. These are quite hardy in our gardens. The Italian Arum deserves a place in the wild garden, from its fine leaves in winter. It should be placed in sheltered places where it would not suffer much from storms. The old Dragon plant (A. Dracontium) grows freely enough about the foot of rocks or walls in

Tall Asphodel in copse.

sandy or dry peaty places. The nearly-allied Arum Lily (Calla æthiopica) is quite hardy as a water and water-side plant in the southern counties of England and Ireland.

Silkweed, *Asclepias.*—Usually vigorous perennials, with very curious flowers, common in fields and on river banks in North America and Canada, where they sometimes become troublesome weeds. Of the species in cultivation, A. Cornuti and A. Douglasi could be naturalized easily in rich deep soil. The showy and dwarfer A. tuberosa requires very warm sandy soils to flower as well as in its own dry hills. A good many of the hardy species are not introduced; some of them are water-side plants, such as A. incarnata, the Swamp Silkweed of the United States.

Starwort, *Aster.*—A very large family of vigorous, often beautiful perennials, mostly with bluish or white flowers, chiefly natives of North America. Many of these, of an inferior order of beauty, used to be planted in our mixed borders, which they very much helped to bring into discredit, and they form a very good example of a class of plants for which the true place is the copse, or rough and half-cared-for places in shrubberies and copses, and by wood-walks, where they will grow as freely as any native weeds, and in many cases prove charming in autumn.

With the Asters may be grouped the Galatellas, the Vernonias, and also the handsome Erigeron speciosus, which, however, not being so tall, could not fight its way among such coarse vegetation as that in which the Asters may be grown. Associated with the Golden Rods (Solidago)—also common plants of the American woods—the best of the Asters or Michaelmas Daisies will form a very interesting aspect of vegetation. It is that which one sees in American woods in late summer and autumn when the Golden Rods and Asters are seen in bloom together. It is one of numerous aspects of the vegetation of other countries which the wild garden will make possible in gardens. To produce such effects the plants must, of course, be planted in some quantity, and not repeated all over the place or mixed up with many other things.

Nearly 200 species are known, about 150 of which form part of the rich vegetation of North America. These fine plants inhabit that great continent, from Mexico—where a few are found—to the United States and Canada, where they abound, and even up to the regions far north of that quarter of the world.

In my own garden, at Gravetye, many thousands of these Asters were massed in picturesque ways for the first time: almost every kind in cultivation in gardens in broken but effective groups between the cedars, yews, and other evergreen trees near the house. The trees were planted in a much more open way than is customary, thus avoiding a crowded growth. The Asters kept the ground quite furnished and clean, and were often very beautiful in the autumn winds. They were never staked and, perfectly hardy, they required no attention after planting. As these plantations, however, were really part of the garden, some more attention was given the Starworts than would have been the case in a wild garden; that is to say that after two or three years in the same place they were moved, to encourage growth and a longer bloom. The more vigorous of the species— and indeed all of them—may be naturalized in open woods or copses, or by river banks and in hedgerows.

Milk Vetch, *Astragalus.*—A numerous family of hardy plants, little seen in our gardens, though hundreds of them are hardy, and many of them among the prettiest of the Pea-flowers that adorn the mountains. They are best for rocky or gravelly soils, or bare banks, though some of the taller species, like A. galegiformis, are stout enough to take care of themselves among the larger perennials. This plant is valuable for its handsome port and foliage, though its flowers are not such as recommend it for the flower-garden. The species from the Mediterranean region might be successfully introduced on banks in our chalk districts and in rocky places. Astragalus ponticus, a tall kind, and A. monspessulanus, a dwarf one, are both worth growing.

Masterwort, *Astrantia.*—This is an elegant genus, of which few species are known, five being European—found in Italy, Carinthia, Greece, and the centre of Europe—others from Northern Asia. They are among the few umbellates with attractive and distinct flowers, and yet they are rarely seen in gardens. In the wild garden they are quite at home among the

Grass and medium-sized herbaceous plants, and partial shade prolongs their quaint beauty.

Blue Rock Cress, *Aubrietia.*—Dwarf rock plants, with purplish flowers, quite distinct in aspect and hue from anything else grown in our gardens, and rarely perishing from any cause, except from being overrun by coarser plants. They are admirable for association with the Alyssums and Arabises in any position where the vegetation is very dwarf, or in rocky bare places. There are several species and varieties, all almost equally suitable, but not differing much in aspect or stature from each other. The Aubrietias come chiefly from the mountains of Greece, Asia Minor, and neighbouring countries. Wherever there is an old wall, or a sunk fence, or a bare bank, evergreen curtains may be formed of these plants, and in spring they will be sheeted with purple flowers, no matter what the weather.

Great Birthwort, *Aristolochia Sipho.*—A great climbing plant for covering arbours, banks, stumps of old trees, and also wigwam-like bowers, formed with branches of trees. It is American, and will grow as high as thirty feet; A. tomentosa is distinct and not so large in leaf. These will scarcely be grown for their flowers; but for covering stumps or trees they are valuable, and afford a distinct effect.

Virginian Creepers, *Ampelopsis.*—Although this chapter is mostly devoted to herbaceous plants, the Virginian Creeper and its allies are so useful for forming curtains in rocky places, ravines, or over old trees, that they deserve mention here. These plants are not very distant relations of the vine—the wild American vines that are worthy of a place in our groves, garlanding trees as they do in a grand way.

Bamboo, *Bambusa.*—In many parts of England, Ireland, and Wales, various kinds of Bamboos are more hardy, and perhaps near the sea thrive freely. Their beauty is more precious from their being wholly distinct in habit from any other plants or shrubs that we grow. They are so tall and so enduring that they will thrive among the strongest plants or bushes, and the partial shelter of the thin wood saves their leaves from the effects of violent winds. By quiet Grass walks, in sheltered dells, in the shrubbery, or in little glades in woods, the Bamboos will be at home. The commonest kind is that generally known as Arundinaria falcata (sometimes called Bambusa gracilis); but others, such as B. Metake, B. Simmonsi, and B. viridis-glaucescens, are of equal or greater value. They all delight in rich, light, and moist soils, and in our country some shelter helps them.

Baptisia.—A strong Lupin-like plant seldom grown in gardens, but beautiful when in bloom for its long blue racemes of Pea-flowers, growing three to four feet high; it will hold its own in strong soil.

Borage, *Borago.*—A genus seldom seen out of botanic gardens, where they form part of the usual distressing arrangements honoured with the name of 'scientific.' Among the best kinds for our purpose are B. cretica and B. orientalis; even the well-known annual kind will be found a pretty plant, naturalized in stony places, old quarries, and the like.

Bell-flower, *Campanula.*—Beautiful and generally blue-flowered herbs, varying from a few inches to five feet in height, and abundant in northern and temperate countries. All the medium-sized and large kinds thrive very well in rough places, woods, copses, or shrubberies, among grasses and other herbaceous plants; while those smaller in size than our own Hare-bell (C. rotundifolia) are quite at home, and very pretty, on any arid or bare surfaces, such as sandy banks, chalk pits, and even high up on old walls. In such positions the seeds need only to be scattered. Campanula rapunculoides and C. lamiifolia do finely in shrubberies or copses, as, indeed, do all the tall-growing kinds, and where there are white varieties they should be secured. Many people will begin to see the great beauty of this family for the first time when they have them growing among the grass—the effect is far more beautiful than that which they show in the garden border.

Red Valerian, *Centranthus ruber.*—This showy plant is seen best only on banks, rubbish-heaps, or old walls, in which positions it endures much longer than on the level ground, and becomes a long-lived perennial with a shrubby base. Grows apace on old bridges, banks, chalk pits, and on stone heaps.

Knap-weed, *Centaurea.*—Vigorous perennial or annual plants, seldom so pretty as autumn-sown plants of our corn bluebottle (C. Cyanus). They are scarcely important enough for borders; hence the wild garden is the place for them. Among the best are C. macrocephala, C. montana, C. babylonica, and C. uniflora, the last being more suitable for banks.

Mouse-ear, *Cerastium.*—Dwarf plants with many white flowers. Half a dozen or more of the kinds have silvery leaves, and will grow in any position where they are not choked by coarser plants.

Wallflower, *Cheiranthus.*—The varieties of the common Wallflower have great beauty for rocky places and old walls. The clear yellow Erysimum ochroleucum is very like a Wallflower in type, and thrives well in dry sandy places. With these might be associated Vesicaria utriculata.

Meadow Saffron, *Colchicum.*—In addition to the Meadow Saffron, dotted over the moist fields in various parts of England, there are several other species that could be naturalized in grassy places, and they would be useful where plants that flower in autumn are sought.

Crocus.—One or two kinds of Crocus are naturalized in England. They should not be placed where coarse vegetation would choke them up or prevent the sun getting to their flowers and leaves. Some of the pretty

The foliage of the
Meadow Saffron
in Spring.

varieties of C. vernus are well worth planting in grassy places and on sunny slopes. Crocus Imperati is an early kind, and the autumnal Croci are charming. A friend writes:—

> 'In the plantations here on each side of a long avenue, we have the common Crocus in every shade of purple (there are scarcely any yellow ones) growing literally in hundreds of thousands. We have no record of when the roots were originally planted (and the oldest people about the estate say they have always been the same); but they grow so thickly that it is impossible to step where they are without treading on two or three flowers. The effect produced by them in spring is magnificent. I have transplanted a good many roots to the wild garden, to the great improvement of the size of the blooms; they are so matted together in the shrubberies, and have remained so long in the same place, that the flowers are small.'

In my own garden the prettiest early effects are those of Crocuses in the grass, which come up year after year without attention of any kind, and which no manure or 'compost' of any kind has once touched.

Virgin's Bower, *Clematis.*—Mostly climbing or trailing plants, free, often luxuriant, sometimes rampant, in habit, with bluish, violet, purple, white, or yellow flowers, and sometimes deliciously fragrant. They are best suited for covering stumps, planting on rocky places, among low shrubs in copses, for draping over the faces of rocks, sunny banks, or the brows of sunk fences, covering objectionable railings, rough bowers, chalk pits, hedges, &c., and occasionally for isolating in large tufts in open spaces where their effect could be seen from a distance. Not particular as to soil, the stronger kinds will grow in any ground, but the large-flowered new hybrids will thrive best in warm, rich, deep soil. Clematis Viorna, C. flammula, C. montana, C. campaniflora, C. Viticella, and C. cirrhosa must not be omitted from a selection of the wild kinds.

Dwarf Cornel, *Cornus canadensis.*—This charming little plant, beautiful from its white bracts, thrives in moist, sandy, or peaty spots, in which our

native heaths—Mitchella repens, Linnæa borealis, and the Butterworts—
would be likely to thrive.

Mocassin Flower, *Cypripedium spectabile.*—The handsomest of hardy
orchids, found far north in America, and thriving perfectly in England
and Ireland in deep rich vegetable soil. In places where the soil is not naturally peat or rich vegetable matter this fine plant will succeed on the margins of beds of rhododendrons, &c. It should be sheltered by surrounding bushes, and be in a moist position. Others of the genus, and various
other hardy orchids, are worthy of naturalization; the mocassin flower is
the best as well as the most easily tried.

Sowbread, *Cyclamen.*—It was the sight of a grove nearly covered with
C. hederæfolium, near Montargis, in France, that first led me to think of
how many plants might be tried in like ways. Both C. hederæfolium and C.
europæum may be naturalized with ease on light, loamy, or other warm
soil. Cyclamen vernum, C. Coum, and C. repandum are also well worthy of trial. Nothing can be more agreeable to the lover of hardy plants
than endeavouring to naturalize these charming flowers, now rarely seen
out of the greenhouse. The best positions would be among dwarf shrubs
that would afford slight shelter, on banks or sunny open spots in copses
or woods. Bare or dug borders they abhor, and a sunny warm exposure

The White-flowered
European Clematis
(C. erecta).

should be chosen. In the case of C. hederæfolium (and perhaps some of the others), ground under trees, bare, or with a very scant vegetation, would do quite well if the soil were free and warm.

Giant Sea-kale, *Crambe.*—Crambe cordifolia is a fine perennial, but its place is on the turf in rich soil. It has enormous leaves, and small whitish flowers in panicles. It is one of the finest plants in a wild garden in Oxfordshire of about five acres, associated with Rheums, Ferulas, Gunneras, Centaurea babylonica, Arundo Donax, and Acanthus.

Bindweed, *Calystegia.*—Climbers, with handsome white or rosy flowers, often too vigorous to be agreeable in gardens. Calystegia dahurica, larger than the common kind, is handsome trailing through shrubs, in rough places, or over old stumps.

The pretty little Rosy Bindweed that one meets often upon the shores of the Mediterranean is here depicted at home in an English garden, creeping up the leaves of an Iris in Mr. Wilson's garden at Heatherbank, Weybridge Heath.[1] We possess a great privilege in being able to grow the fair flowers of so many regions in our own. This beautiful pink Bindweed is, so to speak, the representative in the south of our own Rosy Field Bindweed, but it is perfectly hardy and free in our own soils. Its botanical name

1. See next page. —Ed.

Cyclamens in the Wild Garden; from nature.

is Convolvulus althæoides. I put the Great Bindweed in the banks when forming fences, as in these it is a harmless as well as a beautiful 'weed.'

Marsh Calla, *Calla palustris.*—A creeping Arum-like plant, with white flowers showing above a low carpet of glossy leaves, admirable for naturalization in muddy places, moist bogs, on the margins of ponds.

Rosy Coronilla, *Coronilla varia.*—On grassy banks, stony heaps, rough rocky ground, spreading over slopes or any like positions. A very fine plant for naturalization, thriving in any soil.

Giant Scabious, *Cephalaria.*—Allied to Scabious but seldom grown. They are worth a place for their fine vigour alone, and the numerous pale yellow flowers will be admired by those who do not limit their admiration to showy colours.

Coral-wort, *Dentaria.*—Showy perennials, the purplish or white flowers of which look like a stock-flower, are distinct in habit and bloom, and too rarely seen in our gardens; they will be found to thrive well and look well in peat soil beneath rhododendrons, and towards the margins of clumps of American shrubs.

Leopard's Bane, *Doronicum.*—Stout, or dwarf perennials, hardy, free, and with very showy flowers; well suited for naturalization among herbaceous vegetation, in any position where the beauty of their early bloom can be enjoyed.

American Cowslip, *Dodecatheon.*—All who care for hardy flowers admire the beautiful American cowslip (D. Meadia), found in rich woods in Pennsylvania, Ohio, to Wisconsin and south-westward, in America. This would be a charming plant to naturalize on rich and light sandy loams, among dwarf herbs, low shrubs, &c., in sheltered and sunny spots. Jeffrey's American cowslip (D. Jeffreyanum), a vigorous kind, is also worth a trial.

Fumitory, *Fumaria, Dielytra.*—Plants with graceful leaves and gay flowers suited for association with dwarf plants on open banks, except D. spectabilis, which in deep peat or other rich soil will grow a yard high. The little Fumaria bulbosa is one of the dwarf plants that thrive under the branches of trees, and Corydalis lutea thrives in almost every position from the top of an old castle to the bottom of a well shaft. I saw Dielytra

A South European Bindweed creeping up the stems of an Iris in an English garden.

eximia naturalized in Buckhurst Park, in a shrubbery, the position being shady. Its effect was charming, the plumy tufts being dotted over with flowers, it thrives and spreads freely in shady spots. The blossoms, instead of being of the usual crimson hue, were a delicate pale rose, no doubt owing to the shade; and, as they drooped over the graceful leaves, they looked like snowdrops of a faint rosy hue.

Larkspur, *Delphinium* perennial species.—Tall and beautiful plants, with flowers of many exquisite shades of blue and purple. They are well suited for rich soil in glades, thin shrubberies, or among masses of dwarf shrubs, above which their fine spikes of bloom might here and there arise.

One of the prettiest effects I have ever seen among naturalized plants was a colony of tall Larkspurs (Delphiniums). Portions of old roots of various kinds had been trimmed off where a bed of these plants was being dug, and in the autumn the refuse had been thrown into a near shrubbery, far in among the shrubs and tall trees. Here they grew in half-open spaces, which were so far from the margin that they were not dug and were not seen. When I saw the Larkspurs in flower they were certainly the loveliest things that one could see. They were more beautiful than they are in borders or beds, not growing in such close stiff tufts, and they mingled with and were relieved by the trees above and shrubs around. This suggests that we might make wild gardens from the mere parings and thinnings of the borders in autumn, where there is a collection of hardy plants.

Pink, *Dianthus.*—Beautiful dwarf mountain plants, with flowers mostly of shades of rose, sometimes sporting into other colours in gardens. The finer alpine kinds would be likely to thrive only on bare stony ground, and with plants of like size. The bright D. neglectus would thrive in any ordinary soil. Some of the kinds in the way of our own D. cæsius grow well on old walls and ruins, as does the single carnation; indeed, many kinds of Pink would thrive on old walls far better than on the ground.

Foxglove, *Digitalis.*—It need not be said here that our own stately Foxglove should be seen in the wild garden, in districts where it does not naturally grow wild; there are a number of exotic species for which a place might be found—some of them are not very satisfactory elsewhere. The most showy hardy flowers of midsummer are the Foxglove and the French Willow (Epilobium angustifolium), and in rough places in plantations their effect is beautiful. In such half-shady places the Foxglove thrives best; and, as the French Willow is too rampant a plant for the garden proper, the place for it too is the wild garden. It is a most showy plant, and masses of it may be seen great distances off. The spotted varieties of the Foxglove should be sown as well as the ordinary wild form.

Hemp Agrimony, *Eupatorium.*—Vigorous perennials, with white or purple fringed flowers. Some of the American kinds might well be associated with our own wild one—the white kinds, like E. aromaticum and E. ageratoides, being beautiful and distinct.

Sea Holly, *Eryngium.*—Distinct and beautiful perennials, with usually spiny leaves, and flowers in heads, sometimes surrounded by a bluish involucrum, the stems of a fine amethystine blue. They are handsome on margins of shrubberies and near wood-walks, thrive in ordinary free soil, and will take care of themselves among grasses and all but the most vigorous plants. They often come freely from self-sown seed and may be easily naturalized on warm soils and in sunny places.

Heath, *Erica, Menziesia.*—The brilliant Erica carnea is so charming that it well deserves naturalization among our native kinds. The beautiful St. Daboec's Heath (Menziesia polifolia), found wild in the west of Ireland, is to the majority of English gardens an exotic plant. It will grow almost anywhere in peaty soil. In the country place no kind of gardening is more delightful than the growth in rather bold groups and masses of all hardy Heaths, native or other. It is gardening that may be done in a bold and careless way, and the growth after a few years left to mingle with the grass and other vegetation around. The Heath beds after a year or two's growth look well throughout the year, and are often beautiful with bloom. Such bold groups would seldom come into the flower-garden, and they are best placed by grass-walks in the pleasure ground, preferring open and raised ground. The natural soil for such plants would seem to be peat, but it is not necessary for their culture. At Gravetye where there is no peat I planted many Heaths which did well.

A Sea Holly
(Eryngium).

Barren-wort, *Epimedium.*—Interesting perennials, with pretty flowers, and finely formed leaves. They like peaty or free moist soils, among low shrubs or on rocky banks. The variety called E. pinnatum elegans, when in deep peat soil, forms tufts of leaves nearly a yard high, and in spring bears long racemes of handsome yellow flowers.

Globe Thistle, *Echinops.*—Large perennials of fine port, from three to six feet high, with spiny leaves and numerous flowers in spherical heads. These thrive in almost any position, and hold their ground amid the coarsest vegetation. Of a 'type' distinct from that of our native plants, they are also well fitted for naturalization—E. exaltatus and E. ruthenicus are among the best kinds.

May-Flower, *Epigæa repens.*—A small creeping shrub, with pretty and fragrant flowers, which come soon after the melting of the snow in North America, and are there as welcome as the Hawthorn with us. In its native country it inhabits woods, mostly in the shade of pines; and wherever I saw it, it seemed to form a carpet under three or four layers of vegetation,— that is to say, it was beneath pines, medium-sized trees, tall bushes, and dwarf scrub, the plant itself was not more than one or two inches high. It can be naturalized in Pine woods on a sandy soil.

Dog's-tooth Violet, *Erythronium.*—This beautiful plant, some years ago rarely seen in our gardens, adorns many a dreary slope in the Southern Alps, and there is no difficulty in the way of adding its charms to the wild garden.

The Winter Aconite, *Eranthis hyemalis.*—Classed among British plants but really naturalized. Its yellow buttons peeping through the moss and grass in snowdrop time form one of the prettiest aspects of our garden vegetation in spring. It will grow almost anywhere, and is one of the plants that thrives under the spreading branches of summer-leafing trees, as it blooms and ripens its leaves before the buds open on the beech. On many lawns, spring gardens might be formed by planting some spring-flowering plants that finish their growth before the trees are in leaf. Another advantage of such positions is that the foliage of the trees prevents coarse plants taking possession of the ground, and therefore these little spring plants have the ground to themselves, and wander into natural little groups in the moss and grass. The Winter Aconite does not thrive in some cool soils.

Plantain Lilies, *Funkia.*—The conditions in the wild garden are sometimes more suitable to many plants than borders, the plants remaining longer in bloom in the shade and shelter of shrubby places than when exposed. As an instance of this, I saw Funkia cœrula showing great size and beauty in a shady drive at Beauport, near Battle. The plant was over a yard high, and bore many stately stems hung with blue flowers. The Plantain Lilies are plants for the wild garden, not being liable to the accidents that are fatal to Lilies and other plants exposed to the attacks of slugs and rabbits.

Snake's-head, *Fritillaria.*—The beautiful British Snake's-head (F. Meleagris) grows wild, as most people know, in meadows in various parts of England, and should be established in the meadows of many a country seat. Various other Fritillarias not so pretty as this, and of a peculiar livid

Groups of
Siebold's
Plantain Lily.

dark hue, which is not likely to make them popular in gardens, would be worthy of a position also. Of such is F. tristis, and the Crown Imperial would do on the fringes of shrubberies. The Golden Fritillary is charming, and when plentiful will be lovely in the wild garden.

Giant Fennel, *Ferula.*—Noble herbaceous plants of the parsley family, with exquisitely cut leaves; forming magnificent tufts of verdure, like the most finely-cut ferns. The leaves rise very early in spring, and go at the end of summer, and the best way to plant them is in places occupied by spring flowers, among which they give a fine effect. With the Giant Fennels might be grouped various other plants of this distinct family of plants, so far very little seen in gardens.

Ferns.—No plants may be naturalized with more charming effect than ferns. The Royal Ferns, of which the bold foliage is reflected in the marsh waters of North America, will do well in the many places where our own Royal Fern thrives. The graceful Maidenhair Fern of the rich woods of the Eastern States and Canada thrives in any cool place, or dyke, or in a shady wood, but the soil must be leafy and good. The small ferns that find a home on arid alpine cliffs may be established on old walls and ruins. Cheilanthes odora, which grows on the sunny sides of walls in Southern France, might be grown in the south of England, the spores to be sown in mossy chinks of the walls. The climbing fern Lygodium palmatum, which I saw with great pleasure running through native shrubs in cold New Jersey, and which goes as far north as cold Massachusetts, will climb up the undershrubs in England.

There is no fern of the numbers that inhabit the northern regions of Europe, Asia, and America that may not be tried with confidence. One could form a rich and stately type of fern vegetation without employing one of our native kinds at all, though the best way will be to associate all so far as their habits will permit. Treat them boldly; put strong kinds out in glades; imagine colonies of Daffodils among the Oak and Beech Ferns, fringed by early Aconite, in the spots overshadowed by the branches of summer-leafing trees. There are few kinds of gardening more interesting than naturalizing the fine hardy ferns of North America. Those having peaty and leafy soils have a great advantage, as many of the plants grow in these soils naturally; though the ferns will often grow in loamy soils they do not endure so long or spread so rapidly. The great ferns, like the Feather Ferns that live in the ditches and wet hollows in American woods, are not so difficult, and will grow in any moist deep peat.

Geranium, *Geranium, Erodium.*—Handsome perennials, mostly with bluish, pinkish, or deep rose flowers. Some of the stouter kinds of the hardy geraniums, such as G. ibericum and G. Armenum, are the very plants to take care of themselves in open places. With them might be grown the fine Erodium Manescavi; and where there are very bare places, on which they would not be overrun by coarser plants, the smaller Erodium, such as E. romanum.

Goat's Rue, *Galega.*—Tall and graceful perennials, with numerous pink, blue, or white flowers, G. officinalis and its white variety are among the pretty tall border flowers, and they are useful for planting in rough places, as is also the blue G. orientalis and G. biloba, being all free growers.

Gypsophila, *Gypsophila.*—Neat perennials, hardy, and with myriads of flowers, mostly small, and of a pale pinkish hue. They are best suited for rocky or sandy ground, or even old ruins, or any position where they will not be smothered by coarser vegetation. Like them in character is the

A hardy Geranium.

pretty little Tunica Saxifraga, which grows on the tops of old walls and sand heaps in Italy and in Southern Europe, and will thrive on bare places with us.

Gentian, *Gentiana.*—Dwarf, and usually evergreen, alpine or high-pasture plants, with large and numerous flowers often handsome, and frequently of the most vivid blue. The large Gentianella (G. acaulis) would grow as freely in moist places on any of our own mountains as it does on its native hills; indeed, it would flourish in all moist loams, where it could not be choked by coarse and taller subjects. The tall Willow Gentian (G. asclepiadea) is a handsome plant, which, in the mountain woods of Switzerland, I have often seen blooming among long grass in shade of trees, and this fact is suggestive as to its use in this country.

Snowdrops, *Galanthus.*—The charms of our own Snowdrop when naturalized in the grass are well known to all, but many of the new kinds, such as G. Elwesi and G. plicatus, have claims also in that respect, all of which would be as easily naturalized as the common Snowdrop. For some account of the various kinds of Snowdrop that have come into our gardens of recent years, see the article in *The English Flower-Garden*.

Cow Parsnips, *Heracleum.*—Giant herbaceous plants, mostly from Northern Asia, with huge leaves, and umbels (sometimes a foot across) of white or whitish flowers. They are very suitable for rough places on the banks of rivers or artificial water, islands, or for any place where bold foliage may be desired. In planting them it should be borne in mind that their foliage dies down and disappears at the end of summer. When established they often sow themselves, so that seedling plants in abundance may be picked up around them; but it is important not to allow them to become giant weeds. To prevent this, it may, in certain positions, be desirable to prevent them seeding.

Day Lily, *Hemerocallis.*—Vigorous plants of the Lily order, with long leaves and large and showy red-orange or yellow flowers, often scented delicately. There are two types, one large and strong like H. flava and H. fulva, the other short and somewhat fragile like H. graminea. The larger kinds are valuable plants for the wild garden, thriving in any rich soil.

Christmas Rose, *Helleborus.*—Stout dwarf perennials, with showy blooms appearing in winter and spring when flowers are rare, and with handsome leathery leaves. They thrive in almost any soil; but to get their early bloom good, it is well to place them on sunny banks in groups, and not far from the eye. They form beautiful ornaments near wood-walks, where the spring sun can reach them. There are various kinds useful for naturalization, especially on warm chalky soils.

Sun Rose, *Helianthemum.*—Dwarf spreading shrubs, bearing myriads of flowers in a variety of colour. The most satisfactory way of employing these in our gardens is to naturalize them on banks or slopes in half-wild parts of our pleasure grounds, where there is sandy or warm soil. They are best suited for chalk or rocky districts, where they thrive and make a brilliant display.

Perennial Sunflower, *Helianthus, Rudbeckia, Silphium.*—Stout and very tall perennials with showy yellow flowers, the best known of which is Helianthus multiflorus fl. pl., of which plenty may be seen in Euston Square and other places in London. As a rule these are all better fitted for rough places than for gardens, where, like many other plants mentioned in these pages, they will tend to form a vigorous herbaceous covert. Helianthus rigidus is a brilliantly showy plant, running very freely at the root, and an excellent subject for naturalization. Helianthus giganteus, common in thickets and swamps in America, and growing as high as ten feet, is also desirable. The showy and larger American Rudbeckias, such as R. laciniata, R. triloba, and also the small but showy R. hirta, belong to the same type. All these plants, and many others of the tall yellow Composites that one sees among herbaceous vegetation in America, would give showy effects in autumn, and might perhaps interest those who only visit their country seats at that time of year. The Silphiums, especially the Compass plant (S. laciniatum), and the cup plant (S. perfoliatum), are in general character like Helianthus.

St. John's Wort, *Hypericum.*—The well-known St. John's Wort does only too freely in many places; there is scarcely one of its numerous brethren which will not thrive in rough places, in any soil. They have all the same bright yellow flowers as the St. John's Wort, and are nearly all taller. Some of the newer kinds have handsome flowers like the St. John's Wort. It should be noted that the common St. John's Wort so exhausts the soil of moisture that it sometimes is the cause of the death of trees. Many places have too much of it, as they also have of the common Laurel.

Rocket, *Hesperis.*—The common single Rocket (Hesperis matronalis) is a showy plant in copse or shrubbery, and very easily raised from seed.

Evergreen Candytuft, *Iberis.*—Compact little evergreens, forming spreading bushes from three to fifteen inches high, and sheeted with white flowers in spring and early summer. There are no plants better for naturalization in open or stony places, or, indeed, in any position where the vegetation is not strong enough to overrun them. They, however, attain greatest beauty when fully exposed to the sun, and are admirable for every kind of rocky or stony ground and banks.

Iris, *Fleur de Lis.*—These plants, once so well known in our gardens, rivalling (or rather exceeding) the lilies in beauty, are varied and numerous enough to make a wild garden by themselves. The many beautiful varieties of I. germanica will grow in almost any soil, and may be planted in woods, copses, by wood-walks, or near the margin of water, though the water-rat often eats the roots. Iris sibirica will grow in the water, as will the Japanese and the beautiful Asiatic Irises such as I. aurea and I. Monnieri. On the other hand, I. pumila, and the varieties of I. germanica, are often seen on the tops of old walls and thatched roofs, in France, flowering well.

Common Lupine, *Lupinus polyphyllus.*—Amidst the handsomest hardy plants, grouped where they may be seen from grass drives or wood-walks, or in any position or soil. Excellent for islets or on river banks, in the soil of which it spreads freely.

Honesty, *Lunaria.*—This, which approaches the Stocks in the aspect of its fine purplish violet flowers, is one of the best plants for naturalization. Sows itself freely in dryish ground or on chalk banks, and is one of the prettiest plants in early summer.

Lily, *Lilium.*—There are hardy lilies that may be naturalized. The places that these grow in, from the high meadows of Northern Italy dotted with the orange lily, to the woody gorges of the Sierras in California, rich with tall and handsome kinds, are such as make their chances in copses and rough grassy places, hopeful. In woods where there is rich vegetable soil the fine American lilies will do. The European lilies, dotted in the grass in the rough unmown glades, would not grow nearly so large as they do in the rich borders of our cottage gardens; but the effect of the single large blooms of the orange lily just level with the tops of the grass, in early summer, where it grows wild, is as good as any effect it gives in gardens. Along the bed of small rivulets, in the bottom of narrow gorges densely shaded by great Pines, Arbutus trees sixty feet high, and handsome evergreen oaks on the Sierras of California, I saw in autumn numbers of lily stems seven, eight, and nine feet high, so one could imagine what pictures the flowers formed in early summer. No mode of cultivating lilies in gardens is equal to that of dotting them through beds of rhododendrons and other American plants usually planted in peat, the soil of these beds, usually and very unwisely left to the rhododendrons alone, being peculiarly suited to the majority of the lily tribe. As for Lilies in the wild garden, Mr. G. F. Wilson sent me a stem of Lilium superbum, eleven and one-half feet high, grown in a rich woody bottom; this fine lily—the swamp lily of North America— should be planted in rich boggy bottoms where these occur in the wild garden.

Snowflake, *Leucojum.*—I have rarely seen anything more beautiful than a colony of the summer Snowflake on the margin of a tuft of rhododendrons at Longleat. Some of the flowers were on stems nearly three feet high, the partial shelter of the bushes and good soil causing the plants to be unusually vigorous. Both the spring and summer Snowflakes (L. vernum and L. æstivum) are valuable plants for wild grassy places, and the last grows freely in the good soil in the islets in the Thames near Wargrave.

Gentian Lithosperm, *Lithospermum prostratum.*—A very distinct and pretty plant, with many flowers of as fine a blue as any gentian. Thrives in any deep sandy soil, and in such well deserves naturalization among dwarf rock plants, in sunny spots.

Lychnis.—Handsome perennials, with showy blooms, mostly of a brilliant rose or scarlet colour. If the type were represented by the rose campion only it would be a valuable one, as this is a beautiful plant in dry soils, on which it does not perish in winter. The Lychnises are most fitted for association with medium-sized perennials, in open places and in rich soil.

Honeysuckle, *Lonicera.*—Such favourites as these must not be omitted. Any kind of climbing Honeysuckle will find a happy home in the wild garden, either rambling over stumps or hedgerows, or planted by themselves on banks. Our woods are graced by our wild Honeysuckles, and where garden varieties or new kinds of Honeysuckle from other countries are plentiful, it is well to add them to the wild garden.

Pea, *Lathyrus.*—Most cultivators of flowers are aware of the rambling habits of the greater number of plants of the pea tribe, but in that particular L. pyrenaicus eclipses them all. It produces an immense quantity of bright orange blossoms, but a strong plant of this species will ramble over, and by its density of growth prevent every plant and shrub that comes within its reach from thriving; indeed, it is a greater rambler than the Hop, the Bindweed, or the Bryony, and is very handsome. Tying up or training such a plant is out of the question; but there are many rough places in the wild garden where it would be quite at home. Every kind of Everlasting Pea is excellent for the wild garden, either for scrambling over hedgerows, stumps, or growing among the grass.—J. W. in *Garden.*

Monkey-flower, *Mimulus.*—'Wandering one day in the neighbourhood of "Gruigfoot," a queer-shaped hill in Linlithgowshire, my eye was attracted by a small burn whose banks were literally jewelled throughout its visible course with an unfamiliar yellow flower. A nearer approach showed me that it was the garden Mimulus (Monkey-flower), the seed of which must have escaped from some cottage garden, and established itself here, in the coldest part of the British Isles. I took the hint, and have naturalized it by the banks of a small stream which runs at the foot of my garden, and I strongly recommend your readers to do the same. It mingles charmingly with the blue Forget-me-not.'—S. in *Garden.*

Grape-Hyacinth, *Muscari.*—These free and hardy little bulbs are eas-

Everlasting Pea, creeping up stem in shrubbery.

ily naturalized and very handsome, with their little spikes of flowers of many shades of blue. At Gravetye I used to throw the bulbs in little hollows in grassy places, and then fill up level with a couple of inches of soil, thus saving the trouble of lifting the turf to plant. We had some very pretty effects, my only trouble was in not being able to get these things by the million.

Forget-me-not, *Myosotis.*—There is one exotic species, M. dissitiflora, not inferior in beauty to any of our handsomest native kinds, and well worthy of naturalization everywhere. It thrives best on moist and sandy or rocky soil.

Molopospermum cicutarium.   A very fine plant, with large deeply-divided leaves of a lively green colour, forming a dense irregular bush. Many of the umbellate plants, while very elegant, perish by the end of June, but this is firmer in character, of a fine rich green, growing more than three feet high. It is hardy, and increased by seed or division, and loves a deep moist soil, but will thrive in any good garden soil. It is a fine plant for grouping with other hardy and graceful-leaved plants.

Stock, *Matthiola.*—Showy flowers, mostly fragrant, peculiarly well suited for old ruins, chalk pits, and stony banks. Some of the annual kinds are pretty. With the Stocks may be associated the single Rocket (Hesperis matronalis), which thrives on woody banks and in copses.

Bee Balm, *Monarda.*—Large and very showy herbaceous plants, with scarlet or purple flowers, beautiful in American and Canadian woods in autumn, and good plants for naturalization in woods and shrubberies, copses, or anywhere among medium-sized vegetation. They thrive best in light or well-drained soils. Few plants have given me more pleasure than wide groups of the scarlet Bee Balm, which are splendidly effective, and form pictures from various points of view in the same place. Even in the broiling summer of 1893 we enjoyed their beauty for many weeks.

Mallow, *Malva, Althæa, Malope, Kitaibelia, Callirhoë, Sida.*—Plants of several distinct genera may be included under this type, and from each very showy plants. They are for the most part too coarse for gardens generally; but among the taller vegetation in rough shrubberies, and glades in

The Bee Balm (Monarda). American wood plant.

woods, they give good effect. Some of the Malvas are vigorous-growing plants, mostly with rosy flowers. The Althæas, close allies of the common single Hollyhock, are fine, as are also the Sida and Kitaibelia vitifolia. The Malopes are among the best of the annual flowers. The Callirhoës are dwarf, handsome trailers, brilliant too, and are the only ones of the type that should be planted amidst dwarf vegetation, as all the others are of vigorous character.

Type of fine-leaved umbellate plants seldom grown in gardens.

Mulgedium Plumieri.—A plant of distinct port, with purplish-blue blossoms. Till recently it was generally seen in botanic gardens only, but it has many merits as a wild garden plant, and for groups in quiet green corners of pleasure grounds or shrubberies. It does best in rather rich ground, and in such will pay all who plant it, being a hardy and long-lived perennial. The foliage is sometimes over a yard long, and the flower-stems over six feet high in good soil.

Water Lily, *Nymphæa* and *Nuphar.*—Two noble North American plants well deserve naturalization in our waters, associated with our own beautiful white water lilies the large Nuphar advena, which thrusts its great leaves well out of the water in many parts of North America, and the sweet-scented Nymphæa odorata, which floats in crowds on many of the Pine-bordered lakes and lakelets of New England, looking very like our own water lily. These and the new and beautiful hybrid water lilies have been dealt with fully in the chapter on water-plants.

Daffodil, *Narcissus.*—Most people have seen the common Daffodil in a wild state in our woods and fields. Apart from varieties, there are more than a score of species of Daffodil that could be naturalized quite as easily as this in all parts of these islands. Of all the planting I have ever made, the planting of these in the grass has given the greatest pleasure and the most lasting. They were put in by thousands, in the meadows mown for hay as well as in the less shaven parts of the pleasure ground, and no kind that we tried failed save the Bayonne Daffodil. We did not try the southern and Hoop Petticoat kinds, as the soil was not warm or sandy enough.

Bitter Vetch, *Orobus.*—Banks, grassy unmown margins of wood-walks, rocks, fringes of shrubberies, and like places, with deep and sandy loam, well drained, will grow the beautiful spring Bitter Vetch or any of its varieties or allies perfectly.

Evening Primrose, *Œnothera.*—Among the handsomest of hardy flowers. The yellow species, and varieties allied to the common Evening Primrose (Œ. biennis), may be readily naturalized in any soil. These noble and fragrant flowers are easily grown and beautiful. They, however, from their boldness, are suited for shrubberies, copses, and the like, sowing themselves freely.

Cotton Thistle, *Onopordon.*—Large thistles, with very handsome hoary and silvery leaves, and purplish flowers on fiercely-armed stems. No plants are more distinct than these, and they thrive freely in rough open places and on rubbish heaps, and usually come up freely from self-sown seeds.

Star of Bethlehem, *Ornithogalum.*—Various handsome hardy species of this genus will thrive as well as the common Star of Bethlehem in any turf; other less popular kinds have a quiet graceful beauty, and not being generally admitted to the gay company of showy Tulips and the like, there is all the more reason to give them a home in the grass.

Creeping Forget-me-not, *Omphalodes.*—The creeping Forget-me-not (Omphalodes verna) is one of the prettiest plants to be naturalized in woods, copses, or shrubberies, running about with freedom in moist soil. It is more compact in habit and lives longer on good soils than the other Forget-me-nots, and should be naturalized round every country place.

Wood Sorrel, *Oxalis.*—Dwarf plants with clover-like leaflets and pretty rosy or yellow flowers. Two of the species in cultivation, viz. O. Bowieana and O. floribunda, thrive on sandy soils amidst plants not more than six inches high; the family is so numerous that probably other members of it will be found equally free-growing.

Knotweed, *Polygonum.*—Vigorous herbaceous plants, two at least very precious for our present aim (i.e., P. cuspidatum and P. sachalinense). These are among the plants that cannot be put in the garden without fear of their overrunning other things, while outside in the pleasure ground or plantation, or by the water-side where there is enough soil, they may be very handsome indeed. I find P. sachalinense is often very beautiful in foliage in the autumn when in the sun, and P. cuspidatum is most effective in flower in autumn. They are fine plants for deep soils and certainly can take care of themselves.

Pæony.—Vigorous herbaceous plants, with large and splendid flowers of various shades of crimson, rosy-crimson, and white. There are many species and varieties, the flowers of some of the varieties being very sweet-scented, double, and among the largest flowers we have. Fringes of shrubberies, open glades in copses, and indeed almost any rough place, may be adorned by them; and they may also be on the grass in the rougher parts of the pleasure ground. I never felt the beauty of the fine colour of Pæonies till I saw a group of the double scarlet kind flowering in the long grass in Oxfordshire. The owner had placed a large group of this plant in an unmown glade, quite away from the garden proper; and yet, seen from the lawn and garden, the effect was most brilliant. To be able to produce such effects in the early summer is a gain from a landscape point of view, apart from the beauty of the flowers when seen close at hand.

Poppy, *Papaver*, in var.—The huge and flaming Eastern Poppies, Papaver orientale, P. bracteatum, and P. lateritium, are the most important of this type. They will thrive and live long in almost any position, but the proper place for them is in open spots among strong herbaceous plants. For the

The Great Japan
Knotweed
(Polygonum
cuspidatum).

wild garden the Welsh Poppy (Meconopsis cambrica) is one of the best plants. It is a cheerful plant at all seasons; perched on some old dry wall its masses of foliage are very fresh, but when loaded with a profusion of large yellow blossoms the plant is handsome; it is a determined colonizer, ready to hold its own anywhere. Its home is the wall, the rock, and the ruin. It even surpasses the Wallflower in adapting itself to out-of-the-way places; it will spring up in the gravel walk under one's feet, and is happy among stones in the courtyard. It looks down on one from crevices in brick walls, from chinks where one could scarcely introduce a knife-blade, and it delights most in shady places. No plant can be better adapted for naturalizing on rough stony banks, old quarries, and gravel pits.

Phlomis.—Showy and stately herbaceous or half-shrubby plants, with a profusion of handsome yellow or purplish flowers. Excellent for naturalization in warm open woods, copses, banks, growing well in ordinary soil. Some kinds carpet the ground very closely and keep away weeds.

Virginian Poke, *Phytolacca decandra.*—A robust perennial, with long dense spikes of purplish berries. It will grow anywhere and in any soil; but is most imposing in rich deep ones. The berries are relished by birds, and it is fine for association with the stoutest herbaceous plants in rough places.

Lungwort, *Pulmonaria.*—Dwarf plants of the borage family, with showy blue or pinkish blossoms. Easily established in woods or copses, in which position the common blue one must be familiar to many in the woods of England and France. The plants are common in cottage gardens; they grow in any soil.

The Tall Ox-eye Daisy, *Pyrethrum serotinum.*—This fine autumn flowering plant, for years left in the botanic gardens, is one of the handsomest flowers. It grows five or six feet high, and flowers late in autumn. It is picturesque in habit.

Bramble, *Rubus.*—Although we have nearly fifty kinds of bramble native in Britain, some of the exotic species, entirely distinct from our own, are well worthy of naturalization among low shrubs and tall herbaceous plants; for shady woods there is the large white R. Nutkanus, and the deep rose-coloured R. odoratus, and the early spring-flowering

Phlomis.—Type of handsome Labiates; flowers admirably suited for the Wild Garden.

R. spectabilis; while the very striking white-stemmed R. biflorus is a good plant for warm slopes, sunny sides of chalk and gravel pits.

The Great Reed, *Arundo Donax.*—This noble reed I do not like to omit here, it is so beautiful in the southern counties of England, though in cold soils and hard winters it may perish. Where the hardier Bamboos find a place this will be welcome, though in our country it is only in the warmer parts that it attains the dignity it shows in the south of Europe.

Rhubarb, *Rheum.*—There are several species of Rhubarb in cultivation in addition to those commonly grown in gardens. They are much alike in port and in the size of their leaves, Rheum palmatum and R. Emodi being the most distinct. The Rhubarbs are fine plants for association with large-leaved herbaceous plants in deep soils.

Rose, *Rosa.*—As in the case of brambles, we have many more kinds of Wild Roses in England than is commonly supposed, but nobody ever thinks of planting such things in gardens or shrubberies, where such ill-smelling and ugly things as Privet make up the underwood. There are scores of the roses of northern and temperate countries which would thrive as well in our woodlands; but as these are not to be obtained in our nurseries, it is useless to mention them. Any species of rose from a northern country might be tried; whilst of roses commonly cultivated, the climbing races—such as the Boursault, Ayrshire, and Sempervirens—are the most likely to be satisfactory. The Damask, Alba gallica, and vigorous climbers, being hardy, would do, as would Félicité-Perpétue, Banksiæflora, the Garland roses, Austrian brier, R. berberifolia, and R. microphylla rubra plena. Pruning, or any other attention after planting, should of course not be thought of in connexion with these. Rosa Brunoniana is a very fine free and hardy species from India. See the Chapter on Roses.

Sea Lavender, *Statice.*—Vigorous hardy plants with a profusion of bluish lavender-coloured bloom, thriving freely on all ordinary garden soils. Statice latifolia, and some of the stronger kinds, thrive in any position.

Meadow Sweet, *Spiræa.*—Usually vigorous herbaceous plants, with white or rosy flowers. Such beautiful kinds as S. venusta and S. palmata are good among the medium-sized perennials. Spiræa Aruncus is,

The tall Ox-eye Daisy (Pyrethrum serotinum).

The Great Reed of
Southern Europe
(Arundo Donax).

perhaps, the finest plant for the wild garden. Mr. Ellam planted out some spare stock of S. japonica in a wood at Bodorgan, and with the happiest effect. The plants grow and flower freely, the flowers appearing a fortnight later in the moist cool wood than on plants of the same kind on a north garden border; and so prolong the season of this favourite flower.

Golden Rod, *Solidago.*—Tall perennials with yellow flowers, showy when in bloom, and attractive when seen in America in autumn, mingled with the Starworts of that country, but rarely pretty as grown in gardens. These, like the worst of Asters, used to be grown to excess in the old borders; but the positions they are best for are rough places, where in many cases it would be easy, with their aid and that of the Asters, to form that mixture of Golden Rod and Michaelmas Daisies which is one of the prettiest effects in American woods in autumn.

Catch-fly, *Silene.*—Dwarf or spreading plants, allied to the Pinks, and generally with white or rosy flowers. The choice mountain kinds, such as S. Lagascæ, S. alpestris, S. Schafta, &c., are among the most charming subjects that can be naturalized on rocky places or banks, associated with very dwarf plants. Such fine annual or biennial kinds as S. Armeria or S. pendula are among the best, and might be easily established by scattering a few seeds in likely places.

Bloodwort, *Sanguinaria canadensis.*—This little plant, which abounds in the woods of Canada and North America, and which is very rarely indeed seen well grown in our gardens, will thrive under the branches of deciduous trees as well as the Winter Aconite, and in spring will give a beautiful effect.

Squill, *Scilla.*—Several kinds of Scilla, closely allied to the common Bluebell, would do quite as well in our woods as that well-known native plant, notably S. campanulata, S. bifolia, and S. sibirica. Scilla bifolia and S. sibirica would be better on sunny banks or sheltered fringes of shrubberies. The tall kinds would do in woods or copses like the Bluebell. With the dwarfer Scilla might be associated the Grape-Hyacinth and the Amethyst Hyacinth (Hyacinthus amethystinus).

Comfrey, *Symphytum.*—Herbaceous plants of the borage order, usually with handsome blue flowers. One of the handsomest spring flowers is S. caucasicum, and it is also one of the easiest things to naturalize, running about in shrubby places. Coarse kinds, like S. asperrimum (unfit for garden culture), thrive apace among the largest plants in ditches and rich bottoms, and look beautiful when in flower.

Scabious, *Scabiosa, Cephalaria, Knautia.*—Sometimes handsome and free-growing herbaceous plants, bluish, purplish, or yellowish in colour of flowers. Among these may be seen, in botanic and other gardens, plants suited for naturalization, but scarcely worthy of a place in the garden. The fine S. caucasica would thrive in warm soil, as would the Knautias in any soil.

Stonecrop, *Sedum.*—Small and usually prostrate plants, with white, yellow, or rosy flowers, and occurring in multitudes on most of the mountain chains of northern and temperate countries. There are few of these pretty plants that would not grow on the top of an old wall, or thatched house, or stony bank, or bare ground, as well as our common Stonecrop. All grow in any soil, are as easily increased as any weed, and grow anywhere if they are not too much overshadowed by trees and coarser vegetation. Such kinds as S. spurium, S. pulchellum, kamtschaticum, and S. spectabile are among the best.

Rockfoil, *Saxifraga.*—A very extensive family of plants, abundant on mountains in northern countries. For our purpose they may be thrown into five sections—the Mossy section, represented in Britain by S. hypnoides; the Silvery section, represented by S. Aizoon; the London Pride section, by the Kerry saxifrages; the Megasea section, by the large S. crassifolia; and the Oppositifolia section, distinguished by its rosy-purple flowers. With the exception of the Megasea and Oppositifolia sections, which have rosy flowers, most of the Saxifrages have white blossoms spotted with red; a few are yellow, and all are very hardy, and the easiest to grow of all Alpine flowers. The mossy, silvery, and purple saxifrages may be naturalized with the greatest ease on bare rocky or mountainous grounds, amidst dwarf vegetation; but, as the places in which this kind of ground occurs are comparatively few, the Megaseas and the Kerry saxifrages are probably the most generally useful, as they can fight their way amongst grass and other common herbs. There are probably nearly 150 species in cultivation in England.

Houseleek, *Sempervivum.*—Very dwarf and succulent plants, with their fleshy leaves arranged in dense rosettes, and mostly with curious but seldom conspicuous flowers. They abound in mountainous regions, and are very hardy. The greater number of these grow quite as freely as the common Houseleek in any arid soil, and in any position where the vegetation is not taller than themselves, such as on bare sandy banks, gravelly heaps, &c. There are about fifty hardy kinds in cultivation in this country.

Meadow Rue, *Thalictrum.*—Tall herbaceous plants, often affording a pleasing effect when seen in groups, and hence pretty for this mode of gardening. They grow in any soil, and should be placed among rank vegetation. There are many kinds not differing much in aspect; some of the smaller ones, like our British T. minus, deserve a place among dwarf plants for the elegance of their leaves. With these last may be associated the Italian Isopyrum thalictroides, which is handsome in flower and leaf.

Spiderwort, *Tradescantia virginica.*—A handsome North American perennial, with purple, blue, or white flowers, attaining a height of one and a half or two feet. A good plant for naturalization on almost any soil, thriving often on the wettest, and therefore suited for many places where other perennials would make little progress.

Woody Lily, *Trillium.*—Very singular and beautiful American wood plants, of which T. grandiflorum is worthy of special mention, thriving in shady places in moist rich soils, in woods and copses, where some vegetable soil has gathered.

Globe Flower, *Trollius.*—Beautiful plants of vigorous habit, with handsome yellow flowers, of a fine colour, like those of the Buttercups, but turning inwards so as to form an almost round blossom, quite distinct in aspect. Few plants are more worthy of a position in grassy glades where the soil is rich, although they will grow in ordinary soil. There are several distinct kinds suitable, though there is little difference in their effect. I have established them without trouble

Telekia. Type of the larger Composites, excluded from gardens proper.

in wettish places foul with Crowfoot and other bad weeds, and planting them without any preparation of the ground.

Tulip, *Tulipa.*—Various species of Tulips might be naturalized by wood-walks and in the rougher parts of the pleasure grounds. In such positions they would not attain such a size as the richly-fed garden flowers, but that would make them none the less attractive to those who care about the wild garden.

Telekia, *Telekia cordifolia.*—A vigorous herbaceous plant, suited for association with Echinops, Rheum, and plants grown for their foliage. It is very free in growth, and has large leaves and sunflower-like flowers.

Flame-Flower, *Tritoma.*—Flame-Flowers are occasionally planted in excess, so as to neutralize the good effect they might otherwise produce, and they, like many other flowers, have suffered from being, like soldiers, put in straight lines and in other geometrical formations. It is only where a fine plant or group of plants is seen in some green glade that the true beauty of the Flame-Flower is seen. Although not always hardy plants,

Group of Tritoma,
in grass, by the
lake at Longleat.

Tall Mullein (Verbascum).

they are so free in many soils that they might with confidence be planted in the wild garden, and our sketch shows a picturesque group of them planted in this way.

Showy Indian Cress, *Tropæolum speciosum.*—Against walls, among shrubs, and on slopes, on moist banks, or bush banks near the hardy fernery, in deep, rich, and light soil, this brilliant plant is well worth any trouble to establish. Many fail with it in the garden, but moist, sandy, and bushy places will suit it better, and, in the south of England and on warm soils, the north sides of houses and walls, rocks and beds of shrubs should be chosen.

Mullein, *Verbascum.*—Verbascum vernale is a noble plant, which has been slowly spreading in our collections of hardy plants for some years past, and it is one of peculiar merit. I first saw it in the Garden of Plants,[2] and brought home some roots which gave rise to the stock now in our gardens. Its peculiarity, or rather its merit, is that it is a true perennial species—at least on warm soils—and in this respect quite unlike other Mulleins that are sometimes seen in our gardens, and oftener in our hedgerows. It also has the advantage of great height, growing to a height of ten feet, or even more. Then there are the large and green leaves, which come up rather early and are extremely effective. Finally, the colour is good and the quantity of yellow flowers with purplish filaments that are borne on one of these great branching panicles is enormous. The use of such a plant cannot be difficult to define, it being so good in form and so distinct in habit. Another good kind is V. phlomoides, which I saw last autumn abundantly wild in Touraine, in stony places about Chenonceau, and which might be sown with us in like places.

Periwinkle, *Vinca.*—Trailing plants, with glossy foliage and blue flowers, well known in gardens. They grow in any position, shady or sunny. There are variously-coloured and very pretty varieties of V. minor, while the variegated forms of both species are pretty.

Speedwell, *Veronica.*—Herbaceous and alpine plants, usually rather tall

2. The Garden of Plants probably refers to the botanical garden in Paris known as the Jardin des Plantes. —Ed.

(one and a half to three feet), in some cases dwarf alpine plants with blue flowers in various shades; they are among the hardiest of plants, and will grow in any soil. All the taller kinds are admirably suited for naturalization among long grass and other herbaceous vegetation. Very many that are in cultivation in borders are fit only for the wild garden. The dwarf kinds are equally suitable for bare places, or among other dwarf plants.

Violet, *Viola.*—A numerous race of dwarf and interesting plants, thriving freely in our climate, in half-shady places, rocky spots or banks, fringes of shrubberies, or almost any position. The very handsome bird's-foot Violet of North America (V. pedata) would thrive in sandy level places or on rocky banks. In this family occur a good many kinds, such as V. canadensis, which, not being fragrant, or not possessing sufficient charms to ensure their general cultivation in gardens, are best suited for wild gardening. Our own sweet Violet should be abundantly planted wherever it does not occur in a wild state.

Selections of Hardy Exotic Plants
for the Wild Garden

——◆◆——

AN IMPORTANT POINT IS THE GETTING of a stock of plants to begin with. In country or other places where many good old border flowers remain in the cottage gardens, many plants may be found. Nursery beds should be formed in which such plants could be increased. Free-growing spring-flowers, like Aubrietia, Alyssum, and Iberis, may be multiplied to any extent by division or cuttings. Numbers of kinds may be raised from seed sown rather thinly in drills, in nursery beds in the open air. The best time for sowing is spring, but any time in summer will do. Many perennials and bulbs must be bought in nurseries, and increased as well as may be in nursery beds. As to soil, the best way is to avoid the trouble of preparing it; the point is to adapt the plant to the soil—in peaty places to place plants that thrive in peat, in clay soils those that thrive in clays, and so on.

Roof tiles made of local stone have kept Gravetye Manor dry inside for more than four centuries.

A SELECTION OF PLANTS FOR NATURALIZATION IN PLACES WITH DWARF VEGETATION, ON BARE BANKS, AND IN POORISH SOIL

Acantholimon glumaceum
Achillea aurea
Ajuga genevensis
Alyssum saxatile
Anthyllis montana
Arabis albida
Armeria cephalotes
Aster alpinus
Astragalus monspessulanus
Astrantia major
Athamanta Matthioli
Aubrietia, in var.
Campanula cæspitosa
Campanula carpatica
Campanula fragilis
Campanula garganica
Cerastium Biebersteinii
Cerastium grandiflorum
Cerastium tomentosum
Cornus canadensis
Coronilla varia
Dielytra eximia
Dielytra formosa
Dodecatheon Meadia
Dondia Epipactis
Doronicum caucasicum
Euphorbia Cyparissias
Genista sagittalis
Gentiana acaulis
Geranium cinereum, and others
Geranium striatum

Geranium Wallichianum
Gypsophila repens
Hedysarum obscurum
Helianthemum, in var.
Hieracium aurantiacum
Iberis corifolia
Iberis correæfolia
Iberis sempervirens
Iris cristata
Iris graminea
Iris nudicaulis, and many others
Iris pumila
Iris reticulata
Linum alpinum
Linum arboreum
Linum flavum
Lithospermum prostratum
Myosotis dissitiflora
Œnothera Missouriensis
Œnothera speciosa
Œnothera taraxacifolia
Orobus lathyroides
Orobus vernus
Oxalis floribunda
Pentstemon procerus
Phlox amœna
Phlox stolonifera
Phlox subulata
Physalis Alkekengi
Plumbago Larpentæ
Polygonum Brunonis

Polygonum vaccinifolium
Potentilla
Prunella grandiflora
Pulmonaria grandiflora
Pulmonaria mollis
Saponaria ocymoides
Saxifraga Aizoon
Saxifraga cordifolia
Saxifraga Cotyledon
Saxifraga crassifolia
Saxifraga crustata
Saxifraga longifolia
Saxifraga rosularis
Scabiosa caucasica
Scutellaria alpina
Sedum dentatum
Sedum kamtschaticum
Sedum Sieboldii
Sedum spectabile
Sedum spurium
Sempervivum calcareum
Sempervivum hirtum
Sempervivum montanum
Sempervivum sedoides
Sempervivum soboliferum
Silene alpestris
Silene Schafta
Stachys lanata
Symphyandra pendula
Teucrium Chamædrys
Thlaspi latifolium

Tunica Saxifraga
Tussilago fragrans
Veronica austriaca
Veronica candida

Veronica taurica, and many others
Vicia argentea
Vinca herbacea
Viola cornuta

Viola cucullata
Waldsteinia trifolia
Zietenia lavandulæfolia

PLANTS OF VIGOROUS HABIT FOR THE WILD GARDEN

Acanthus latifolius
Acanthus spinosissimus
Acanthus spinosus
Achillea Eupatorium
Aconitum, in var.
Alfredia cernua
Althæa ficifolia
Althæa nudiflora
Althæa taurinensis
Asclepias Cornuti
Asclepias Douglasii
Aster elegans
Aster ericoides, and any strong and pretty kinds
Aster Novæ Angliæ
Aster Novi Belgii
Astilbe rivularis
Astilbe rubra
Astragalus ponticus
Bambusa, hardiest kinds
Campanula, all the tall and showy kinds
Centaurea babylonica
Crambe cordifolia
Datisca cannabina
Delphinium, in var.

Dipsacus laciniatus
Echinops bannaticus
Echinops exaltatus
Echinops purpureus
Echinops ruthenicus
Eupatorium purpureum
Ferula communis
Ferula glauca
Ferula sulcata
Ferula tingitana
Galega biloba
Galega officinalis
Harpalium rigidum
Helianthus angustifolius
Helianthus multiflorus
Helianthus orgyalis and others
Heracleum, any exotic kinds
Lathyrus grandiflorus, and any others
Lathyrus latifolius
Lavatera Olbia
Lupinus polyphyllus
Macleaya cordata
Molopospermum cicutarium
Mulgedium Plumieri
Onopordon, any

Pæonia, in var.
Papaver bracteatum
Papaver orientale
Peucedanum involucratum
Peucedanum longifolium
Peucedanum ruthenicum
Physostegia imbricata
Physostegia speciosa
Phytolacca decandra
Polygonum sachalinense
Polygonum Sieboldii
Rheum Emodi
Rheum palmatum
Silphium perfoliatum
Spiræa Aruncus
Statice latifolia
Telekia cordifolia
Thalictrum aquilegifolium
Thermopsis barbata
Trollius, any kind
Veratrum album
Verbascum Chaixii
Verbascum phlomoides
Yucca flaccida
Yucca recurva

HARDY PLANTS WITH FINE FOLIAGE OR GRACEFUL HABIT
SUITABLE FOR NATURALIZATION

Acanthus, several species
Actæa, in var.
Alfredia cernua
Althæa taurinensis
Aralia edulis
Aralia japonica
Arundinaria falcata
Asclepias syriaca
Astilbe rivularis
Astilbe rubra
Bambusa, several species
Carlina acanthifolia
Centaurea babylonica
Cimicifuga racemosa
Crambe cordifolia

Datisca cannabina
Dipsacus laciniatus
Echinops exaltatus
Echinops ruthenicus
Elymus arenarius
Eryngium, several species
Euphorbia Cyparissias
Ferula, several species
Helianthus orgyalis, and others
Heracleum, several species
Macleaya cordata
Onopordon Acanthium
Onopordon arabicum
Onopordon tauricum

Panicum bulbosum
Panicum virgatum
Phytolacca decandra
Polygonum cuspidatum
Polygonum sachalinense
Rheum Emodi, and other kinds
Silybum eburneum
Silybum Marianum
Spiræa Aruncus
Statice latifolia
Telekia cordifolia
Veratrum album
Verbascum Chaixii
Yucca, several species

PLANTS FOR HEDGE-BANKS AND LIKE PLACES

Aconitum, in var.
Anemone japonica, and vars.
Aristolochia Sipho
Asparagus Broussoneti
Asparagus officinalis
Aster, in variety
Astilbe rivularis
Astragalus ponticus
Baptisia australis
Calystegia dahurica
Calystegia pubescens
Campanula, in great var.
Chrysanthemum maximum, and
    allied kinds
Clematis, the wild species, in var.

Coronilla varia
Delphinium, in var.
Ferula, in var.
Fritillary, in var.
Galega biloba
Galega officinalis, both white and
    pink forms
Honeysuckles, in var.
Kitaibelia vitifolia
Lathyrus grandiflorus
Lathyrus latifolius
Lathyrus latifolius albus
Lathyrus rotundifolius
Leocojum, in var.
Lilies, common kinds

Macleaya cordata
Narcissus, common kinds
Œnothera Lamarckiana
Phlomis Herba-venti
Phlomis Russelliana
Physostegia speciosa
Physostegia virginica
Phytolacca decandra
Rubus biflorus
Scillas, in var.
Thalictrum aquilegifolium
Tropæolum speciosum
Verbascum Chaixii
Veronica, tall kinds in var.
Vitis, in var.

TRAILERS AND CLIMBERS

The selection of plants to cover banks and old trees suitably is important, particularly as the plants fitted for these purposes are equally useful for rocks, precipitous banks, sides of bridges, river-banks, ruins, covering out-houses, or rough sheds in pastures.

Ampelopsis bipinnata
Ampelopsis cordata
Ampelopsis hederacea
Ampelopsis tricuspidata
Aristolochia Sipho
Aristolochia tomentosa
Boussingaultia baselloides
Calystegia dahurica
Cissus orientalis
Cissus pubescens

Clematis, in var., species
Hablitzia tamnoides
Jasminum nudiflorum
Jasminum officinale
Jasminum revolutum
Lonicera, in variety
Menispermum canadense
Menispermum virginicum
Passiflora cœrulea
Periploca græca

Vitis æstivalis
Vitis amoorensis
Vitis cordifolia
Vitis Isabella
Vitis Labrusca
Vitis laciniosa
Vitis riparia
Vitis Sieboldii
Vitis vulpina
Wistaria sinensis

SPRING AND EARLY SUMMER FLOWERS FOR NATURALIZATION

Allium ciliatum
Allium neapolitanum
Alyssum saxatile
Anemone alpina
Anemone apennina
Anemone blanda
Anemone coronaria
Anemone fulgens
Anemone Hepatica
Anemone ranunculoides
Anemone trifolia, and many others
Aquilegia, various
Arabis
Arenaria montana
Aubrietia, various
Bulbocodium vernum

Centaurea montana
Corydalis capnoides
Corydalis lutea
Crocus aureus
Crocus speciosus
Crocus susianus, and many others
Crocus versicolor
Cyclamen europæum
Cyclamen hederæfolium
Dielytra eximia
Dielytra spectabilis
Dodecatheon Jeffreyanum
Dodecatheon Meadia
Doronicum caucasicum
Epimedium pinnatum
Eranthis hyemalis

Erica carnea
Fritillaria, in var.
Galanthus, in var.
Gentiana acaulis
Helleborus niger
Helleborus olympicus and many
    other kinds
Hesperis matronalis
Hyacinthus amethystinus
Iberis corifolia
Iberis correæfolia
Iberis sempervirens
Iris amœna
Iris cristata
Iris De Bergii
Iris flavescens

Iris florentina
Iris germanica
Iris graminea
Iris ochroleuca
Iris pallida
Iris sambucina
Iris sub-biflora, and many other
    kinds
Leucojum pulchellum
Leucojum vernum
Muscari botryoides
Muscari moschatum, and various
    others
Myosotis dissitiflora
Narcissus angustifolius
Narcissus bicolor
Narcissus incomparabilis
Narcissus major
Narcissus montanus
Narcissus poeticus & vars. (All the
hardy kinds are fitted for the
    wild garden.)
Narcissus odorus
Omphalodes verna
Ornithogalum, various
Orobus cyaneus
Orobus flaccidus
Orobus lathyroides
Orobus variegatus
Orobus vernus
Pæonia, many kinds
Papaver bracteatum
Papaver orientale
Paradisia Liliastrum
Phlox reptans, and other alpine
    Phlox
Primula, in var.
Pulmonaria grandiflora
Pulmonaria mollis
Ranunculus aconitifolius
Ranunculus amplexicaulis
Ranunculus montanus
Saponaria ocymoides
Scilla altaica
Scilla amœna
Scilla bifolia
Scilla campanulata
Scilla italica
Scilla sibirica
Silene alpestris
Symphytum bohemicum
Symphytum caucasicum
Thlaspi latifolium, and others
Tulipa Gesneriana
Tulipa scabriscapa, and many
    others
Tulipa suaveolens
Vicia argentea
Vinca major
Viola cornuta

PLANTS FOR NATURALIZATION
BENEATH TREES ON LAWNS

Where the branches of trees, both evergreen and deciduous, sweep the turf, a great number of pretty spring flowers may be naturalized beneath the branches, where they will thrive without attention. It is chiefly in the case of deciduous trees that this could be done; but even in the case of conifers and evergreens some graceful little spring flowers might be dotted beneath the outermost points of their lower branches. We know that many of our spring flowers and hardy bulbs mature their leaves and go to rest early in the year. They enjoy the sun in spring, under the deciduous tree; they have time to flower and develop their leaves under it before the foliage of the tree appears; then, as the summer comes, they are gradually overshadowed and go to rest; the leaves of the trees once fallen, they soon begin to appear again and cover the ground with beauty.

Take a spreading old summer-leafing tree, and scatter a few tufts of the Winter Aconite beneath it, and leave them alone. In a very few years they will have covered the ground; every year afterwards they will spread a pretty carpet beneath the tree; and when the carpet fades there will be no eyesore from decaying leaves as there would be on a border—no need to replace the plants with others; the tree puts forth its leaves, covering the ground till autumn, and in early spring we again
see our little friend in his glossy coat and yellow buttons.

There are other plants of which the same is true. We have only to imagine this done in a variety of cases to see to what a beautiful result it would lead. Given the bright blue Apennine Anemone under one tree, the spring Snowflake under another, the bright and many coloured Crocuses, and so on, we should have a spring garden of the most beautiful kind. The plan could be carried out under the branches of a grove as well as under those of specimen trees. Pretty mixed plantations might be made by dotting tall plants, like the large Jonquil and other Narcissus, among dwarf spreading plants like the blue Anemone.

The following are selected as among the most suitable for such arrangements as that just described, with some little attention as to the season of flowering and the kind of soil required by some rather uncommon species. A late-flowering kind, for example, should be planted under late-leafing trees, or towards the points of their branches, so that they might not be obscured by the leaves of the tree before perfecting their flowers.

Anemone angulosa
Anemone apennina
Anemone blanda
Anemone Coronaria
Anemone fulgens
Anemone Hepatica
Anemone stellata
Anemone sylvestris

Anemone trifolia
Arum italicum
Bulbocodium vernum
Corydalis solida
Corydalis tuberosa
Crocus biflorus
Crocus Imperati
Crocus reticulatus

Crocus versicolor, and many others
Cyclamen in variety
Eranthis hyemalis
Erythronium Dens-canis
Ficaria grandiflora
Iris reticulata
Muscari, any of the numerous
  kinds

Narcissus, in var.
Puschkinia scilloides
Sanguinaria canadensis
Scilla bifolia

Scilla campanulata
Scilla sibirica
Snowdrop, many kinds

Snowflake, all the kinds
Trillium grandiflorum
Tulipa, species in var.

PLANTS FOR VERY MOIST RICH SOILS

Althæa, in var.
Aralia edulis
Aralia nudicaulis
Asclepias Cornuti
Asphodelus ramosus
Aster, in var.
Astilbe rivularis
Baptisia exaltata
Caltha palustris fl. pl.
Campanula glomerata, and large
    kinds
Colchicum, in var.
Convallaria multiflora
Crinum capense
Datisca cannabina
Echinops, in var.
Elymus, in var.
Epilobium, in var.

Eupatorium, in var.
Galax aphylla
Galega officinalis
Gentiana asclepiadea
Helianthus multiflorus
Helianthus orgyalis
Helianthus rigidus
Helonias bullata
Hemerocallis, in var.
Heracleum, in var.
Iris ochroleuca
Liatris, in var.
Lythrum roseum superbum
Mimulus, in var.
Mulgedium Plumieri
Narcissus, stronger kinds
Œnothera, large kinds
Onopordon, in var.

Phlomis Herba-venti
Phlomis Russelliana
Physostegia speciosa
Phytolacca decandra
Polygonum, in var.
Ranunculus amplexicaulis
Ranunculus parnassifolius
Rudbeckia, in var.
Sanguinaria canadensis
Silphium, in var.
Solidago, in var.
Spiræa Aruncus
Swertia perennis
Telekia speciosa
Thalictrum, in var.
Trollius, in var.
Vaccinium, in var.
Veratrum, in var.

PLANTS SUITED FOR PEAT SOIL

Alstrœmeria, in var.
Calluna, in var.
Chimaphila maculata
Chrysobactron Hookeri
Coptis trifoliata
Cornus canadensis

Cypripedium spectabile
Daphne Cneorum
Dentaria laciniata
Dryas octopetala
Epigæa repens
Epimedium, in var.

Funkia grandiflora
Funkia Sieboldii
Galax aphylla
Gaultheria procumbens
Gentians, in var.
Hardy Heaths, in var.

Helonias bullata
Iris nudicaulis, and vars.
Iris pumila, and vars.
Jeffersonia diphylla
Lilies, in var.

Linnæa borealis
Podophyllum Emodi
Podophyllum peltatum
Polygala Chamæbuxus
Pyrola, in var.

Ramondia pyrenaica
Sisyrinchium grandiflorum
Spigelia marilandica
Trientalis europæa
Trillium grandiflorum

PLANTS SUITED FOR CALCAREOUS SOIL

Adenophora, in var.
Æthionema, in var.
Alyssum, in var.
Anemone, in var.
Anthyllis montana
Antirrhinum, in var.
Campanula, in var.
Carduus eriophorus
Cheiranthus, in var.
Cistus, in var.
Coronilla, in var.
Dianthus, in var.
Echium, in var.
Erodium, in var.
Genista, in var.
Geranium, in var.

Geum, in var.
Gypsophila, in var.
Hedysarum, in var.
Helianthemum, in var.
Lunaria biennis
Onobrychis, in var.
Ononis, in var.
Ophrys, in var.
Othonna cheirifolia
Phlomis, in var.
Prunella grandiflora
Santolina, in var.
Saponaria ocymoides
Saxifraga (the encrusted and the
    large-leaved kinds)

Scabiosa, in var.
Sedum, in var.
Sempervivum, in var.
Symphytum, in var.
Thermopsis fabacea
Thymus, in var.
Trachelium cœruleum
Trifolium alpinum
Triteleia uniflora
Tunica Saxifraga
Vesicaria utriculata
Vicia, in var.
Vittadenia triloba
Waldsteinia geoides
Waldsteinia trifoliata

PLANTS SUITED FOR DRY AND GRAVELLY SOIL

Achillea, in var.
Æthionema cordifolium
Agrostemma coronaria
Alyssum saxatile
Antennaria dioica
Anthyllis montana
Antirrhinum rupestre

Arabis albida
Armeria cephalotes
Artemisia, in var.
Aubrietia, in var.
Carlina acanthifolia
Cerastium, in var.
Cheiranthus, in var.

Chrysopsis Mariana
Cistus, in var.
Corydalis, in var.
Dianthus, in var.
Dielytra eximia
Dorycnium sericeum
Dracocephalum, in var.

Echium, in var.
Erodium, in var.
Eryngium, in var.
Euphorbia Myrsinites
Fumaria, in var.
Geranium, in var.
Gypsophila, in var.
Helianthemum, in var.
Helichrysum arenarium
Hypericum, in var.
Iberis, in var.
Jasione perennis
Lavandula Spica

Linaria, in var.
Linum, in var.
Lupinus polyphyllus
Modiola geranioides
Nepeta Mussinii
Onobrychis, in var.
Ononis, in var.
Ornithogalum, in var.
Plumbago Larpentæ
Polygonum vaccinifolium
Rosemary
Santolina, in var.

Saponaria ocymoides
Scabiosa, in var.
Sedum, in great var.
Sempervivum, in great var.
Stachys lanata
Teucrium Chamædrys
Thlaspi latifolium
Thymus, in var.
Trachelium, in var.
Tussilago fragrans
Verbascum, in var.
Vesicaria utriculata

SELECTION OF PLANTS FOR GROWING ON OLD WALLS, RUINS, OR ROCKY SLOPES

Achillea tomentosa
Alyssum montanum
Alyssum saxatile
Antirrhinum majus
Antirrhinum Orontium
Antirrhinum rupestre
Arabis albida
Arabis petræa
Arenaria balearica
Arenaria cæspitosa
Arenaria ciliata
Arenaria graminifolia
Arenaria montana
Arenaria verna
Asperula cynanchica
Campanula Barrelieri

Campanula fragilis
Campanula fragilis lanuginosa
Campanula garganica
Campanula pumila
Campanula pumila alba
Campanula rotundifolia
Centranthus albus
Centranthus coccineus
Centranthus ruber
Cheiranthus alpinus
Cheiranthus Cheiri
Cheiranthus Cheiri plenus
Coronilla minima
Corydalis lutea
Cotyledon Umbilicus
Dianthus cæsius

Dianthus deltoides
Dianthus monspessulanus
Dianthus petræus
Draba aizoides
Erinus alpinus
Erodium Reichardii
Erodium romanum
Gypsophila muralis
Gypsophila prostrata
Helianthemum, in var.
Hutchinsia petræa
Iberis, in var.
Ionopsidium acaule
Königa maritima
Linum alpinum
Lychnis alpina

Lychnis Flos-Jovis
Lychnis lapponica
Malva campanulata
Santolina lanata
Saponaria ocymoides
Saxifraga bryoides
Saxifraga cæsia
Saxifraga caryophyllata
Saxifraga crustata
Saxifraga cuscutæformis
Saxifraga diapensioides
Saxifraga Hostii
Saxifraga intacta
Saxifraga ligulata
Saxifraga longifolia
Saxifraga pectinata
Saxifraga pulchella
Saxifraga retusa
Saxifraga Rhei
Saxifraga Rocheliana
Saxifraga rosularis

Saxifraga sarmentosa
Sedum acre
Sedum Aizoon
Sedum album
Sedum anglicum
Sedum arenarium
Sedum aureum
Sedum brevifolium
Sedum californicum
Sedum cœruleum
Sedum dasyphyllum
Sedum elegans
Sedum Ewersii
Sedum farinosum
Sedum globiferum
Sedum Heuffelli
Sedum hirtum
Sedum hispanicum
Sedum kamschaticum
Sedum montanum
Sedum multiceps

Sedum piliferum
Sedum pulchrum
Sedum sempervivoides
Sempervivum arachnoideum
Sempervivum sexangulare
Sempervivum sexfidum
Sempervivum soboliferum
Sempervivum spurium
Sempervivum tectorum
Silene alpestris
Silene rupestris
Silene Schafta
Symphyandra pendula
Thlaspi alpestre
Thymus citriodorus
Trichomanes, and vars.
Tunica Saxifraga
Umbilicus chrysanthus
Veronica fruticulosa
Veronica saxatilis
Vesicaria utriculata

A SELECTION OF ANNUAL AND BIENNIAL PLANTS FOR NATURALIZATION

Agrostis nebulosa
Alyssum maritimum
Amberboa moschata
Amberboa odorata
Arabis arenosa
Blitum capitatum
Briza, in var.
Bromus brizæformis
Campanula Medium and vars.

Clarkia elegans
Clarkia pulchella
Collinsia bicolor
Collinsia verna
Collomia coccinea
Dimorphotheca pluvia
Dipsacus laciniatus
Dracocephalum moldavicum
Dracocephalum nutans

Erysimum asperum
Erysimum Peroffskianum
Eschscholtzia californica
Gilia capitata
Gilia tricolor
Godetia, various
Gypsophila elegans
Hedysarum coronarium
Hesperis matronalis

Ophrys, in grass.

Iberis coronaria
Iberis umbellata
Leptosiphon androsaceus
Leptosphon densiflorus
Limnanthes Douglasii
Lunaria biennis
Malcolmia maritima
Malope trifida
Matthiola, in var.
Matthiola annua
Matthiola bicornis
Nicandra physaloides
Œnothera Jamesi
Œnothera Lamarckiana

Œnothera odorata
Ononis viscosa
OnoQuepordon, in var.
Panicum capillare
Papaver somniferum
Platystemon californicum
Polygonum orientale
Saponaria calabrica
Silene Armeria
Silene pendula
Silybum eburneum
Verbascum phlomoides
Viscaria oculata

GRASSES FOR NATURALIZATION

Agrostis nebulosa
Briza maxima
Brizopyrum siculum
Bromus brizæformis

Hordeum jubatum
Milium multiflorum
Panicum bulbosum
Panicum capillare

Panicum virgatum
Polypogon monspeliensis
Stipa gigantea
Stipa pennata

Some of our nobler grasses, like the Pampas and the New Zealand reeds, have not the qualities of perfect hardiness and power of increase without care in our climate that would entitle them to a place in these selections.

HARDY BULBS FOR NATURALIZATION

Allium ciliatum
Allium fragrans
Allium Moly
Allium neapolitanum

Brodiæa congesta
Bulbocodium vernum
Camassia esculenta
Colchicum, in var.

Crocus, in great var.
Cyclamen, in var.
Erythronium, in var.
Fritillaria, in var.

Gladiolus, hardy European species
Hyacinthus amethystinus
Leucojum, in var.
Lilium, in var.
Merendera Bulbocodium

Muscari, in var.
Narcissus, in great var.
Ornithogalum, in var.
Scilla, in var.
Snowdrops, in var.

Sternbergia lutea
Trichonema ramiflorum
Triteleia uniflora
Tulipa, in var.

LIST OF PLANTS FOR NATURALIZATION IN LAWNS AND OTHER GRASSY PLACES

Anemone apennina
Anemone blanda
Anemone ranunculoides
Anemone trifolia
Antennaria dioica rosea
Anthyllis montana
Bulbocodium vernum
Colchicum, in var.

Crocus, many
Dianthus deltoides
Fumaria bulbosa
Hyacinthus amethystinus
Leucojum, various
Merendera Bulbocodium
Muscari, in var.
Narcissus, many kinds

Scilla alba
Scilla amœna
Scilla bifolia
Scilla italica
Scilla sibirica
Snowdrops, all
Trichonema ramiflorum

CLIMBING AND TWINING PLANTS FOR THICKETS, HEDGEROWS, AND TREES

Ampelopsis bipinnata
Ampelopsis cordata
Ampelopsis hederacea
Ampelopsis tricuspidata
Apios tuberosa
Aristolochia Sipho
Aristolochia tomentosa
Calystegia dahurica
Cissus orientalis
Clematis flammula
Clematis montana

Clematis Viticella, and others
Hablitzia tamnoides
Jasminum nudiflorum
Jasminum officinale
Lathyrus grandiflorus
Lathyrus latifolius
Lathyrus rotundifolius
Lathyrus tuberosus and others
Lonicera, in variety
Menispermum canadense

Menispermum virginicum
Periploca græca
Roses, single, in great var.
Smilax, hardy kinds
Tamus communis
Tropæolum pentaphyllum
Tropæolum speciosum
Vitis, various
Wistaria frutescens
Wistaria sinensis

These selections are proposed only as aids to those dealing with special positions. The selection and best guide to the material for the beginner will be found in the Chapter on the principal types of Hardy Exotic Plants for the wild garden.

RABBITS

This sad subject has been kept for the last, as the only disagreeable one in connexion with the wild garden.

It is incalculable the injury rabbits do to young trees alone; indeed, where they prevail there is no chance of getting up cover except at an extravagant cost. Hares are less destructive, if they damage trees at all; and it is said by experienced gamekeepers that they never thrive so well where rabbits abound. And as regards pheasants, rabbits drive them away by eating down the evergreen cover so necessary for shelter in winter. Pheasants will not remain in a wood where there is not shelter of this kind; and nothing are they more partial to than the Holly, which ought to abound in every wood, but which the rabbits destroy first. Here are two sorts of game—hares and pheasants—which many can never have enough of, and the existence of which is directly interfered with by the rabbits; not to speak of the expense incurred year after year making up losses in plantation, and the expense of wire-netting in protecting the trees.

The extermination of rabbits is not such a difficult matter as might be imagined. When it was determined here a few years since to reduce their numbers to a minimum on the farm lands and woods, it did not require more than a couple of years to do so by shooting and ferreting during the season; and they are now principally confined to one part of the estate— an extensive tract of waste land not of much use for any other purpose. I feel pretty certain that a few active poachers would undertake to clear an estate of its rabbits in short time, and would be glad to pay for the right of doing so. In whatever degree rabbits contribute to our food supply—and it is not much—they certainly destroy a great quantity of our crops, are no profit to game-preservers, and there is little excuse for their existence.

Hungry rabbits, like hungry dogs or starving men, will eat almost anything that can be got. Rabbits, as a rule, prefer to nibble over a pasture that contains short, sweet, wholesome grass, and a proportion of Clover, Dandelion, and Daisies; but in and about woods where rabbits are numerous, the grass, from being closely and constantly eaten off, gradually disappears, and at the approach of winter is succeeded by Moss, a very cold, watery, and innutritious substitute; then rabbits are driven to seek food from other sources than grass, and the bark of small trees, the leaves, stalks, and bark of shrubs, are eaten almost indiscriminately.

Amongst evergreen shrubs, Rhododendrons and Box are generally avoided, but I have known newly-planted Rhododendrons to be eaten by rabbits. The Elder is distasteful, and American Azaleas are avoided. I have frequently seen Yew trees barked; Mahonias are devoured in these woods as soon as planted; and Periwinkle, which is named amongst rabbit-proof plants, is generally eaten to the ground in severe winter.

Where rabbits are permitted, the fact that they require food daily, like other creatures, should be recognized. A certain portion of grass land should be retained for them and managed for them; a few acres might be wired round, or, surrounded with wire-netting, to the exclusion of rabbits, until the approach of wintry weather, when it could be thrown open for them. If this cannot be done, and frosty weather sets in, when the mischief to shrubs is done, trimmings of Quick hedges should be scattered about, and an allowance of turnips, carrots, or mangold wurzel[1] made and doled out daily in bad weather. Rabbits prefer newly-planted trees and shrubs to those established. I have even had the fronds of newly-planted Athyrium Filix-fœmina eaten, while other ferns have been untouched: certain breeds of wild rabbits are much more prone to bark trees than others. The barking of trees is more done by north-country rabbits.—J. S.

A correspondent who has given much attention to the subject (Salmoniceps) gives the following, as among the most rabbit-proof of plants:—'Most of the Lily family are,' he says, 'rejected by them, including Daffodils, Tulips, Snowdrops, Snowflakes, Lilies, Day Lilies, Asphodels, and others, and they cannot be too extensively planted; but even in that tribe the Crocus is greedily devoured.'

1. Mangold wurzel (*Beta vulgaris*) is a beet relative whose large yellow root was used for animal fodder. —Ed.

Androsæmum officinale
Anemone coronaria
Anemone japonica
Arabis
Artemisia Abrotanum
Asphodelus albus
Aubrietia
Berberis Darwinii
Canterbury Bells
Cineraria maritima
Columbine
Common Yews
Deutzia scabra
Dog's-tooth Violet
Elder
Euonymus
Fuchsia

Hibiscus syriacus
Honesty (Lunaria)
Iris
Lilies (common orange and white kinds)
Lily of the Valley
Lonicera, in var.
Lycium barbarum
Mahonia Aquifolium
Monkshood
Muscari
Narcissus
Ornithogalum
Pansies
Periwinkle (large and small)
Phlox, in var.

Poppy
Primrose
Ruscus aculeatus
Ruscus racemosus
Scilla
Snowberry
Solomon's Seal
Stachys lanata
Syringa persica
Syringa vulgaris
Tritoma
Violets
Weigela rosea
Winter Aconite
Woodruff
Yucca gloriosa

Lists, however, and considerations of the above sort, are a poor substitute for what is really required in such cases—the extermination of pests which are destructive alike to field crops, to trees and shrubs, and to plants, and which offer at best a very scanty return for the havoc they commit.

Large-leafed Rockfoil in the Wild Garden.

CHAPTER XVI
The Garden of British Wild Flowers and Trees

———••———

My learned and travelled friends who tell me I cannot natural-ize Narcissus in thick grass, will hardly say we cannot grow our own lovely British tree Willows, or have our own native Heaths in all their delight-ful variety growing near us in picturesque tangles, and some of our own more beautiful Wild Roses in the hedge! The passion for the exotic is so universal that our own finest plants are never planted, while money is thrown away like chaff for worthless exotic trees like the Wellingtonia, on which tree alone fortunes have been wasted. Once on the bank of a beau-tiful river in Ireland, the Barrow, I was shown a collection of ornamental Willows, and very interesting they were, but among them not one of our native Willows, which are not merely as good as any of the garden Wil-lows but as good in beauty as the Olive tree—even where the Olive is most beautiful.

We search the world over for flowering shrubs—not one of which is prettier than the Water Elder (Viburnum Opulus), common in Sussex woods, and often seen near the water-side in Surrey. Mr. Anthony Waterer, who has the finest nursery in England in our own day, told me that when asked for a number of it he could not find them in his own nursery, or in any other.

Robinson favored growing red valerian, *Centranthus ruber*, on old walls, as here on the south steps at Gravetye Manor in late May.

As many of our beautiful wild flowers, and even our trees and shrubs, are strangers to our own gardens, I cannot do better than try to show, so far as I may, what beautiful things may be gathered from our British flora that may have charms for our gardens and wild gardens. However well people may know the beauty of our fields and woods in spring or summer, few have any idea of the great number of flowers that are wild in our own country, and worth a home in gardens—at least in those of a picturesque nature. Few of us have much notion of the great variety of beauty that may be culled from British flowers alone. Many of us have full opportunity of seeing the beauties of the fields and hedges; not so many the mountain plants, and few, such rare gems as Gentiana verna, which grows wild in Teesdale, and here and there on the western shores of Ireland; or the mountain Forget-me-not, a precious little dwarf Alpine that is found but rarely in the north. It is only by a good choice of the plants of the British Isles that we can hope to arrive at a 'garden of British plants.'

It is not only the curious and rare that may afford us interest among the plants of Britain; among them are plants of much beauty. Even for the sake of plants for lakes, rivers, ponds in parks, pleasure grounds, or gardens, the subject is worthy attention. For the rock-garden, too, many of our wild flowers are fitted. In any part of the country where the soil or surface of the ground suits the habits of a variety of native plants, it would prove interesting to collect kinds not found in the neighbourhood, and naturalize them therein; and wherever the natural rock crops up, much beauty may be added by planting these rocky spots with wild mountain flowers.

'Botany,' says Emerson,[1] 'is all names, not powers'; to press and dry wild plants is necessary for botanists, but it is not likely to cause any wide human interest in such things; and therefore I propose that we look through our British wild flowers with a view of giving some of them a home in the garden. It will be well to have a complete list of our wild flowers, which would be found in the index to Syme's, Bentham's, Babington's, or any other good book on our flora; but best is a list called *The London Catalogue of British Plants*, which was published by Pamplin of Soho, and

1. From 'Beauty' in *The Conduct of Life*, 1860. —Ed.

is now published by Bell in Covent Garden. This gives a full list of all the species, and by means of numbers indicates their distribution. The compilers adopted Mr. Hewett Watson's division of Britain into a number of botanical districts, and after the name of each species a number is placed, which tells the number of districts in which that particular plant is found.

Those who wish to work at wild flowers should get one of these lists, as on them may be at once marked the kinds we have or want; by their aid in part we may exchange the Orchids of the Surrey hills for the Alpines of the higher Scotch mountains, and so on throughout the country. Every admirer of British plants should have a manual to aid in identifying the species. Another aid would be a 'local flora,' a list of the plants growing in any particular neighbourhood or county; such, for instance, as the *Flora of Reigate*, Baines's *Flora of Yorkshire*, and Mackay's *Flora Hibernica*, or the *Cybele Hibernica*.

We will next turn to the plants, beginning with the natural order of Crowfoots. The Crowfoot order is the order which brightens the moist hollows in the spring with the glittering of the lesser Celandine, the meadows in May with Buttercups; when 'those long mosses in the stream'[2] begin to assume a livelier green, 'and the wild Marsh Marigold shines like fire in swamps and hollows grey.'[3] 'Those long mosses in the stream' of 'The Miller's Daughter' are the Water Crowfoots that silver over the pools with their pretty white cup-like blossoms in early summer; and it is the same family which burnishes our meadows with a glory of colour not equalled by any tropical flowers. But in considering British plants from a garden standpoint only, we can only seek those that are worthy of garden culture, and certain to reward us for giving them a place in the garden.

The first plant named in books of British Plants is the Traveller's Joy (Clematis Vitalba), the well-known common Clematis that streams over the trees, and falls in graceful folds from trees in many parts of the south of England, having in autumn heads of feathery awns. It is well known as a garden plant, and from its rapidity of growth nothing is better adapted for quickly covering rough mounds or bowers. However, it may be best used in the shrubbery, and particularly so on the margin of a river, or

2. From 'The Miller's Daughter' by Alfred Lord Tennyson. —Ed.

3. From 'The May Queen' by Alfred Lord Tennyson. —Ed.

water, where the long streamers of its branchlets are graceful. It is the only native plant that gives an idea of the 'bush ropes' that run in wild profusion through tropical woods.

We have the Meadow Rues, of one of which in this book is a figure [4] as showing plants of some claim to beauty not often seen in the ordinary garden: the elegant lesser Meadow Rue (Thalictrum minus), so like the Maidenhair Fern that some say it is as pretty for the open air as the Maidenhair Fern is for the greenhouse. It is wild in many parts of Britain, in Scotland and North-Western England, and rather abundant on the island of Ireland's Eye, near Dublin, and in many parts of the limestone districts of Clare and Galway. There are several other species, natives of Britain, but none of them showing any gain on this kind.

NATIVE WINDFLOWERS. Next come the Windflowers, or Anemones, four kinds, at least two of them—Anemone nemorosa, the Wood Anemone, and A. apennina, the blue Anemone—indispensable for our garden. The Wood Anemone is pretty either in its wild or cultivated state, and besides the common white variety there are a reddish and a double white variety.

The most beautiful form of our Wood Anemone which has come into the garden in our day is the large sky-blue form. I first saw it as a small tuft at Oxford, and grew it in London where it was often seen with me in bloom by Mr. Boswell Syme, author of the third edition of Sowerby, who had a great love for plants in a living state as well as in their merely 'botanical' aspects, and we were often struck with its singular charm about noon on bright days. There is reason to believe that there is both in England and Ireland a large and handsome form of the Wood Anemone—distinct from the common white of our woods and shaws in spring, and that my blue Anemone is a variety of this. It is not the same as the blue form wild in parts of North Wales and elsewhere in Britain, this being more fragile looking and not so light a blue.

As for the Apennine blue Anemone, it is one of the loveliest of spring flowers, both in the borders and scattered here and there in woods and shrubberies and grass. The flowers are freely produced, and of the loveliest

4. See page 102. —Ed.

Robinson's Blue Windflower. A large sky-blue form of the Wood Anemone.

blue. It is not a true but a naturalized native flower, so to speak, its home being the hills of South Europe, having escaped out of gardens into our land.

The Pasque Anemone, or Pasque-flower, is a beautiful native plant bearing large flowers of a lovely violet purple, silky outside. It grows on limestone pastures, and occurs in several districts in England, though it is wanting in Scotland and Ireland. The Pasque-flower is one of those that are more beautiful in a wild than in a cultivated state, for though it grows freely in light and chalky soils in gardens, it has not half the beauty it shows in spring on the Downs. I never saw any plant more charming than this in the woods and hills and even on walls in Normandy in spring.

Another kind, Anemone ranunculoides (yellow), is a doubtful native found in one or two spots, and pretty for chalky soils, on which it flowers freely. Being uncommon it is just the sort of plant to which those who have the right soil may give the hospitality of the garden.

Adonis autumnalis is the pretty pheasant's-eye, an annual plant found in corn-fields, and of which the seed is offered in catalogues under the name of Flos Adonis.

The Ranunculi, or Crowfoots, begin with Ranunculus aquatilis and its several varieties, and several other species of Water Ranunculi with divided leaves. Few gardens offer any facilities for cultivating these. The most we can do is to introduce them to a pond or stream in which they are not already found, or add one of the long-leaved or rarer kinds to the common kind or kinds; but their home is in the fresh stream, 'hither, thither, idly'[5] playing, or in the lake, and therefore they hardly come among garden plants.

I have tried to grow all the kinds I could get, but the Canadian weed or the common Ranunculus aquatilis soon exterminated them. Ranunculus Ficaria is the pretty shining-leaved yellow kind, which abounds in moist and shaded places in spring; R. Flammula (the Spearwort) is a native of wet marshes and river-sides in all parts of Britain, and is well suited for planting by the water-side, though not so handsome as the greater Spearwort, R. Lingua, which is two or three feet high, and has large showy,

5. From "The Miller's Daughter" by Alfred Lord Tennyson. —Ed.

yellow flowers. It is very fine near water, and is freely scattered over the British Isles, though not often plentiful. These plants must usually be collected in a wild state, though they are grown in some botanic gardens. Ranunculus acris pleno and R. repens pleno are double forms of the wild kinds, and worth growing, from their pretty 'bachelor's-button' flowers, bright yellow, neat, double, lasting longer in flower than the single kinds.

Then we have the Marsh Marigold (Caltha palustris), which makes such a glorious show in spring along moist bottoms, or by river banks in rich soil—notably on the banks of the Thames, where, when in high tide, the ground for many feet under water looks as if strewn with gold, the water having overflowed numbers of these showy flowers. Even where common, in the woods and fields, this handsome plant, single or double, deserves a home beside all garden waters, or even in moist ground, because it makes a truly fine spring-flowering plant. There is a double variety sold in Covent Garden in early summer, bearing double flowers of large size, which, like the double Crowfoots, last longer than the single bloom. Apart from the double garden forms of the Marsh Marigold, these are the kinds now recognized as belonging to our flora.

Caltha
    palustris (Linnaeus)
        a. *vulgaris* (Schott)
        b. *Guerangerii* (Boreau)
        c. *minor* (Syme)
    radicans (Forster)

Trollius europæus is the Globe Flower, well worthy of a garden home from its fine form, colour, and sweetness. Not a common plant in England, but frequent in the North and West, and in Ireland, it will grow in moist places and in clayey hollows often hopeless from weeds. I planted a large group in such a spot, and it has kept the weeds in check ever since, and gives us its welcome bloom every May.

That pretty early spring flower, the Winter Aconite (Eranthis hyemalis), also belongs to this order, and is well worthy of culture. It is naturalized here and there, and is beautiful in light and chalky soils under trees in spring.

The common Columbine (Aquilegia vulgaris) is often pretty. It is not common in the wild state, but a true native in several counties of England. In one gorge on Helvellyn I have seen it ascend almost to the top of that mountain, flowering beautifully in almost inaccessible spots; it is rather common in gardens, but in many and varied garden forms.

The common poisonous Aconite (Aconitum Napellus) is a fine native plant; it is, however, very common in gardens, where it should be kept quite isolated from any roots likely to be used as food, owing to its poisonous roots.

Lastly, in the Buttercup order we have our native Helleborus (H. viridis and H. fœtidus), which will adorn rough banks with their evergreen leaves.

The common Berberis vulgaris, which is rather widely distributed, must not be forgotten, for there is no more beautiful sight afforded by any shrub than by this when draped over with its bright racemes of fruit.

The white Water Lily, so common in our rivers, should be seen in all garden waters, not thickly planted, but a single specimen or group here and there. It is most effective when one or a few plants are seen alone on the water; then the flowers and leaves have full room to develop and float right regally; but when a dense crowd of water lilies are seen together, they crowd each other out. With it should be associated the yellow Water Lily (Nuphar lutea), and if it can be had, the smaller and rare Nuphar pumila.

Among the Poppies, the one best worth growing as a garden plant is the Welsh Poppy (Meconopsis Cambrica), which grows so abundantly along the road sides in the lake district. It is a perennial of a fine yellow, and thrives well at the bottom of walls and on stony banks. Some might care to grow the large Opium Poppy (Papaver somniferum); its finer double varieties are handsome, but these are scarcely British, the plant is naturalized. The field Poppy is everywhere in our corn-fields, and from it we get pretty races of Poppies, double and single. The Horned Poppy of our seashores is distinct and may be grown in a garden.

Corydalis bulbosa is a dwarf early flower, scarcely a native, or rare; and the yellow fumitory (Corydalis lutea) is almost wonderful in its way of adorning walls and stony places, with the greatest differences as to soil and moisture.

In the natural order Cruciferæ, Thlaspi alpestre (a pretty Alpine), Iberis amara (a fine white annual), Draba aizoides (a rare and beautiful Alpine), Königa maritima, the sweet Alyssum, and Dentaria bulbifera, rare, and curious; the Ladies' Smock and its double variety; Arabis petræa (a sweet dwarf Alpine); the common Wallflower, and the single Rocket (Hesperis matronalis), and the Sea-kale of our shores are worth growing.

All the British Helianthemum or Sun Roses, and the annual kind, H. guttatum of the Channel Islands, are pretty plants. Many do not know we have a list so full as this of native kinds:—

Helianthemum
    guttatum (Miller)
    Breweri (Planchon)
    marifolium (Miller)
      b. *vineale* (Persoon)
    Chamæcistus (Miller)
    polifolium (Miller)

These of course apart from the garden forms of the common Sun Rose which are numerous.

Of the Violets, in addition to the sweet Violet, which should be grown on a north aspect, Viola lutea and V. tricolor will be found the most distinct and worthy of culture. Apart from the many garden varieties there are the white and various wild forms. The interesting little Milkworts, which are so pretty on our sandy and chalky hills, are very rarely grown—though they well might be in a garden of native rock or heath and down plants. The very dwarf trailing Frankenia lævis (Sea Heath) runs over stones, and looks neat and mossy on a rock-garden.

In the Pink tribe, the scarce, single, wild Carnation (Dianthus Caryophyllus), D. plumarius, the parent of the garden pink, and the Cheddar Pink, which thrives on an old wall, D. deltoides, the maiden pink, the

Native Sun Rose in Somerset at Combe.

soapwort (Saponaria officinalis), the Sea-bladder Campion (Silene maritima), Silene acaulis, the beautiful little Alpine that clothes our higher mountains, the Corn Cockle (Lychnis Githago), the Ragged Robin, and the Alpine Lychnis; the vernal sandwort (Arenaria verna), Arenaria ciliata, found on Ben Bulben, in Ireland, and Cerastium alpinum are among the prettiest. The last is as shaggy as a Skye terrier, and does not grow more than an inch high.

A pretty species of Flax is not a common plant in British gardens, but one occurs wild in some of our eastern counties—Linum perenne, a blue-flowered plant, of which there is a pure white variety, both very pretty plants, quite hardy and perennial. The perennial Flax, or any of its varieties, will be found to thrive in any place where the grass is not mown as well as on borders. The field Flax is sometimes found wild with us, but it is not a true native.

Among the Malva tribe we have several showy plants, but less worthy of garden cultivation, except it be Lavatera arborea (the tree Lavatera), sparsely found along the south and west coasts. It is a plant of fine habit, growing five or six feet high. The best of the Mallows is the Musk Mallow (Malva moschata), which has showy flowers, and is a charming native flower by streams and on banks: it is a very good garden plant, especially the white form.

The St. John's Worts (Hypericum) have some beauty, and might find a place among low shrubs; the best perhaps is H. calycinum, or St. John's Wort, a kind which is not perhaps truly British, but which is now naturalized in parts of England and Ireland. The showy flowers of this and its habit fit it for the garden; and it is particularly adapted for rough banks, or will crawl freely under and near trees, though it will best show its beauty when fully exposed to the sun and air. It should not be used as a 'carpet' under old or favourite trees, as it will sometimes starve and kill trees.

In the Geranium order there are a few pretty plants for the garden—notably, G. pratense, G. sylvaticum, and G. sanguineum, with its fine variety G. lancastriense. This variety was originally found in the Isle of Walney, in Lancashire, and some writers have made it a species under the name of G. lancastriense. Both plants are well worth growing in a garden. Geranium sanguineum makes a very pretty border plant, or for forming groups between shrubs.

The stubwort (Oxalis Acetosella) is the prettiest among its British allies; and a chaste little plant it is, too, when seen in shady, woody places, along hedge-banks, and over mossy stumps; in gardens where there is a little diversity of surface, or half-shady spots, it might be grown with advantage where it does not come of itself. Some say it is the Shamrock of the ancient Irish, but they are wrong. Custom among the Irish, during the experience of the oldest people, and everything that can be gleaned, point to the common Trifolium repens as the true Shamrock.

In the Pea order there are a few plants of great merit, and the first we meet with is the very pretty dwarf shrub Genista tinctoria, or Dyer's genista. This is a little shrub, but vigorous in the profusion of its yellow flowers, and would be at home on any rough banks or grassy places, or among dwarf shrubs. It is frequent in England, but rare in Scotland and Ireland. Its two allies, G. pilosa and G. anglica, are also neat little shrubs, both worth a place among dwarf British shrubs.

Many who care for wild flowers must have been struck with the beauty of the common Restharrow, which spreads such delicate colour over many a chalk cliff and sandy pasture. It bears garden culture well, and is prettier when in flower than numbers of New Holland plants, which require protection. There is a smoother and more bushy form of this sometimes admitted as a species, Ononis antiquorum, which is also a fine plant, growing freely from seed, and of the easiest culture.

The Bird's-foot trefoil, though common, is so beautiful that it must not be forgotten, flowering as it does nearly the whole summer. There are several forms of it and few better plants for the front edge of borders.

The Lady's Fingers (Anthyllis vulneraria) is a pretty plant found in chalky pastures and dry stony places in England.

The three native kinds of Astragalus are worthy of cultivation, and so are the allied plants, Oxytropis. Both O. campestris and O. uralensis are dwarf plants, the foliage of the last being silvery. The first is found only in one spot among the Clova mountains in Scotland; the second is rather common on the Scotch hills.

Hippocrepis comosa is rather like the Bird's-foot trefoil, both in habit and flower, and is worth a place among rock plants.

Of the Vetches two at least are worthy of culture—Vicia Cracca and V. sylvatica. The first makes a charming border plant if slightly supported on stakes, so that it may have hidden its supports by the time the flowers appear. The wood Vetch is of a climbing habit, and very elegant when seen running up the stems of young trees or over bushes. This is found in most woody hills of Britain and Scotland, and V. Cracca is common everywhere.

Among native peas the best is the Sea Pea (Lathyrus maritimus), a handsome plant in rich ground. It occurs on the coast of Southern and Eastern England, of Shetland, and of Kerry, in Ireland.

In the Rose order both the Spiræas should interest us—certainly S. Filipendula, which has leaves cut somewhat like a fern. The double variety is pretty. Dryas octopetala, a plant found on the limestone mountains of North England and Ireland, and abundantly in Scotland, is a pretty little rock evergreen bush.

NATIVE BRIERS AND WILD ROSES

As for the Blackberry, Raspberry, Dewberry, and Cloudberry, some may desire to cultivate them, and it is very interesting to observe the differences between some of the sub-species and varieties of blackberries, and the beauty, both in fruit and flower, of the family. Many people, even among those who care for trees and shrubs, have little idea of the variety existing among our native Brambles. Over ninety species and their varieties and wild forms are given in the last edition of the *London Catalogue*! The question of whether these are true species or merely varieties need not trouble us, for plants showing very slight distinction to a botanist may be essentially distinct in beauty and effect. A man might do a more foolish thing than get these together and grow them on some rough bank or corner or even in newly-made banks of hedgerows. There is much beauty of leaf among the plants, and variety in the quality of the fruit, some of the kinds being valuable for their fruit.

Whatever we may do with brambles, however, our native Wild Roses deserve a place in fence or hedgerow, or rough banks if convenient. Some indeed come of themselves, but it would be very interesting to grow many of the less common kinds and consider them for their beauty. Botanic gardens might well show us such fine families as these, instead of rivalling the pastry-cook 'bedding' of the private gardener, and I do not remember ever seeing any attempt to grow them except in the Cambridge Botanic Garden, the curator of which writes as follows of our Wild Roses.

'We all allow the Roses of the florist to be without rival among flowers of the garden, and we can but admit that Wild Roses are perhaps the most lovely flowers of the field. But there are numbers of the wildings, and all beautiful, and some of surpassing charm. We want to see them more often grown in our gardens. Sometimes we admire a chance seedling, as, for instance, in the Cambridge Botanic Garden, where some years ago Rosa dumalis (a form of the Dog Rose) took possession of a Spruce Fir, and now attains to a height of about twenty feet, forming wreaths of blossom in summer. The Spruce is dead, but the Rose still clings to the old stem, which forms just the right kind of support. Such an object as this, or Rosa arvensis, in the collection, makes us wonder why these single Roses have not received more attention. They are usually so robust, just what is wanted for pleasure grounds and the wild garden, and then in autumn we frequently have their brilliant red fruit. At this moment in some of the hedges of the neighbourhood are shrubs with quantities of fruit, which in a garden would help considerably in colour effect.

'To show what material there is, I may mention that the many forms of our native roses fall under seven distinct aggregate groups.

'We have first the well-known Scotch or Burnet Rose (Rosa

spinosissima), lovely with white or pink flowers; next, R. villosa, which in various forms makes a large bush, with erect or arching branches, very hairy leaves and densely glandular sepals. It is distinguished from the last-mentioned by its larger size and equal prickles, and from R. canina by its straight prickles. Under it we have R. tomentosa, with a large pale pink flower, and R. mollissima, with a smaller, deeper-coloured flower.

'The succeeding species is R. involuta, under which are numerous kinds, small and erect, with short branches and crowded prickles, passing into bristles. Among them we may note R. Wilsoni, with bright red flowers, and R. Sabini, with ample foliage and pale pink flowers.

'Next is our fragrant R. rubiginosa, the Sweet Brier, which, however, is less fragrant, as it approaches R. canina and R. villosa. Near to this species we may mention R. macrantha and R. sepium, both of which have rather pretty flowers, though they are somewhat small.

'Rosa hibernica is the next species to refer to, and it is intermediate between R. spinosissima and R. canina, though most like the latter. It is small and erect, with short, sometimes arching branches and erect globose naked fruit. It is figured with pale pink flowers.

'Rosa canina is the familiar Dog Rose, of which the varieties are very numerous. It has long arching branches, with stout hooked prickles, having a thickened base, and in the common form is the strongest growing of British Roses. It is often very beautiful, and, all things considered, some of the best results may no doubt be got from this species. Rosa cæsia and R. incana, belonging to this species, have glaucous leaves. The foliage of R. Bakeri is very pretty, and R. dumalis is a fine tall kind, but the varieties of this species are so numerous, that it is difficult to specify.

'Our last species is R. arvensis, known from R. canina by the union of the styles into a long slender column, that species having

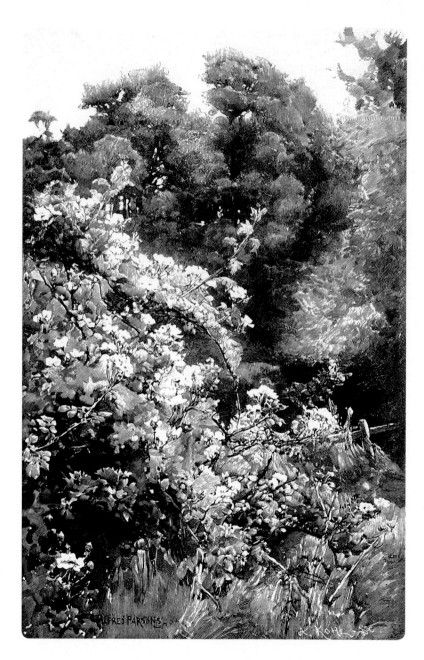

The Field Rose
(R. arvensis). Engraved from
a picture in the possession
of Mrs. L. Maxse.

the styles free. There are two subspecies, R. arvensis proper (R. repens) having the leaflets glabrous, glaucous beneath, and R. stylosa with leaflets pubescent beneath. This last connects R. arvensis with R. canina, and under it the several varieties occur. The variety Monsoniæ, found in a hedge at Watford, has very large red flowers and sub-globose, orange-red fruit. It is our present R. arvensis proper to which the Ayrshire Rose must be referred. The flowers are more cup-shaped than those of any other British Rose, and Lindley says that Sabine had a variety with pink flowers. No illustration has before appeared in any journal, but a figure in *English Botany* shows to some extent what a fine thing it is. The plant has long, trailing shoots, with small, scattered prickles, oval leaflets, glabrous on both surfaces, and glaucous or whitish green beneath. The flowers are of elegant outline, with pure white corolla, except the throat, which is yellow, and have a purple calyx; and the fruit is scarlet when ripe.'

SLOE, BULLACE, WILD CHERRY, ROWAN, WILD SERVICE, WHITE BEAM, WILD PEAR, CRAB, MEDLAR, MAY

These are native trees—some of them of much beauty, taking great share in the landscape beauty of our country, and a place in its literature—some of them also being the source of our best hardy fruits. I wish to plead for their use in the wild garden, if not in the garden itself. What is more beautiful in the landscape than a snowy wreath of old Sloe trees in spring, seen beyond the wide fields, or more delicate in bud when seen at hand? The Wild Cherry, Rowan, White Beam, and Crab do their own part in adorning our woods, but we need not leave them wholly there. I find the Medlar charming for its leaves in the fall as well as for the large simple flowers in spring, and make groups of it on the grass. The May is the one loved tree that all enjoy: there are several wild forms in Britain besides the garden varieties:—

Cratægus
  Oxyacantha (Linnaeus)
    a. *oxyacanthoides* (Thuillier)
    b. *laciniata* (Wallroth)
    c. *kyrtostyla* (Fingerhuth)
    d. *monogyna* (Jacquin)

To remind the reader of how much tree beauty there is in this now obscure corner of our flora—so far as gardens go—I print here the names of the wild kinds of these trees so far as known to us now, with their English names where they have any.

Prunus
  communis (Hudson)—Sloe
    b. *fruticans* (Weihe)
  insititia (Linnaeus)—Bullace
  Avium (Linnaeus)—Gean
  Cerasus (Linnaeus)—Wild Cherry
  Padus (Linn.)—Bird Cherry

Pyrus
  torminalis (Ehrhart)—Wild Service
  Aria (Smith)—White Beam
    b. *rupicola* (Syme)
  latifolia (Syme)
  scandica (Syme)
  hybrida (Linnaeus)
  Aucuparia (Gærtner)—Rowan
  communis (Linnaeus)—Pear
    a. *Pyraster* (Linnaeus)
    b. *Achras* (Gærtner)
    c. *cordata* (Desvaux)
  Malus (Linnaeus)—Apple
    a. *acerba* (De Candolle)
    b. *mitis* (Wallroth)
  Germanica (Linnaeus)—Medlar

The Cloudberry can be grown best in a wet, boggy soil, and is difficult of culture as a garden plant, except in moist and elevated spots.

The Dewberry, distinguished principally by the glaucous bloom on the fruit when ripe, is of easy culture.

Of the Potentillas, P. rupestris, white-flowered, found on the Breiddin Hills in Montgomeryshire, and the large yellow P. alpestris, from the higher limestone mountains, are the best. Potentilla fruticosa, of the north of England, and in Clare and Galway, in Ireland, is a free-flowering low bush; and the marsh potentilla (P. Comarum) will do well in boggy ground, if we have it, though it is more distinct than pretty.

The common Willow Herb (Epilobium angustifolium), so showy, and so apt to become a bad weed, is well known. But, in a wood or out-of-the-way spot, where it cannot overrun rarer plants, it is very pretty. Even the botanist, in describing it, says, 'a handsome plant'—an expression very seldom used by gentlemen who write on English botany.

The Evening Primrose (Œnothera biennis) deserves a place from its fragrance; and it is as well to sow it in some out-of-the-way spot. It often covers waste building ground in London.

Next we have the Loosestrife (Lythrum Salicaria), a water-side plant, abundant in many parts of Britain. There is a variety of this plant known in gardens by the name of L. roseum superbum, which should be in and by every pond.

The common Herniary (Herniaria glabra) and Scleranthus perennis are two very dwarf green spreading plants, found in some of the southern and central counties of England, and which give a neat Lycopodium-like effect in the rock-garden.

Then we come to the Rose-root (Sedum Rhodiola) and the tribe of pretty Stonecrops (Sedum), every one of which is worthy of a place on the rock-garden—from the common Stonecrop, which grows on the thatch of cottages and abundantly in many parts of Britain, on rocky places, to that little gem for a wall, S. dasyphyllum of the south of England. The Rose-root is so called from the drying root-stock smelling like roses.

The Orpine or Livelong (Sedum Telephium) is also a fine old plant of this order. If you have any olds walls or buildings, try and establish a few of the smaller kinds on these; it is interesting to have rare plants established in such places, and the tenderer kinds will always survive on walls, whereas they may get cut off by the winter on the ground.

Fern-growers find it difficult to establish the little Wall Rue (Asplenium Ruta-muraria) in pots, pans, or any way in the fernery; but by taking a few of the spore-bearing fronds, and shaking a little of the 'fern-seed' into the chinks of an old wall, we may soon establish it; and in like manner it is quite possible to cultivate the Ceterach and the graceful Spleenwort, only that the wall must be somewhat older, so to speak, to accommodate these than the Wall Rue, as this little fern will grown on a wall that is in perfect condition, as may be seen at Lord Mansfield's at Highgate, where the high garden-wall that runs for some distance parallel with the road running from Hampstead to Highgate is covered in its upper part with this plant. In gardening few things are more interesting than an old wall covered with ferns and rock and mountain plants.

The Stonecrops are followed in the natural classification of British plants by the Rockfoils (Saxifraga), like the Stonecrops in size, but more valuable for the garden. First, there is the Irish group of Saxifrages, the London Pride and its varieties; and the Killarney Saxifrage, S. Geum and its interesting varieties, both species very pretty for the rock-garden and borders. Next we have the mountain S. stellaris and S. nivalis, and the yellow marsh S. Hirculus, and the yellow S. Aizoides, which fringes the rills and streams on the hills and mountains in Scotland, and the north of England and Ireland, all interesting, but surpassed in beauty by the purple S. oppositifolia, which opens its bright flowers soon after the snow melts in the Scotch Highlands, and as far north, among the higher mountains of Europe and Asia, as the Arctic Circle. It bears garden culture well, on the rock-garden, or in patches in the front of a border, planted in the full sun.

The meadow (Saxifraga granulata) differs in most respects from most of the other Rockfoils, and is worth growing; its double variety, seen in cottage gardens, is used for the spring garden. It flowers so well that the very leaves are hidden by large double flowers. It is frequently found in small cottage gardens in Surrey.

The dense green mossy Rockfoils are precious for the garden, from the living green which they take on in winter, when all else fades—when the fallen leaves rush by, driven by the winds of autumn—and when Geraniums and all the fleeting flower-garden things are cut off. These mossy Rockfoils grow on almost any soil or situation, and may be grown with ease even in towns. They are dotted over with white flowers in early summer, the stems of which should be cut off as soon as the flowers perish, but their greatest charm is in winter. Saxifraga hypnoides, abundant in Scotland, Wales, and Northern England, with its varieties, is our best plant in this way; and S. cæspitosa, found on some of the higher Scotch mountains, is allied to it, and also good. In towns shrubs do not keep their verdure, through various adverse influences; in all places these mossy Rockfoils charm us with their verdure if we take the trouble to put them in bold flakes on the rock-garden or on borders, or to use them as a carpet beneath tea and other roses. There are many forms of the mossy Rockfoil, natives of Britain.

Next we have the beautiful Grass of Parnassus (Parnassia palustris), a distinct and charming native plant, rather frequent in Britain in bogs and moist heaths. I have grown it very successfully in a small artificial bog, and still better in six-inch pots in peat soil, the pots being placed in a saucer of water during summer, and preserved in a cold frame in winter. It is, however, much better to 'naturalize' it in moist grassy places than to grow it in this way.

The Spignel or Baldmoney (Meum athamanticum) of the Scotch Highlands, Wales, and the north of England, having elegantly divided leaves, and being very neat in habit, is an interesting border or rock plant.

Among the plants of the umbelliferous order there are not many native plants worthy of cultivation, except the Sea Holly (Eryngium maritimum), and the sweet Cicely (Myrrhis odorata), often cultivated in old times and gardens for various uses; not a rare plant, but most plentiful in the hilly parts of the north of England. This for its odour and foliage is welcome in the garden, and groups of it are pretty between shrubs. The sweet Fennel, which is often seen wild in the south on chalk banks, is a graceful plant, and typical of the great beauty of form, which belongs to many plants of the order. For the rest of this numerous order they are best seen in a wild state where their effects are often striking—particularly in some rich woods. The Twin-flower (Linnæa borealis) is one of the most charming among our native plants, trailing as it does so prettily in fir woods in the north. It is found, though rarely, in Scotland; and it may be grown easily in gardens in moist peat, or cool sandy parts of the rock-garden or cool borders, and may indeed be naturalized in peaty soil with a sparse growth.

Of our native Dogwoods (Cornus), one (C. sanguinea) is an excellent native shrub, the beauty of which is very effective in gardens where it is grouped in bold and artistic ways. The winter effect is bright and good, and the plant fine for association with our handsomer native willows: this Dogwood being used as undergrowth near the largest willows. The little

Natural growth of
umbellate plants.

native Cornel is a charming alpine and bog plant. Our native woodbine appeals to all, so I need hardly tell of its beauty: the value of our native Viburnums is not so well known—few shrubs of any countries are so handsome in blossom and berry as the Water Elder (V. Opulus)—so called in some of the home counties, from its frequence on river banks, though common too in underwoods. The other is the wayfaring tree (V. Lantana) common in hedgerows in the south, its berries conspicuous in autumn.

OUR NATIVE HEATHS. Of the variety and beauty of our native heaths few have much idea. The wild species are beautiful; from time to time varieties have appeared amongst them which nurserymen have preserved; and in a collection of these, the variety of gay colour is charming. I had no idea of the beauty of colour afforded by the varieties till I visited the Comely Bank nurseries at Edinburgh a few years ago, and there found a large area of ground covered with their exquisite colours, and looking like a beautiful flower-garden. But if all this beauty did not exist, the charms of the common species, as spread out even on our southern heaths, should lead us to give the heaths a good place in the picturesque garden.

All species and varieties are worthy of a place, beginning with the varieties of the common Ling (Calluna vulgaris)—the commonest of all heaths. It has 'sported' into a great number of varieties, many of which are preserved in nurseries. Some of them are bright and distinct in colour; others differ distinctly in habit, some close to the ground in dense bushes.

There is no more beautiful shrub than the native Heather in its commonest form, so that it is easy to judge of the value of the fine white and other forms if we use them well: as to vigour, the plant may be often seen flourishing on banks with little soil on them, and the same fine vigour is true of the varieties—excluding merely monstrous and variegated forms.

Then we have the Scotch heather (Erica cinerea), the reddish purple showy flowers of which are very attractive, but surpassed in beauty of colour by a variety of the same plant, coccinea; and there is also a white variety, as there is of the Bell Heather (E. tetralix), to which is also closely related the Irish E. Mackaiana. Next we have the ciliated Heath (E. ciliaris), a pretty kind, with flowers nearly as large as those of St. Daboec's Heath, and the Irish Heath (E. hibernica), found in some of the western counties of Ireland.

Finally, we have among these interesting plants the Cornish Heath (Erica vagans), and from what has been said of the family it will be seen what interesting beds or groups might be made from these alone, grown almost anywhere. Our object should be to make the most of natural advantages, and as many persons must have gardens suited for what are called American plants, they would find it worth while to devote a spot to our Heaths and their varieties. It is charming to form a garden of bold beds of these, as the late Sir W. Bowman did so well in Surrey, but the most artistic way is to form bold masses of these Heaths without the garden proper, on rough banks and the outer parts of the grounds.

It is an error to suppose that peat is required for these plants. Even in 1893—the year of many sunny months and days—I often saw the Heather in bloom on stony railway banks in Sussex, often facing the sun; and that same year too when staying at Coolhurst I saw the prettiest possible foreground to a house in the home counties at Newells—a field of Heather in full bloom with the rich weald seen across it. This field had, I think, come of itself.

Where we seek to establish the heaths in the way named above it is best to get them in some quantity from growers who offer them in liberal numbers: to set by picturesque beds I plant in large masses in well-dug ground, but once established leave the beds alone, and allow them to grow together in their own way. I must state here, for those who will not take the trouble to understand, that these Heath beds are *not* in my flower-garden.

Nearly allied to the Heaths we have the interesting bog Vaccinium, which may be cultivated in marshy or peaty ground. To these belong the Cranberry, Bilberry, and Whortleberry; and for some of these and the American kinds, people have ere now made artificial bogs in their gardens. The little creeping evergreen, Arctostaphylos uva-ursi, or Bearberry, is neat in the rock-garden. It is found in hilly districts in Scotland, northern England, and Ireland. Then the Marsh Andromeda (A. polifolia), found chiefly in central and northern England, bears very pretty pink flowers, and grows freely in peat. The very small English Azalea (Rhododendron procumbens) is also a very interesting native plant, forming a cushiony bush not more than a couple of inches high. In Britain it is found only in the Scotch Highlands. I have only once seen this well established in a garden.

Few people who admire what are called peat shrubs can have failed to notice from time to time the beautiful St. Daboec's Heath (Menziesia polifolia), a plant found abundantly on the heathy wastes of the Asturias and in south-western France, and also in Connemara, in Ireland. It is usually associated with 'American plants' in our nurseries and gardens, liking peat soil, and is a beautiful plant. The flowers are usually pink, and there is a white variety even more beautiful. The very rare blue Menziesia of the Sow of Athol, in Perthshire, is also charming.

The Pyrolas, or Winter Greens, are very pretty native plants, some of them fragrant. Pyrola rotundifolia and P. uniflora are among the best, and both are rare, flourishing in moist sandy soils, as they do between the sand-hills on the coast of Lancashire.

The periwinkles, Vinca minor and V. major, and their forms, are well known, and they often garland banks and hedgerow bottoms.

One of the most precious gems in the British flora is the vernal Gentian (Gentiana verna), which grows in Teesdale and on the western shores of Ireland. The blue of this flower is most vivid; it is one of the most charming of all Alpine flowers, and should be in every garden of hardy plants, on the rock-garden, or borders where only dwarf plants are grown. It may be grown well in sandy loam mixed with broken limestone or gravel, and indeed is not particular as to soil, provided that it be mixed with sharp sand or grit, and kept moist, and left for several years undisturbed. It is best suited for a level spot on the rock-garden with a good body of soil into which its roots may descend. It may be grown in rock-gardens, the surface of the ground being studded here and there with small stones, among which this lovely plant will grow and flower. It is abundant in mountain pastures in Central and Southern Europe; it is, in fact, a true Alpine, and may now be had in various nurseries.

It cannot be too well known that 'rock-works,' as generally made, are ugly, unnatural, and quite unfit for a plant to grow upon. The stones or 'rocks' are piled up, with no sufficient quantity of soil or any preparation made for the plants, so that all delicate rock-plants die upon them, and the 'rocks' are taken possession of by rank weeds. These rock-gardens are generally made too perpendicular, even in the best gardens in England—masses of rock being used merely to produce an effect, or masses of stone piled up without any of those chinks of soil into which rock-plants delight to root. The best way is to have more soil than 'rock,' to let the latter suggest itself rather than expose its uncovered sides, and to make them very much flatter than is the rule, so that the moisture may freely enter in every direction, and that the rock-garden may more resemble a cropping out of stone or rocks than the ridiculous wall-like structures which pass for rock-gardens.

The Vernal Gentian. (Engraved from a photograph.)

The Marsh Gentian (Gentiana Pneumonanthe) is also a lovely plant, which should have a moist spot in a border, and is not difficult to find in the north of England; also, less plentifully, in central and southern England. The Brighton Horticultural Society is in the habit of giving prizes for collections of wild plants, and thereby doing much harm by causing a few rude collectors to gather bunches of the rarest wild flowers, and perhaps exterminate them. When at one of its meetings a few years ago, I observed among the collections competing for a trifling prize large bunches of this beautiful Gentian, which had been pulled up by the roots, to form one of one hundred or more bunches of wild flowers torn up by one individual.

In the Gentian order we have also the beautiful Bog-bean (Menyanthes trifoliata), a plant that will grow on the margin of water or ditches or ponds; it will also grow and flower in a moist border. It is a well-known plant almost everywhere in Britain; a beautiful native flower elegantly fringed on the inside with white filaments, and its unopened buds tipped with apple-blossom red.

Villarsia nymphæoides is also another pretty water-plant, with floating, small, water-lily-like leaves, and, in July, many yellow flowers—so many as to give a very showy effect; and it associates well with the white Water Lily. One of the prettiest effects I have ever seen was produced by this plant lining a small bay with a group of Water Lilies on its outer side. Seen from the opposite shore the effect was charming—large Water Lilies in front, then a wide-spreading mass of green sprinkled with starry yellow, and behind the shrubs which came to the water's edge on the shores of the little bay.

Jacob's Ladder, or Greek Valerian as it is sometimes called, also belongs to the Gentian order, and is a border plant, and its variegated variety (Polemonium cæruleum variegatum) is much used in fine flower-gardens.

Most worthy of notice, in the Galium tribe, is the little white-starred Woodruff (Asperula odorata), which grows profusely in many British woods in spring. Where not wild, it should be grown in gardens, even if only for its fragrance. It is as sweet as the new hay, and continues to give forth its odour for a long time. When green, the 'haulm'[6] of this plant

6. Stalk. —Ed.

betrays no very noticeable fragrance, but begins to emit it very soon after being cut, and merely requires to be placed on some dry shelf or half-open drawer, where it may get quite dry.

The common Red Valerian, as it is called, or Centranthus ruber botanically, is a handsome plant, on banks, borders, or rocky places and walls. As it may be readily raised from seed, there can be no difficulty in procuring it, and it should be noted that there is a fine deep red as well as the ordinary variety, and also a pure white one. Like the Wallflower, they do well on old walls and bridges, and thus have become 'naturalized' in many parts of the country. It is the first plant that comes up in newly-opened chalk pits.

The Hieraciums are often beautiful plants, as may be well seen in Mr. Hanbury's book now in progress. Many of them may be grown on rock-gardens or on well-exposed borders of dwarf plants. Such plants as these, the beauty of which is so little known in gardens, should be taken up by persons who like to get out of formal tracks, as botanical books rarely or never show the beauty of plants as they grow, and as very few have opportunities of seeing the plants on the hills when in flower. One who grew the more beautiful species might give rare pleasure to people who cared for our native mountain plants.

Silybum Marianum, the Milk thistle; Carduus eriophorus, a noble thistle—found chiefly in the limestone districts of the south of England—and the great, woolly, silvery Cotton thistle, as it is often called, are handsome plants. One isolated plant or a group or two will be sufficient for ordinary gardens; but where there is sufficient space these, with many other fine wild plants, might be naturalized by sowing a few of the seeds in any waste place, or in the shrubbery. The Milk thistle, with its shining green leaves and white markings, is very desirable among the British plants, though scarcely so much so as the great Cotton thistle.

The common Corn-flower (Centaurea Cyanus) is a beautiful garden plant, if sown in autumn: sown in spring, it is not so strong. I know of nothing more beautiful than a bold group of the Corn-flower in spring and early summer; the bloom is so lasting, the flowers so pretty for cutting.

One of the prettiest of dwarf trailing silvery plants is the woolly Diotis maritima, which is found on the southern shores of England, coming up as far as Anglesea on the west and Suffolk on the east, but generally a rare plant in this country. The double variety of the Pyrethrum, now so frequent in our flower-gardens, is a native plant—or, at least, the single or normal form of the species is. The Sea Wormwood (Artemisia maritima) forms a silvery bush, common on our shores, and worthy a corner now and then in our gardens. There is a deep rose-coloured variety of the common Yarrow, which should be in every garden, and there is a very pretty double white variety of the Sneezewort (Achillea Ptarmica) which comes from British parents.

The Mountain Everlasting (Gnaphalium dioicum) is a beautiful dwarf plant, admirable for rocks or the front of a border, or in any way amongst alpine plants; it abounds on mountains in Scotland, Wales, and many parts of England. There is a variety called G. dioicum roseum that has its dwarf flowers delicately tinted with rose; neat edgings are sometimes made of this plant, so that there should be no difficulty in procuring it, even supposing we cannot find it wild; it is a popular plant wherever Alpine flowers are grown.

We will now turn to the extensive Harebell order, where we shall find much beauty, from the Harebell which swings its pretty blue above the wind-beaten turf on many an upland pasture, to the little prostrate Ivy Campanula (C. hederacea), plentiful in moist spots in Ireland and western England.

The giant Campanula (C. latifolia) is one of the handsomest and is pretty frequent. The spreading Campanula (C. patula), of the central and southern counties of England, is also very ornamental. Campanula Trachelium is also good, and indeed nearly all the plants of the family are pretty; but none of them surpass in beauty the common Harebell, which, although it may struggle for existence on poor or exposed pastures, yet, when transferred to a garden, makes a vigorous plant and flowers profusely—a mass of pleasing colour.

The little Ivy Campanula had better be grown in a pan of peat soil, or in some moist and slightly shaded spot where it may not be overrun by tall plants. Both this plant and the even more interesting Linnæa borealis may be grown well on the outside of the window, with a north or shady aspect, during the seven warmest months of the year, by planting them in pots of peat earth, and standing these in pans of water.

The Ivy-leaved Cyclamen, or the common Cyclamen (Cyclamen hederæfolium), a native of Southern Europe, but not supposed to be truly British, has been found in several places, apparently wild, and as such is generally included among British plants. Being a beautiful plant, it is worthy of a place. We cannot easily find it wild in England, but it is not difficult to obtain, and a lovely plant it is when seen in flower. A ring of it planted round a small bed of choice shrubs forms a pretty sight, and it may be naturalized, in bare places, in woods and shrubberies.

The Water Violet (Hottonia palustris) with its whorls of pale purple flowers is a pretty plant for ponds or ditches.

I had almost forgotten our native Primroses and Cowslips, but there is no need to plead for these and their numerous and beautiful varieties. The Bird's-eye Primrose of Northern England—one of the sweetest of our native plants—is, however, very rarely seen in gardens. It would thrive well in wet spots on pastures and heaths, and also in bare moist spots by the side of rivulets, and in the bog bed, as would the smaller and beautiful Scotch Bird's-eye Primrose.

The Loosestrifes, or Lysimachias, are pretty for cultivation; L. Nummularia, the Creeping Jenny of the London windows, trailing its luxuriant leaves where few other plants would thrive so well. The upright-growing species L. thyrsiflora is good for the margin of water, in consequence of the curious habit it has of half-hiding its flowers among the green of its leaves; a mass of it by a river, or pond, or ditch looks very distinct and pleasing.

Finally, we have in the Primula order the beautiful Trientalis of the north, a wood plant, and somewhat difficult to cultivate, but one that may be grown in shady and half-shady spots in peat soil.

Of the Thrift family, certainly the most valuable plant is a deep and charming rose-coloured variety of the common Thrift (Armeria vulgaris).

Everybody knows the Thrift of our seashores, and of the tops of some of the Scotch mountains, with its pale pink flowers; but the variety named here is of a showy rose, and one of the plants we can use in the spring garden as an edging plant, or in borders. This kind is sold and known as Armeria vulgaris rubra.

Any of the British Statices that may be collected are worthy a place in a collection of wild flowers.

Euphorbia Lathyris is the stately Caper Spurge, which is established here and there with us; it is worthy of a place, though not for the beauty of its flowers. Nor must we forget the common Hop (Humulus lupulus) which is graceful when well grown over a bower.

The beautiful Poet's Narcissus (Narcissus poeticus), hawked about the streets of London so abundantly in spring, is generally included in native plants, though not considered truly British; but whether it be so or not, such a distinctly beautiful plant should be in every garden.

The Snowflake (Leucojum æstivum) occurs in several of the south-eastern counties, and makes a handsome border plant; the dwarf, sweet, and fine vernal Snowflake has been recently found in Dorsetshire in some abundance; while the common Snowdrop is freely naturalized in various parts of the country. These, it need hardly be said, should all be in any collection of British wild flowers, and with them the Daffodil and the Wood Tulip (Tulipa sylvestris). This last is found most frequently in some of the eastern counties of England, but may be had readily from the nurserymen, who sell it as T. florentina and T. cornuta. Lloydia serotina is an extremely rare little bulbous plant, found in North Wales. It is also known as Anthericum serotinum.

Among native bulbs there are some very interesting. The Snake's-head (Fritillaria meleagris) is abundant in some parts of the south and east of England, and it is worthy of a place in a garden. I know of nothing prettier in the spring garden than the singular suspended bells of the English Fritillary, often so prettily spotted, and occasionally white. The white form is a plant to encourage in every garden, the large white bells being so distinct.

The two British Scilla, though not so pretty as some of the continental species, so conspicuous among spring flowers, must not be forgotten in a full collection, nor the varieties of the wood hyacinth, and there are several of interest, both white and pink.

The Two-leaved Lily of the Valley (Convallaria bifolia) is a diminutive and sweet little herb, found in only a few localities, and thriving on rocky borders and banks among dwarf plants. It is common on the Continent, and may be readily had from some nurseries, and in all botanic gardens in this country. The common Lily of the Valley is a true native plant, abundant in some counties, though wanting in others. The graceful Solomon's Seal (Polygonatum multiflorum) and the Lily of the Valley should be planted to establish themselves in a semi-wild state in every place which has a shrubbery or wood.

Snowflake at Longleat.

The Star of Bethlehem (Ornithogalum umbellatum) and the drooping O. nutans are established in several parts of the country. The first is a well-known old garden plant; the second a handsome kind with drooping flowers.

To these we may add the Meadow Saffron (Colchicum autumnale), abundant in parts of Ireland and England, and frequently cultivated as a garden plant, commonly under the name of the Autumn Crocus, which name properly belongs to our blue Crocus nudiflorus.

A Gladiolus (G. illyricus) has recently been found in the New Forest, near Lyndhurst; it is worthy of culture, and indeed is, or was, a favourite plant in many gardens before it was discovered as a British plant, having come to our gardens from Southern Europe.

The Spring Crocus (C. vernus) is abundant in the neighbourhood of Nottingham, and other parts of England and Ireland; and the less known but equally beautiful Autumn Crocus (C. nudiflorus) is also naturalized in Derbyshire, about Nottingham, and in a few other places. The Vernal Crocus is in nearly every garden, but the Autumnal Crocus is uncommon in gardens, and should be introduced to all, because it opens its handsome flowers when most others have perished. It is as easy of culture as the Spring Crocus, but, being so much scarcer, deserves good soil, and some watchfulness, to prevent its being dug up.

Those who have seen the Flowering Rush (Butomus umbellatus) in flower, are not likely to omit it from a collection of water-plants, as it is handsome and distinct. It is a native of the greater part of Europe and Asia, and the central and southern parts of England and Ireland. Plant it near the margin, it likes rich muddy soil. The common Sagittaria, frequent in England and Ireland, but not in Scotland, might be associated with this; and there is a very much finer double kind which is to be had here and there, and is probably a variety of the common kind.

Among picturesque plants for the water-side, nothing equals the great Water Dock (Rumex Hydrolapathum), which is rather generally dispersed over the British Isles, and has leaves quite sub-tropical in aspect and size, becoming of a lurid red in the autumn. It forms a fine mass of foliage on rich muddy banks. The Reed Maces (Typha) must not be forgotten, but they should not be allowed to run everywhere. The narrow-leaved one is more graceful than the common kind.

Carex pendula is good for the margins of water, its drooping spikes being so distinct. It is rather common in England, more so than Carex Pseudo-cyperus, which grows well in a foot or two of water, or on the margin of a muddy pond. Carex paniculata forms a strong and thick stem, sometimes three or four feet high, somewhat like a tree-fern, and with luxuriant masses of falling leaves, and on that account is transferred to moist places in gardens, though the larger specimens are difficult to remove and soon perish.

Scirpus lacustris (the Bulrush) is too distinct a plant to be omitted, as its stems, sometimes attaining a height of more than seven and even eight feet, are very singular; Cyperus longus is also a handsome water-plant, reminding one of the aspect of the Papyrus when in flower. It is found in some of the southern counties of England. Cladium Mariscus is also another distinct and rather scarce British aquatic which is worth a place.

The Great Horse-tail, which grows pretty commonly in the greater part of England and Ireland, attains its greatest development in rich soil, reaching a height of four or five feet, and the numbers of slender branches depending from each whorl look most graceful. The wood Equisetum (E. sylvaticum), common all over Britain, is smaller, but even more graceful. The long simple-stemmed Equisetums, or Horse-tails, are also interesting to cultivate in marshy spots.

BRITISH WILLOWS

Our Willows are as beautiful as Olives, perhaps much more beautiful, as after one has enjoyed their slender wands and silvery leaves against the summer sky they are the prettiest things in the winter landscape when they have lost all their leaves. Few even among the very men whose business it is to study trees, and plant them (i.e., landscape gardeners) have any idea of the noble effects that may be got by the artistic (i.e., natural)

Giant Horse-tail (Equisetum Telmateia).

White Willow in Hampshire.
(From drawing in possession
of Lady Carnarvon.)

massing of our native Willows, and their best varieties, in fitting situations. These occur often in this river-veined land, where there is so much marsh and estuary and shoreland, in which the hardy Willows of our country and northern lands are at home.

I say again, nothing in tropical or other lands is so effective in the landscape, so simple to secure, and so enduring as the pictures we may make from Willows. Take the White Willow (Salix alba) alone—a stately and very large tree with its mass of silvery leaves so graceful in movement, and also a tree of much value for its timber. Around this tree, naturally grouped so to say, there are various forms of even greater value, of which the shoots assume yellow, red, and other hues—trees which are almost as large as the common White Willow in good soil by rivers, or in marsh land. But in effect and colour they are even more important, one of them, the scarlet form, glowing with splendid colour in the winter sun.

The better known yellow form (Salix vitellina) is most delicate and charming in colour in the winter or in the sun after showers, and indeed in all lights. The colour in the summer is beautiful certainly, but it is the change from the silvery foliage of the summer to the bright decisive colour of winter that is so charming in this and its allies. Simply massed in groups, as things arrange themselves, these Willows give us all we could desire in the way of pictures and beautiful effects in places where there is any breadth or expanse of marsh; but these great spaces are not necessary for single trees; Red and Yellow Willows may be grown in a small garden and be there beautiful. By putting in a few cuttings in the dykes of many farms these Willows will soon give a living picture.

Among British Willows there are some that claim our attention more than others. No doubt every one is interesting from the botanical point of view, but what we seek are effective and picturesque things that can take their place among the trees of the land, finer than any of which they are in colour.

The earliest flowering British Willow is what is called the Goat Willow, or 'pussies' by the children in spring. Next in importance is the Crack Willow or Withy, which also becomes a very fine handsome tree nearly a

Crack Willow in Kennet Valley.

hundred feet high, with a trunk sometimes twenty feet in girth, as in the specimen drawn by Alfred Parsons and engraved herein. There is a variety with the twigs orange or crimson in colour. The Bedford Willow also is a handsome tree and is supposed to be a hybrid between the White and the Crack Willow. The Goat Willow is not so handsome a tree as the others though precious for its beauty, but in almost every woodland district so common that there is no need to plant it. The Violet Willow is the next to claim our attention, being a graceful tree with violet shoots, very free and with a pretty grey bloom upon the leaves.

Then we have the common Osier with its long wavy leaves silvery beneath—this Willow is very common in wet places and in Willow beds; it does not give us such beautiful trees as the White Willow in its various forms. Of the Osier there are numerous varieties; and, lastly, we have the purple Osier, which is not quite a tree but a shrub attaining ten feet or so, with the advantage of being so bitter that rabbits will not eat it. Of this, as of all the others, there are various forms.

Although from a landscape point of view the best are the tree Willows, there is scarcely one which is not right by the water side; and for all who live in cool or mountain districts and have any kind of rock-garden, the dwarf Willows of our own mountains are charming, such as the Creeping Willow in its various forms, and the Woolly Willow, a dwarf silvery shrub of easy culture and a very pretty rock shrub: also the Netted Willow.

BRITISH ORCHIDS. Orchids everywhere beautiful and singular, whether showy, as in the hot or moist east, or tiny on the Kent and Surrey hills, where the Bee Orchis is often frequent—it is most interesting to collect our native Orchids and to cultivate them. If we can succeed in growing the British Orchids, we are not likely to fail with any other hardy plants. They are the most difficult to cultivate, but amongst the most interesting things which can be grown.

I have cultivated the Bee Orchis and the Fly Orchis and the Hand Orchis, and a number of other British Orchids, for several years, and flowered them annually. Devoting a small bed to their culture, in an open spot, digging some chalk into the bed, so as to give the plants the soil in which they are found most abundantly, I succeeded with all except those kinds that are parasitic on the roots of trees.

The difficulty was to imitate the state of the surface of the ground which exists where they live in a wild state. I knew that the surface-dressing of stunted, storm-beaten grass among which they nestle prevents the ground from cracking and drying, and also shelters the plants in winter—in short, keeps the surface open and healthy. To plant grass over a bed in a garden would not do, as the shelter and richness of the ground would induce it to grow so strong that unless we were to look after and shorten it very frequently there would be no chance of keeping it within bounds; and if we did not do that, it would soon smother all the Orchids. A good substitute is cocoa-fibre with a little sand to give it weight. An inch or two of this was spread over the bed, and it prevented cracking and evaporation, and kept the surface in a healthy state. The roots should be inserted firmly but without injuring their fibres—a great point.

Few people know how to plant anything beyond a strong bedding plant. If one of these Orchids which are accustomed to send their fleshy roots down into moist broken chalk in search of food were to be planted without care, it would soon perish.

Well, in this way I have grown and freely flowered the most curious and beautiful Bee Orchis, the Spider Orchis, the Fly Orchis, and a dozen others less difficult to cultivate. The marsh Epipactus palustris is one of the easiest native Orchids to cultivate, growing well in an artificial bog or moist border; whilst most of the Orchises will do well under the treatment above described. The Bee, Fly, and Spider Orchids belong to the genus Ophrys.

The common spotted Orchis (O. maculata), found almost everywhere in the British Islands, is one of the freest to grow in a garden; it makes large tufts of great beauty in stiff ground. Lately nurserymen have been offering a plant described as a variety of this, under the name of O. maculata superba. This is in reality the true British Orchis latifolia, a noble species, easy to grow in a moist spot, and having large spikes of bloom. Orchis militaris and O. fusca are among the handsomest of our Orchids;

but all are interesting, from the early spotted O. mascula to the Butterfly Orchis, both of which are of easy culture in a garden.

Perhaps the rarest and finest of all the British Orchids is the Lady's Slipper, nearly if not extinct. Some of our nurserymen supply it, and they get their supplies from the Continent, where it is a widely distributed plant. It should be planted in broken limestone and fibrous loam, on the eastern side of a rock-work. When well grown it is a beautiful plant, quite as much so as some of the Cypripediums grown in the Orchid house, but, being perfectly hardy, is far more interesting for the British garden.

The most important thing with regard to the Orchids is the procuring of them in a suitable state for planting. When they are gathered in a wild state, the roots should be taken up as carefully as possible, and transferred to their garden home quickly and safely. They are very often sold in markets, but the roots are mutilated, not only from careless taking up, but from being tightly bound with matting.

In the Grass family the common Ribbon Grass (Phalaris arundinacea), Hierochloë borealis (a rare northern plant, sweet-scented when dried), Milium effusum (a handsome wood grass), the exquisitely graceful Apera Spica-venti of the eastern counties, the Hare's-tail Grass of the Channel Islands (Lagurus ovatus), the Quaking Grasses (Briza), the variegated Cock's-foot Grass, and Elymus arenarius (a stout grey grass) are interesting or beautiful.

OUR NATIVE POPLARS

While there is little space to tell of all our native trees, many of which, in nature at least, are as well worthy our attention as any exotic ones, a few words on our native Poplars—among the hardiest of trees and the easiest to increase and grow—may not be amiss. When we think of the rapid growth and the good effect both of single trees and groups in the landscape, we find much to encourage us to plant Poplars—even our native kinds. They will grow in soils not so good for Oak or Ash or Pine, and this is important for a country like ours where there is so much swampy or

The Black Poplar
in Kennet Valley.

low-lying land by rivers and estuaries, and also inland bog land, where the effect of Poplars will be beautiful and their growth profitable.

The White Poplar or Abele, a native tree, is so fine in form and in all ways that it is not neglected, and about country houses we see noble trees of it nearly or quite one hundred feet high. It is excellent for planting by rivers and in spots likely to be under water betimes, and very handsome in the colour of the stems, especially where a number of old trees are seen picturesquely grouped. The Grey Poplar comes near this but is not so fine a tree. I love our true native Aspen (Populus tremula), best of all Poplars: though not uncommon in some underwoods, we rarely see it in England planted either as a garden or woodland tree—a great mistake, as in some countries of North Europe it is a large and useful tree, and always a beautiful one. There is a weeping form and one or two wild ones. The Black Poplar (P. nigra) is a tree of rapid growth and good effect in the landscape.

OUR NATIVE EVERGREENS

When after a very hard winter we see the evergreen trees of the garden in mourning, and perhaps many of them dead, as happens to Laurels, Laurustinuses, and often even the Bay, it is a good time to consider the hardiness and other good qualities of our British evergreens and the many forms raised from them.

If we are fortunate enough to have old Yew trees near us, we do not find that a hard winter makes any difference to them, even winters that sear the evergreen Oak. We have collected within the past two hundred years evergreen trees from all parts of the northern world, but it is doubtful if any of them are better than the common Yew, which when old is often picturesque, and which lives green for a thousand years. Of this great tree we have many varieties, but none of them quite so good as the wild kind when old. In the garden little thought is given to the Yew, and it is crowded among shrubs; while in graveyards the roots are cut by digging, so that one seldom sees it in its fine character when old, which is very beautiful. The Golden Yew is a form of it, and there are other slight variegations which are interesting from a merely garden point of view. The Irish Yew is a well-known form; its prim shape is too often seen. Other seedling variations of the common Yew are better than the Irish variety.

After the ever-precious Yew, the best of our evergreen trees is the Holly, which in no country attains the beauty it does in our own; no evergreen brought over the sea is so valuable not only in its native form, often attaining forty feet even on the hills, but in the almost innumerable varieties raised from it, many of them being the best of all variegated shrubs in their silver and gold variegation; in fruit, too, it is the most beautiful of evergreens. Not merely as a garden tree is it precious, but as a most delightful shelter around fields for stock, in paddocks and places which we wish to shelter. A big wreath of unclipped Holly on the cold sides of fields is the best protection, and a grove of Holly north of any place we want to shelter is the best thing we can plant. As to the garden, we may make beautiful evergreen gardens of the forms of Holly alone; the only thing we have to fear are rabbits, which when numerous make Holly difficult to establish by barking the little trees, and in hard winters even killing many old trees.

Notwithstanding the many conifers brought from other countries within the past few generations, it is very doubtful if as regards beauty, more than one or two equal our native Fir, which when old is so fine in its stem and head. Few things in our country are more picturesque than old groups and groves of the Scotch Fir; few indeed of the conifers we treasure from other countries will ever give us anything so good as the ruddy stems and frost-proof crests of this northern and British tree.

Again, the best of evergreen climbers is our native Ivy, and the many beautiful forms allied to it or that have arisen from it. Ivy in our woods arranges its own beautiful effects, but in gardens it might be made more delightful use of. The form most commonly used in Britain—the Irish Ivy—is by no means so graceful as some others, and there are a great number of delightful kinds varying in form and even in colour. These for edgings, banks, forming screens, covering old trees, and forming summerhouses should be made far larger use of. In many northern countries our

Ivy will not live in the open air, and it is so common with us, that we rarely take advantage of our privileges in such a possession in making bold shelters, wreaths, and many beautiful things of it that would need little care. It requires care in trimming when on our houses and on cottage roofs; but there are many pretty things to make of it away from buildings, and among them Ivy-clad and Ivy-covered wigwams, summer-houses, and covered ways, the Ivy supported on a strong open frame-work, and trained over sticks and mats till it takes hold.

The Box tree, which is a true native on certain dry hills in the south of England, is so crowded in shrubberies that one seldom sees its beauty as it is on the hills full in the sun, where the branches take a charming plumy toss. To wander among natural groves of Box is a great pleasure, and there is no reason why we should not plant it in groups or colonies by itself full in the sun, so that one might enjoy the same charm of form that it shows when wild. In some heavy soils it barely lives, but many soils suit it perfectly. A bower of one of the handsome-leaved Ivies in a grove of Box would be charming, and its charms would last long.

Also among our native evergreens is the common Juniper, a scrubby bush in some places, but on heaths in Surrey, and favoured heaths elsewhere, often growing over twenty feet high and very picturesque, especially where mingled with Holly. There is an upright form, called the Irish Juniper, in gardens.

The Arbutus, which borders nearly all the streams in Greece, ventures into Ireland, and is abundant there in certain parts in the south. This beautiful shrub, though tender in inland districts, is very precious for the seashore and mild districts, not only as an evergreen, but for the beauty of its flower and fruit. Still, it is the one British evergreen which has to be planted with discrimination in places where the winters are severe in inland districts.

We have thus glanced rapidly at the garden of British Wild Flowers and Trees, from showy Buttercups to modest Grasses; but it would require much greater space to do justice to the many delightful aspects of vegetation to which they give rise.

INDEX
to the Fifth Edition

———•◆•———

This index is derived from the one published by William Robinson in the fifth edition of *The Wild Garden*. The terms are Robinson's but the arrangement has been modified (for example, common and scientific names are now kept separate). A separate index of plants, people, and places mentioned in Rick Darke's new chapters begins on page 351. *Italics* indicate illustrations.—Ed.

Gravetye Manor in silhouette at sundown in late May.

THE END

BOTANICAL NAMES AND REVISIONS

Alfredia cernua = *Carduus nutans*
alkanet, evergreen = *Anchusa sempervirens*
Althæa taurinensis = *Althaea officinalis*
Alyssum maritimum – *Lobularia maritima*
Amberboa moschata = *Centaurea moschata*
Androsaemum officinale = *Hypericum androsaemum*
anemone, Apennine = *Anemone apennina*
Anemone japonica = *Anemone ×hybrida*
Aralia edulis = *Aralia cordata*
Aralia japonica = *Fatsia japonica*
Aristolochia Sipho = *Aristolochia macrophylla*
Armeria vulgaris = *Armeria maritima*
Arundinaria falcata = *Drepanostachyum falcatum*
Athamanta Matthioli = *Athamanta turbith*
Atragene alpina = *Clematis alpina*

balm = *Melissa officinalis*
Bambusa metake = *Pseudosasa japonica*
Bambusa viridis-glaucescens = *Phyllostachys viridiglaucescens*
barberry, common = *Berberis vulgaris*
bell-flowered scilla = *Hyacinthoides hispanica*
Betonica = *Stachys*
bird's-foot trefoil = *Lotus corniculatus*
blood-root, Canadian = *Sanguinaria canadensis*

bog-bean – *Menyanthes trifoliata*
Borago Cretica = *Trachystemon orientale*
box = *Buxus*
brier, sweet = *Rosa eglanteria*
buttercup, great = *Ranunculus lingua*

Campanula hederacea = *Wahlenbergia hederacea*
Campanula pumila = *Campanula cochleariifolia*
cardinal-flower = *Lobelia cardinalis*
Cephalaria procera = *Cephalaria gigantea*
Cheddar pink = *Dianthus gratianopolitanus*
cherry plum = *Prunus cerasifera*
Clematis graveolens = *Clematis orientalis*
clematis, Indian mountain – *Clematis orientalis*
cockspur thorn = *Cratægus crus-galli*
compass plant = *Silphium laciniatum*
Convallaria bifolia = *Maianthemum bifolium*
cow parsnip, giant – *Heracleum mantegazzianum*
crab = *Malus sylvestris*
crane's bill = *Geranium pratense*
Cratægus oxyacantha = *Cratægus laevigatus*
Cretan Borage = *Trachystemon orientale*
Cypripedium spectabile = *Cypripedium reginae*

Dianthus cæsius = Dianthus gratianopolitanus

Dielytra = Dicentra

Dielytra spectabilis = Dicentra spectabilis

dog's-tooth violet (American) = *Erythronium americanum*

dog's-tooth violet (European) = *Erythronium dens-canis*

Dorycnium sericeum = Dorycnium hirsutum

evening primrose = *Œnothera biennis*

fennel, giant = *Ferula*

fern, beech = *Phegopteris hexagonoptera*

fern, oak = *Gymnocarpium dryopteris*

fern, plume = *Matteuccia struthiopteris*

fern, royal = *Osmunda regalis*

Ficaria grandiflora = Ranunculus ficaria

flowering rush = *Butomus umbellatus*

forget-me-not, water = *Myosotis scorpioides*

forget-me-not, early = *Myosotis ramosissima*

Funkia = Hosta

Funkia coerulea = Hosta ventricosa

Funkia grandiflora = Hosta plantaginea 'Grandiflora'

Geranium armenum = Geranium psilostemon

globe flower = *Trollius*

globe thistle = *Echinops*

Gnaphalium dioicum = Antennaria dioica

gold thread = *Coptis trifoliata*

golden rod = *Solidago*

gout-weed = *Aegopodium podagraria*

Harpalium rigidum = Helianthus rigidus

hazel = *Corylus avellana*

Helianthus orgyalis = Helianthus salicifolius

hellebore, green = *Helleborus foetidus*

herb Paris = *Paris quadrifolia*

Hemerocallis flava = Hemerocallis lilioasphodelus

hibiscus (herbaceous) = *Hibiscus moscheutos*

holly = *Ilex*

honesty = *Lunaria annua*

horned poppy = *Glaucium*

houseleek = *Sempervivum*

Hungarian bindweed = *Calystegia pulchra*

Hyacinthus amethystinus = Brimeura amethystina

Indian poke = *Phytolacca americana*

Iris Kæmpferi = Iris ensata

ivy = *Hedera*

ivy campanula = *Wahlenbergia hederacea*

Japan anemone = *Anemone ×hybrida*

Koniga maritima = Lobularia maritima

Lathyrus pyrenaicus = Lathyrus sylvestris

loosestrife = *Lythrum salicaria*

Magnolia glauca = Magnolia virginiana

marsh marigold = *Caltha palustris*

May apple = *Podophyllum peltatum*

May flower = *Epigæa repens*

meadow rue, large-flowered = *Thalictrum aquilegiifolium*

meadow sweet = *Filipendula ulmaria*

meadow sweet, red = *Filipendula purpurea*

Megasea = Bergenia

Menziesia polifolia = Daboecia cantabrica

Merendera Bulbocodium = Merendera montana

Michaelmas daisy = *Aster novi-belgii (Symphiotricum novi-belgii)*

milkwort = *Polygala*

mocassin flower = *Cypripedium reginae*. Note: Although

Robinson used the common name mocassin flower to refer to *C. reginae* (*C spectabile* in the historic text), this name correctly refers to *C. acaule*. *Cypripedium reginae* is best called showy lady's-slipper.

Molopospermum cicutarium = *Molopospermum peloponnesiacum*

moon daisy = *Leucanthemum vulgare*

moonseed, Canadian = *Menispermum canadense*

mountain clematis = *Clematis montana*

mountain everlasting = *Antennaria dioica*

Mulgedium plumieri = *Lactuca plumieri*

Myosotis dissitiflora = *Myosotis ramosissima*

myrrh, common = *Myrrhis odorata*

Nepeta Mussinii = *Nepeta ×faasenii*

Nootka bramble = *Rubus nutkana*

osier = *Salix viminalis*

osier, purple = *Salix purpurea*

Othonna = *Othonnopsis*

Pasque anemone = *Pulsatilla vulgaris*

periwinkle = *Vinca*

Phytolacca decandra = *Phytolacca americana*

plantain lily, Siebold's = *Hosta sieboldiana*

Plumbago Larpentæ = *Ceratostigma plumbaginoides*

poet's narcissus = *Narcissus poeticus*

Polygonum Brunonis = *Persicaria affinis*

Polygonum vaccinifolium = *Persicaria vaccinifolium*

poplar, grey = *Populus canescens*

poplar, white = *Populus alba*

Pyrenean Erinus = *Erinus alpinus*

Pyrethrum serotinum = *Leucanthemella serotina*

Pyrus Aria = *Sorbus aria*

Pyrus Aucuparia = *Sorbus aucuparia*

Pyrus Germanica = *Mespilus germanica*

Pyrus hybrida = *Sorbus hybrida*

Pyrus latifolia = *Sorbus latifolia*

Pyrus malus = *Malus*

Pyrus scandica = *Sorbus intermedia*

Pyrus torminalis = *Sorbus torminalis*

quick = *Cratægus*

quick, May blossom = *Cratægus oxyacantha*

restharrow = *Ononis repens*

rock cress = *Aubrieta*

rock rose = *Cistus*

rocket = *Hesperis matronalis*

rockfoil = *Bergenia*

Rosa berberifolia = *Rosa persica*

Rosa microphylla rubra plena = *Rosa roxburghii* 'Plena'

Rosa rubiginosa = *Rosa eglanteria*

Rosa spinosissima = *Rosa pimpinellifolia*

rose, American glossy = *Rosa virginiana*

rose, Carolina = *Rosa caroliniana*

rose, dog = *Rosa canina*

rose, Japan = *Rosa rugosa*

rose, Russian wild = *Rosa acicularis*

rose, Scotch = *Rosa pimpinellifolia*

rose, sweet brier = *Rosa eglanteria*

rose, wild yellow = *Rosa foetida*

scabious, giant = *Cephalaria gigantea*

sandwort, Balearic = *Arenaria balearica*

savin = *Juniperus sabina*

Saxifraga crassifolia = *Bergenia crassifolia*

saxifrage, broad-leaved = *Bergenia*

scilla-like plants = *Chionodoxa*

Scilla campanulata = *Hyacinthoides hispanica*

Scolymus = *Cynara scolymus*
seakale = *Crambe maritima*
sea lavender = *Limonium*
skunk cabbage = *Symplocarpus foetidus*
sloe = *Prunus spinosa*
smilax, hardy = *Smilax aspera*
snowflake, longleaf = *Leucojum aestivum*
snowflake, spring = *Leucojum vernum*
Solomon's seal = *Polygonatum ×hybridum*
Spanish broom = *Spartium junceum*
speedwell = *Veronica*
Spiræa aruncus = *Aruncus dioicus*
Spiræa filipendula = *Filipendula ulmaria*
Spiræa palmata = *Filipendula purpurea*
Spiræa venusta = *Filipendula rubra* 'Venusta'
Stachys lanata = *Stachys byzantina*
star of Bethlehem = *Ornithogalum umbellatum*
starwort = *Aster* (*Symphiotricum*)
statice = *Limonium*
stonecrop = *Sedum*
Struthiopteris = *Matteuccia struthiopteris*
sun rose = *Helianthemum*

teazle = *Dipsacus*
Telekia cordifolia = *Buphthalmum speciosum*
Tenby daffodil = *Narcissus obvallaris*
tiger lily = *Lilium tigrinum*
trailing arbutus = *Epigæa repens*
tree pæony = *Paeonia suffruticosa*
Trichomanes = *Asplenium trichomanes*

Trichonema = *Romulea*
Tritoma = *Kniphofia*
Tunica Saxifraga = *Petrorhagia saxifraga*

Veronica candida = *Veronica spicata* subsp. *incana*
vetch, bitter = *Vicia ervilia*
Villarsia nymphaeoides = *Nymphoides peltata*
Virginian creeper = *Parthenocissus quinquefolia*
Vittadenia triloba = *Erigeron mucronatus*

Waldsteinia trifolia = *Waldsteinia ternata*
water crowfoots = *Ranunculus hederaceus, Ranunculus tripartitus*
water lily, (European) white = *Nymphaea alba*
Welsh poppy = *Meconopsis cambrica*
willow, crack = *Salix fragilis*
willow, creeping = *Salix repens*
willow, French = *Epilobium angustifolium*
willow, goat = *Salix capria*
willow, violet = *Salix daphnoides*
willow, woolly = *Salix lanata*
windflower, Robinson blue = *Anemone nemorosa* 'Robinsoniana'
winter aconite = *Eranthus hyemalis*
wood hyacinth (English) = *Hyacinthoides non-scripta*
woodruff = *Asperula odorata*

yarrow, golden = *Achillea eupatorium*
yew = *Taxus*

Zietenia lavandulæfolia = *Stachys lavandulifolia*

BIBLIOGRAPHY

Sources mentioned in Robinson's 1895 edition, which did not include a bibliography, are enclosed in square brackets. All other sources relate to the new chapters accompanying the historic text.

[Babington, C. C. 1856. *Manual of British Botany*. 4th ed. London: John Van Voorst.]

[Baines, H. 1840. *The Flora of Yorkshire*. London.]

[Bentham, George. 1878. *Handbook of the British Flora*. 4th ed. London: Louvell Reeve.]

[Cariot, L'Abbe. 1860. *Étude des Fleurs Botanique*. 3rd ed. Lyon: Girard and Josserand.]

Cronon, William. 1995. "The Trouble with Wilderness; or, Getting Back to the Wrong Nature." In *Uncommon Ground: Toward Reinventing Nature*, ed. William Cronon. New York: Norton.

Grimm, Juan. 2005. From a lecture given at the Australian Landscape and Garden Design Conference 2005, Camberwell, Australia. Synopsis at www.holbrooktravel.com/GardenTours/Itinerary/CH_ITIN.pdf. Accessed 9 March 2009.

[Hanbury, Frederick J. 1889–1899. *An Illustrated Monograph of the British Hieracia*. London.]

Kowarik, Ingo, and Stefan Körner, eds. 2005. *Wild Urban Woodlands: New Perspectives for Urban Forestry*. Berlin: Springer-Verlag.

[Luxford, G. 1838. *Flora of Reigate*. London: Van Voorst.]

[Mackay, James T. 1836. *Flora Hibernica*. Dublin: W. Curry.]

Miller, Wilhelm. 1911. *What England Can Teach Us About Gardening*. New York: Doubleday.

Miller, Wilhelm. 1906. "William Robinson." In L. H. Bailey's *Cyclopedia of American Horticulture*. New York: Doubleday.

[Moore, A. G., and D. More. 1866. *Cybele Hibernica*. Dublin: Hodges and Smith.]

Robinson, William. 1883. *The English Flower-Garden*. London: John Murray.

Robinson, William. 1906. *The Garden Beautiful: Home Woods, Home Landscape*. London: John Murray.

Robinson, William. 1911. *Gravetye Manor: Or, Twenty Years' Work Round an Old Manor House*. London: John Murray.

Robinson, William. 1917. *My Wood Fires and Their Story*. Country Life.

Sargent, Charles S. 1888–1897. *Garden and Forest: A Journal of Horticulture, Landscape Art, and Forestry*.

[Syme, John T. Boswell, ed. 1863–1886. *English Botany, or, Coloured Figures of British Plants*. 3rd ed. 12 vols. London: Robert Hardwicke.]

[Thoreau, H. D. 1906. Journal entry for 23 March 1856. *The Writings of Henry David Thoreau*. Journal VIII. 1 November 1855–15 August 1856. Cambridge: Riverside Press.]

[Watson, Hewett C., and John T. Boswell Syme, eds. 1857. *The London Catalogue of British Plants*. 5th ed. London: W. Pamplin.]

White, Elizabeth. 1941. My Garden of Pine Barrens Plants. From a transcript of the Radio Garden Club (sponsored by the Garden Club of New Jersey), Mutual Broadcasting System, 24 March 1941.

Williams, Raymond. 1980. "Ideas of Nature." In *Problems in Materialism and Culture: Selected Essays*. London: Verso. 67–85.

INDEX
of
Plants, People, and Places

This index covers terms appearing in the new chapters written by Rick Darke. **Boldface** numbers indicate photo pages. A separate index of terms used in Robinson's historic text begins on page 325.